Christians among the Virtues

Christians among the Virtues

Theological Conversations with Ancient and Modern Ethics

Stanley Hauerwas
Charles Pinches

University of Notre Dame Press

Notre Dame, Indiana

Copyright 1997 by
University of Notre Dame Press
Notre Dame, Indiana 46556
All Rights Reserved

Manufactured in the United States of America

Library of Congress Cataloging-in-Publication Data

Hauerwas, Stanley, 1940–
    Christians among the virtues : theological conversations with
ancient and modern ethics / Stanley Hauerwas and Charles Pinches.
        p.   cm.
        ISBN 0–268–00817–5 (alk. paper). — ISBN 0–268–00819–1 (alk.
paper)
        1. Ethics.   2. Aristotle. Nicomachean ethics.   3. Christian
ethics.   4. Virtues.   I. Pinches, Charles Robert.   II. Title.
        BJ1012.H347   1997
        241'.4—dc20   96-26432
                                                                        CIP

Contents

Preface

This book has been a joy to write, not the least because of the debts we have incurred during the writing of it. Our families are of course those to whom we owe the deepest debts. In particular we thank Paula and Robin for their support as well as their wonderful good humor. Our children, moreover, have been wonderful reminders that this is not a game; a book on the virtues should certainly be about the kind of communities necessary for them to live well as Christians. It is therefore with particular gratitude we thank Adam and his wife Laura, and Jody, Nathan, Claire, and Seth.

Perhaps no one has been more important to our work than Alasdair MacIntyre. Through his writings he has taught us ways to think that we are only beginning to appreciate. Thinking, after all, is a learned skill. We are not nearly as skillful as Alasdair, but we appreciate his willingness to allow us to join him in conversation about matters that matter.

We owe a particular debt to Dr. James Fodor for reading and criticizing the manuscript. The care he exercises as a reader is a gift only a few can give. Most of us read, but we are unable to avoid the narcissistic temptation to make what we read conform to what we think. Dr. Fodor has the remarkable ability to read with humility that makes his criticisms all the more important, exactly because they help us discover what we should have said. Also, we wish to thank Marie Gaughan who typed much of the manuscript and kept track of our many changes and reorganizations.

Finally we dedicate this book to Paul Wadell. Paul was a student with Charlie at Notre Dame and is now a well-respected Catholic moral theologian. For us he is a friend whose life is lived without guile. It gives us great joy that he claims us as friends.

Introduction

1. The Return to Virtue

We hope this book represents a new beginning in recent discussions concerning ethics. It is obviously a book about "virtue ethics," but we hope it will subvert such classifications. We certainly do not think of what we have done here as an attempt to provide an alternative to rule- or principle-based ethics. Indeed, the very distinction between virtue ethics and rule-based ethics was the result of theories about the nature of ethics that have been increasingly left behind, and happily. Such theories were veiled attempts to shore up something called "ethics" as an intelligible mode of investigation and analysis independent from the practices of communities of people who carry forward relatively thick notions—such as courage or humility—of how life should be lived. The oddity of such ethical theories is nowhere better seen than in their misshapen result: "applied ethics."

The popularity of centers and courses in "applied ethics" may, of course, reveal that our hope that we are at a new beginning is little more than a pipe dream. On the other hand, the recent substantial and frequently brilliant work of Alasdair MacIntyre, Charles Taylor, Martha Nussbaum, Bernard Williams, and John Casey—as well as others—indicates that a discussion of the matters we take to be vital to our way of construing "ethics" is not only possible but well underway. Our debt to these thinkers is clear throughout, perhaps especially when we disagree with each. Their work is distinguished not only by an extraordinary historical and philosophical depth but also by a willingness to make claims about how our lives should be lived, and this sets it apart from current academic games. As theologians we believe we have a duty to take up the conversation about ethics these philosophers have begun.

Among other things, that is what we have attempted to do in this book. There is a danger, however, in labeling what we have done "ethics," even if the term cannot be entirely abandoned. Such a label might suggest that "ethics" can be distinguished from theology, and so our entrance into the philosophical conversation transforms us from theologians into "ethicists." In this regard, one of the reasons we find a focus on the virtues helpful is that any adequate account of the virtues Christianly considered will, we believe, render the distinction between theology and ethics problematic. The way we are taught to speak as Christians, what it means for us to be in the Christian faith, is not separable from how we are to live. Because the virtues presume what we say and what we do are inseparable they are an indispensable resource for the display of the Christian life.

Of course, we believe that the Christian life is distinctive. One of the main burdens of the book is to argue that the virtues Christianly considered are in fundamental ways different from the virtues associated with quite different practices, communities, and narratives. We do not believe, however, that the differences make a conversation between Christian and ancient pagan or modern liberal accounts of the virtues impossible or irrelevant. Rather we think the differences make the conversation all the more necessary as well as interesting.

It is with this in mind that we focus in the first three chapters on Aristotle's account of the virtues and, in particular, explore his understanding of their temporal character. Admittedly, "temporal character of the virtues" is our construal of Aristotle's position and as such is related to who we are as Christian interpreters of it, but we are convinced it is also appropriate to his account. For Aristotle, the virtues are acquired over a lifetime—or, even more forcefully put, we only know what a proper lifetime looks like as we come to see it as we acquire the virtues. Temporality is therefore intrinsic to Aristotle's account of the virtues, yet that same temporality threatens the success of lives lived virtuously. This threat leads Aristotle to recommend a form of life that can secure the virtues (and friendship) from ill fortune but, as we try to show, the very attempt to provide such security distorts our character.

As a people whose lives are constituted by the cross and resurrection of Jesus of Nazareth, Christians also cannot avoid the temporal character of life. Yet the way that the Christian narrative and its constitutive practices shape our understanding of our temporality requires a different understanding of the virtues (and different virtues as well) than that offered by Aristotle. For Christians our temporal, our bodily, status is not a threat but a gift by which the vulnerability required for the acquisition of the virtues becomes an invitation for friendship.

Of course Aristotle's account of the virtues also requires an account of friendship, but it is one quite different from that of Christians, particularly that given by Aquinas. Aquinas believed we are destined to be friends with God—something unthinkable from Aristotle's point of view. This is an example of the difference that Christians (and others) can know only as they engage with Aristotle himself, or modern appropriations of his thought. How else can we understand our differences? How else can we discriminate between that which is Christian and that which is not? Moreover, learning to note what marks us off from others does not prevent communication and genuine dialogue. Indeed, it creates its very possibility. Distinctiveness, particularly a distinctiveness requiring friendship with the stranger, does not mean isolation.

Yet we would be less than candid if we pretended that the conversations undertaken in this book are entirely polite. Good conversations, after all, are often conflictual; we have not tried to avoid the conflicts we think necessary for better understanding what difference the God Christians worship should make. One of the ways of characterizing such difference is in terms of the different politics which different accounts of the virtues require. Any account of the virtues involves a politics, for the virtues derive their intelligibility from communal practices. The name we Christians give our politics is "church," since we believe it is the determinative community that makes all we do intelligible. Therefore our exploration of the political repercussions of different accounts of the virtues extends the theological task called ecclesiology.

This should reinforce what is already obvious: We are not political liberals. As we and others have argued, the predominance of liberal politics has been a key reason why the virtues have received inadequate attention in recent ethical discussion. Liberalism, of course, presupposes and encourages certain kinds of virtues, but that it does so is often insufficiently acknowledged or articulated. Our title, *Christians among the Virtues,* is meant to echo Walker Percy's wonderful novel *Love among the Ruins.* Like Percy we have a rather dim view of many of the "advances" celebrated as the benefits of liberal political arrangements. Also like Percy, we do not believe we Christians have anyone to blame for the predominance of these arrangements but ourselves. However, we are little interested in blame; rather we seek amid the ruins resources for resistance and hope.

We trust the conversation we attempt in this book instantiates this hope. That many philosophers today are reconsidering the significance of the virtues for understanding how we should live our lives is hopeful. However, while theologians today read philosophers, philosophers seldom read theologians. There are many reasons for this imbalance, but no doubt one of them is the politics in which we exist. Christian speech has lost the sources, in Charles Taylor's terms, necessary for Christian and non-Christian alike to appreciate what difference that being Christian might make. Since precisely this difference is central to our conversation with various philosophers, we are hopeful that this book might attract a wider readership, including some philosophers.

Hope, after all, is a virtue, perhaps the most political virtue in our times. The most profound alternative to Christian hope we believe to be a kind of stoicism that supports as well as is produced by the politics of liberalism. Such stoicism presupposes a metaphysics incompatible with the Christian claim that our existence is bounded, not by fate, but by God's providential care. This reminds us that our differing accounts of the virtues rest on differing claims about the way things are. (Of course, the way things are cannot be properly understood without also understanding the way things have been and the way things will be—hence the claim that truthful existence is inescapably a "tensed" or temporal existence.) While we do not pretend to have given here a full defense of the Christian virtues and their related metaphysical claims, we hope we have at least located their difference from stoicism and its related virtues that govern so much of life in our time.

2. What We Think We Have Done

Our book is organized into three main sections. These do not build on one another as if part of one long, unfolding argument, but they are importantly connected. The first section is a theological commentary on Aristotle's *Nicomachean Ethics*. It establishes the context and agenda for all that follows. Many of the theological suggestions made through the commentary on Aristotle we try to develop and defend in the essays on Alasdair MacIntyre, Martha Craven Nussbaum, and John Casey. We believe, however, that the final section of the book is the more crucial one for the case we are trying to make, for there we try to exhibit central Christian virtues.

Why choose Aristotle? At least one answer is that Aquinas found Aristotle such a fruitful resource for his account of the virtues—and we believe Aquinas's account of the virtues remains unmatched in Christian theology. Though we do not provide any one extensive discussion of Aquinas's position, we use him throughout and like to think our general position is consonant with his understanding of the virtues. This may seem surprising since we do not credit the "natural virtues" to the degree he is often supposed to have done. Yet we believe accounts of Aquinas that make him more a philosopher than a theologian fail to do justice to his understanding of the significance of the theological virtues.

Of course we have also chosen to comment on Aristotle because we think he is more right than wrong about most things having to do with living virtuously. Moreover we think he remains surprisingly accessible to modern readers exactly because his ethics is meant to make us better. Aristotle simply begins by asking us what we want, accepting but nevertheless interrogating our answers to lead us to further discoveries about what in truth we might want. In Aristotle's hands, ethics is not a theory but a mode of inquiry that shapes skills necessary for those who would live well.

Put differently, in contrast to ethics done in the theoretical mode of modernity that tries to begin from nowhere, Aristotle begins his ethics decidedly from "somewhere." That he does so is of great advantage for those who, like us, have theological concerns. For theology necessarily begins from somewhere. Moreover we can learn better where that place is by comparing it with the "somewhere" from which Aristotle began. Finding theology's place in relation to Aristotle is all the more instructive exactly because he had no need to take a position for or against what we have come to call Christianity.

We hope that the reader will find our conversation with Aristotle edifying and perhaps even uplifting. It is our belief that we are starved today for discussions on rich matters such as happiness, virtue, and friendship. Even more we lack the means to understand their interconnection. No doubt there are other sources than Aristotle that can help Christians understand our lives morally; yet for those of us who work within or nearby the Catholic tradition, Aristotle remains an essential conversation partner.

Besides these three themes—happiness, virtue, and friendship—Aristotle's text is replete with others we have neglected. For example, we have said little about Aristotle's moral psychology and in particular his account of habits. This is a omission excusable only by limited space, for we believe the acquisition of the right habits is a subject of extreme importance. Few have understood this better than Aquinas, who drew on and nuanced Aristotle's account of the habits in a manner that has yet to be surpassed. Nor have we discussed in any systematic way how the virtues are individuated and interrelated. That all this remains to be done is a sign of the rich possibilities offered by this way of thinking morally about our lives, or so we would like to think.

The middle section of our book may appear less systematic than our commentary on Aristotle. There we enter into conversation with modern thinkers whose work, like our own, has been shaped by an engagement with Aristotle. Of the three thinkers we engage most directly, Alasdair MacIntyre has taught us the most; it is therefore not surprising that our differences with him are more difficult to delineate than those with either Nussbaum or Casey. Moreover, MacIntyre continues to develop his position in a manner that may require qualification of some of our judgments.

This is true as well of Martha Nussbaum, although her apparent evolution in recent work may make our differences *more* rather than less pronounced. In contrast, MacIntyre's continuing reflections on the interrelation of practices, tradition, and the virtues seem to offer quite interesting theological possibilities. We suspect that our differences with MacIntyre may be more theological than philosophical, although that is difficult to judge just because MacIntyre has been and continues to be rather cagey theologically. Put differently, we remain puzzled by MacIntyre's strong distinction between philosophy and theology.

Casey's work is not as well known as MacIntyre's or Nussbaum's, yet our discussion of his book is a crucial piece in the position we are trying to develop. Casey has the great virtue of beginning with the world as he finds it. As our essay suggests, we are not convinced we live in a world capable of rising as high as the pagan virtues Casey commends, but we admire his effort nonetheless. We do so partly because of his candid acknowledgment of the difficulty of reclaiming pagan virtues in a society that remains shaped, admittedly in distorted fashion, by Christian habits. We are sympathetic with his effort because, ironically, we are in a not dissimilar position. We are trying to reclaim Christian virtues in a context in which people assume that what it means to be a good Christian is little different from what it means to be a good liberal.

The last section of our book is meant to challenge the assumption that there is little difference between Christians and "all people of good will" by examining the Christian virtues of hope, obedience, courage, and patience. We think of these virtues as exhibits of the Christian life rather than ones that constitute it. For example, in our discussion of these virtues we obviously mention other virtues, most prominently charity, of which we offer no extended analysis, even though it is, in Aquinas's language, the form of all the virtues. Yet we hope this section challenges some of the assumptions Christians and non-Christians often make about the virtues central to Christian existence. We affirm the centrality of charity, but contrary to a good bit of recent theological opinion, we believe that charity cannot stand alone. Indeed, any charity lacking the patience derived from the Christian conviction that we live in God's time cannot help but be distorted. Moreover, any patience unshaped by Christian hope too easily becomes stoic acquiescence. And to be hopefully patient requires that we be part of a community of friends in which we are joyfully obedient.

3. A Final Word about Friendship: Or, How This Book Was Written

We do not remember how or when we decided to write this book, but we know it began in friendship. Nor do we remember when our friendship began, though it was during a time and in a relation often thought to inhibit friendship, that is, the relation between teacher (Hauerwas) and student (Pinches). Add to that inequality the inequality of our ages (Hauerwas is a bit older), and there would seem to remain little basis, particularly on Aristotelian grounds, for friendship to flourish. Nevertheless, we happily name ourselves friends, and we are sure that apart from friendship this book would not have been written.

However, that we have written the book together presents a problem for Pinches. Since Hauerwas is better known, Pinches's contribution may appear secondary. It is important, or at least Hauerwas thinks it is important, to make clear that this book is a common effort. If such calculations were possible, we might say each contributed fifty percent; in any case, the venture was genuinely joint.

Placed within the history of our friendship, the book began with an earlier version of the essays that now comprise the first section on Aristotle. Hauerwas wrote that earlier version when Pinches was a graduate student at the University of Notre Dame. We often discussed their content in seminar, and in the many hours we spent jogging together. Hauerwas published them in the *Asbury Theological Journal,* thinking someday he might refine and rework them, but was distracted by other projects. In the meantime, Pinches continued to think about these matters with a care not characteristic of Hauerwas's usual mode of operation. We continued to discuss them occasionally in correspondence or when together at various professional gatherings. As Pinches's own writing developed along related lines, it occurred to us to develop a book together with the commentary on Aristotle as a beginning.

Hauerwas's original Asbury lectures were extensively revised by Pinches, so much so that the present text of the first section is best thought of as jointly authored. In the second section, we wrote "The Renewal of Virtue" in close collaboration, building a common text together. The remaining two chapters in that section, on the views of Martha Nussbaum and John Casey, were essentially written by Pinches with some revision by Hauerwas. In the final section, the chapters on courage and patience were written by Hauerwas but revised extensively by Pinches, who wrote the chapter on obedience with some advice from Hauerwas. The chapter on "Hopeful Virtues" was originally written by Hauerwas, but has been so thoroughly revised by both of us we cannot remember its original shape. As with all the essays, we reworked that essay for the purpose of inclusion in this book—which is to say something important, namely, that the book is by no means a compilation of random essays. On the contrary, since we first conceived the book some years ago, we have continued to discuss and plan the kind of essays we should write to give the book coherence. We took advantage of other occasions to stimulate our writing, but we did so with this book in mind.

In sum, we gladly take joint responsibility for the book. We hope we have become better friends through writing together. Friends do not have to agree about everything, but friendship certainly requires common judgments commonly arrived at. The discussion and argument necessary for the writing of this book has been a joy for us that we hope the reader senses.

Of course the deepest bond that has made this book possible is our common faith. We are members of a people who make us more than we could ever be individually or even as friends. Indeed our friendship with one another connects us with a broader network of friends, many of whom are unknown to one or the other of us, but whose existence in and contribution to both our lives (and this book) we as heartedly acknowledge.

Part I
Theological Reflections on Aristotelian Themes

ONE

On Being Temporally Happy

1. The Problem with Happiness

We are not happy with happiness. We do not trust being happy and we tend not to trust happy people. How can anyone who is happy know what the world is like, a world riddled with suffering and tragedy?

We particularly distrust the notion of happiness when it is associated with religion. For example, when Christianity is recommended as a religion of happiness it seems to lose any critical bite. It becomes a religion promising satisfaction for the well-off such that the radical demands of the gospel are conveniently overlooked. As a religion of happiness, Christianity becomes a general form of religiosity that is so useful the question of whether it is true hardly makes any difference. Moreover, if Christianity is about happiness then what are we to make of the repeated and insistent claims arising within it that suffering is the hallmark of the Christian life?

Because of this general unhappiness with happiness and talk about it, we have worked to avoid it when thinking or writing about moral matters. Notwithstanding that and if the truth be told, no one has influenced us more than Aristotle, whose *Nicomachean Ethics* begins and ends with a seminal discussion of happiness. Moreover, accounts of the moral life that stress the importance of virtue usually involve a teleology which implies some basic notion of self-fulfillment.

So the suspicion must turn on those of us, now, who shy away from addressing happiness in our account of the moral life. This tells all the more against Christians who affirm that God is the creator and sustainer of human life, and that such a life under God is good—and can be lived well and happily.[1]

Happiness, therefore, cannot be avoided, no matter how we try. In this chapter we turn to Aristotle for help in exploring it. It is yet a common assumption that his account in many ways remains unsurpassed. By way of initial qualification, however, while we hope our

4 On Being Temporally Happy

analysis is true to Aristotle, our primary interest is not in interpreting Aristotle correctly—whatever that would mean. Rather, we are concerned to use Aristotle to help Christians (including ourselves) think about happiness.

Of particular interest to us is Aristotle's claim, as puzzling as it is suggestive, that happiness "requires completeness in virtue as well as a complete lifetime" (1100a3–5).[2] Not only is it unclear how we could ever have completeness in virtue, it is even less clear how this relates to a complete lifetime. If there is one sure implication, however, it is that *feeling* happy is no guarantor of happiness. Or, put more strongly, if you think or feel you are happy it is a good indication you are self-deceived. For according to the claim, happiness seems to come not during, but at the end of our life. We have, therefore, all the more reason to fear an untimely death, for it robs us of our one chance at happiness.

Strange as these ideas may sound, we hope to use them to show how happiness is the province of those who live in a manner such that the end of their life confirms the way they have lived. Or more directly, the happy person is one who can claim his death as his own.

Objections to such an account of happiness seem obvious, for on it, apparently, we are truly happy only when it is too late to enjoy that state. Yet we wish to show that Aristotle's account of happiness is not only plausible but important for helping us think about happiness from a Christian perspective. For unlike so many modern moralists, he rightly struggles to take notice of the contingent and temporal character of our existence. This will seem initially insignificant, until we recognize how time can appear the great enemy of morality. To use the simplest example, notice how what once appeared to us to be so clearly morally right often later seems corrupt if not positively pathetic. To combat this apparent fickleness, true morality easily appears as a battle to secure moral consistency—one unaffected by time—which in turn can secure for us a stable happiness.

Recognition of this essential timefulness requires us to deal with questions of moral change and continuity. We usually think we ought to do some changing in our lives, but it is not clear how this thought is compatible with our sense that a person of character has a stability that insures we can trust her to be who she is. As we shall see, Aristotle's analysis of the kind of person we must be in order to be truly happy manifests rather than resolves this ambiguity. But precisely because of this, we take it to be a rich resource for helping us understand what it might mean for Christians to be happy, as we hope to display.

2. Happiness as the Good and Final End

Where do you begin an analysis of the moral life? It has been the tendency of modern ethicists to begin their reflections on morality from as formal and minimal a starting point as possible. They have done so in the hope of finding a foundation for ethics that is non-arbitrary and rationally compelling—that is, one not temporally determined. Aristotle begins in quite a different manner. He simply asks what most people suppose living life well involves. What do folks think is the highest good?[3]

Well, the answer comes back, many assume morality is about being happy, and with this Aristotle is willing to begin. In Socratic fashion, he is careful not to specify what happiness is prior to an investigation, which he invites us to join. Indeed the investigation itself has a temporal character. He presents, one by one, various opinions from his contemporaries. There is among them one general agreement, that happiness is the "highest good attainable by action," although otherwise they disagree when it comes to specifics. Many say that happiness is pleasure or wealth; some identify happiness with different things at different times (thus, when sick it is health, when poor it is wealth, and so on); and some—the more cultivated who have thought about such matters—think happiness cannot consist in a list of goods but must be a good in and of itself which is the cause of all these goods (1095a20–30).

This last suggestion marks another apparent agreement about happiness, namely that it is the good upon which other lesser goods depend. As a good, or *the* good, happiness has a staying power other goods lack. Thus Aristotle maintains that the happy person

> will have the attribute of permanence and he will remain happy throughout his life. For he will always or to the highest degree both do and contemplate what is in conformity with virtue; he will bear

the vicissitudes of fortune most nobly and with perfect decorum under all circumstances, inasmuch as he is truly good and "four-square
beyond reproach." (1100b16–23)

Even more strongly he argues that

no supremely happy man can ever become miserable, for he will
never do what is hateful and base. For in our opinion, the man who
is truly good and wise will bear with dignity whatever fortune may
bring, and will always act as nobly as circumstances permit, just as
a good general makes the most strategic use of the troops at his dis-
posal, and a good shoemaker makes the best shoe he can from the
leather available, and so on with experts in all other fields. (1100b35–
1101a6)

Yet while happiness has a unique staying power capable of with-
standing certain temporal misfortunes, for Aristotle this is by no
means absolute.

Those who assert that a man is happy even on the rack and even
when great misfortunes befall him, provided he is good, are talking
nonsense, whether they know it or not. Since happiness also needs
fortune, some people regard good fortune as identical with happiness. But that is not true, for even good fortune, if excessive, can be
an obstruction; perhaps we are, in that case, no longer justified in
calling it "good fortune," for its definition is determined by its relation
to happiness. (1153b20–24)

The picture has become increasingly complex. Aristotle accepts that
happiness is the satisfaction of our desire, but he is reluctant to say
precisely which specific desires happiness satisfies. He suggests that
happiness has staying power, but is unclear about how much and
about precisely what (besides the rack) might thwart it.

The complexity of happiness is better understood if we turn to Aristotle's claim that it is the final end. As we have seen, Aristotle begins
his account of happiness assuming that it has to do with an end, that
is, the highest good attainable by action. This assumption reflects his
general view that "all knowledge and every choice is directed toward
some good" (1095a15). Every human activity has some good such
that

it is one thing in medicine, another in strategy, and another again in each of the arts. What, then, is the good of each? Is it not that for the sake of which everything else is done? That means it is health in the case of medicine, victory in the case of strategy, a house in the case of building, a different thing in the case of different arts, and in all actions and choices it is the end. For it is for the sake of the end that all else is done. Thus, if there is some one end for all that we do, this would be the good attainable by actions; if there are several ends, they will be the good attainable by action. (1097a17–24)

We cannot infer from this text that there is one single end to human life. Rather, the sense of "final" we need to see in Aristotle's point about *eudaimonia* is that it is to be pursued for itself and not for something else.

[W]e always choose happiness as an end in itself and never for the sake of something else. Honor, pleasure, intelligence, and all virtue we choose partly for themselves—for we would choose each of them even if no further advantage would accrue from them—but we also choose them partly for the sake of happiness, because we assume that it is through them that we will be happy. On the other hand, no one chooses happiness for the sake of honor, pleasure, and the like, nor as a means of anything at all. (1097b1–7)

So more than one single end, happiness is distinguished from other ends as uniquely final; unlike so many other ends, such as power or wealth, we cannot imagine it being pursued for something else.

But what follows? Are we to suppose that as our final end all else is done as a means to happiness? This would seem implausible, on more than one count. We may jog to lose weight, and we may desire to lose weight to better our health, and we may desire to better our health in order to live longer, and we may desire to live longer because . . . well, we're not sure why we desire to live longer. The reason we're not sure why we desire to live longer is not simply because we lack a clear aim in our lives that requires more time, but because "desiring to live longer" is a complex set of desires involving everything from wanting to see the Cubs win a World Series to enjoying a friendship. To describe the final end by any one term simply fails to do justice to the complex nature of our desires.

Moreover, there seems to be something wrong about the idea that any one action is always a means to something else. We may jog for our health, but it is by no means clear that our jogging is best described as a means to health. On the contrary, even as boring as jogging is, we jog because we like to jog. While we are glad that jogging can result in better health, the reason that we jog cannot be so easily transposed to this one end. Indeed, any explanation for why we jog, like any account of why we should desire to live longer, necessarily turns out to be complex.

Although it is easy to be misled by the examples, it is not part of Aristotle's analysis of the final end that there is some particular act to whose end all others are subordinate.[4] The point is rather that happiness, far from being analogous to other goods we desire, is different in the sense that it is sufficient in itself. And by self-sufficient Aristotle means that which "taken by itself makes life something desirable and deficient in nothing" (1097b15). Happiness, therefore, accompanies life; it does not arrive at its conclusion. Yet its accompaniment is final in the sense that it alone, beyond all other goods, makes life deficient in nothing. It is in this sense self-sufficient.

It is apparent why many commentators on Aristotle resist the rendering of *eudaimonia* as "happiness." For Aristotle, happiness is not an "end" that can be pursued or achieved separately from the kind of life we lead. Our life is not a means to some end called happiness. Rather *eudaimonia* is the name Aristotle gives to "the best possible life."[5] But now: what life is this? Aristotle's notion of "final" cannot be understood as a generic state produced variously by various lives, as sadness is generic, felt in similar ways while produced by an infinite variety of circumstances in our various lives. For even as self-sufficient, it accompanies life. What kind of lives? Which specific life? That is, how are we to understand the material content of happiness? To answer these questions, we must turn to Aristotle's understanding of the *ergon* (function) of human beings.

3. What *Eudaimonia* Is and How It Is Received

The ever-candid Aristotle observes that it is "perhaps a little trite" to call *eudaimonia* the highest good; a clearer account is still required.

He launches this by asking what is the proper function (*ergon*) of man (1097b21–25).

> For just as the goodness and performance of a flute player, a sculptor, or any kind of expert, and generally of anyone who fulfills some function or performs some action, are thought to reside in his proper function, so the goodness and performance of man would seem to reside in his proper function. (1097b25–30)

This appeal to "function" has been criticized as either viciously circular or as an intrusive piece of metaphysics. To some, Aristotle merely tells us what we already know: that certain excellences are essential for happiness.[6] Others suppose that the "good of man" that correlates with his function is a single thing and excludes all other goods.

As a criticism of Aristotle's use of "function," the latter interpretation misses the mark. Aristotle, as we have earlier suggested, seems quite prepared to assume that there are many different goods for humans. As to the circularity, we must recall that Aristotle is not finished with his analysis, and talk of "function" is above all a helpful way to proceed further. At the least, a thing's function is distinctive of it. A knife's function, cutting, distinguishes it from a spoon or fork; one might say it makes it a knife. Likewise, the function of a human being cannot be just biological life, a thing shared with nonhuman plants, or perception, shared with nonhuman animals. For Aristotle, human distinctiveness resides in

> an active life of the rational element. The rational element has two parts: one is rational in that it obeys the rule of reason, the other in that it possesses and conceives rational rules. Since the expression "life of the rational element" also can be used in two senses, we must make it clear that we mean a life determined by the activity, as opposed to the mere possession, of the rational element. For the activity, it seems, has a greater claim to be the function of man. The proper function of man, then, consists in an activity of the soul in conformity with a rational principle or, at least, not without it. (1098a2–8)

Here many find fault with Aristotle's concentration on "reason" as the distinguishing mark of the human. It is often pointed out that there are countless distinctively human things people do besides reason.[7] Moreover, if there is any distinctiveness to human activity *qua* human activity, it does not reside in any one "mark" but rather consists in the complex ways people have learned to coordinate the capacities and skills they share with all life. Some parts of Aristotle's text may justify these objections. Taken as a whole, however, his writing does not suggest that the many things people do are inconsequential to understanding human distinctiveness. Rather his point is simpler, namely that "rationality" is not merely one activity among others that men do, rather it pervades all we do. Indeed, it is exactly that power that allows us to coordinate the many capacities and skills we possess.[8]

Yet Aristotle's move to "function" has quite another purpose than to delineate a rationality by means of which humans can be distinguished from plants and animals. For any discussion of function implies a standard, derived from our notion of what functioning *well* amounts to.

Thus in a summary passage Aristotle says,

> On these assumptions, if we take the proper function of man to be a certain kind of life, and if this kind of life is an activity of the soul and consists in actions performed in conjunction with the rational element, and if a man of high standards is he who performs these actions well and properly, and if a function is well performed when it is performed in accordance with the excellence appropriate to it; we reach the conclusion that the good of man is an activity of the soul in conformity with the best and most complete. But we must add "in a complete life." For one swallow does not make a spring, nor does one sunny day; similarly, one day or a short time does not make a man blessed and happy. (1098a12–20)

This suggests that any notion of rationality as the function of humans cannot be detached from the whole span of a human life. Indeed, happiness for humans as beings whose lives and characters extend over time requires a rationality which will work its way into the whole set of virtues humans will need to live well over the long haul.

This idea of rationality is clearly more practical than theoretical. It might be countered from the controversial Book X, where Aristotle ties happiness to theoretical reason's activity (1177b24–26) and suggests that the practical life is happy only in a secondary sense (1178a9). Yet there his argument rings strange. For it seems based on an assumption that contemplation (the supreme activity of theoretical reason) is more similar to what the gods do. But this would be to base human happiness on something godlike rather than human, a move seemingly already closed off by the discussion of *ergon* we have just had. (Perhaps that is why Aristotle says that "happiness is *some kind* of study or contemplation" [1178b31], thereby leaving vague the kind of activity he takes as his ideal.)

Reference to Book X makes plain that it is possible to mount an attack based on parts of Aristotle's text against our interpretation thus far. We frankly acknowledge the force of this other train of thought in Aristotle.

Yet let us not think so much of a contradiction in Aristotle as a struggle. Contemplation, as an activity focused on those things which cannot be other than they are, seems to promise the kind of permanence that can make us impervious to outrageous fortune. This makes it extremely tempting to Aristotle, who searches, as we have noted, for something that will last and will be self-insuring. Yet never does Aristotle yield entirely to contemplation as temptation. As late as Book X, the conclusion of the *Nicomachean Ethics,* he yet maintains that *even* the contemplative man

> will need external well-being, since we are only human. Our nature is not self-sufficient for engaging in study: our body must be healthy and we must have food and generally be cared for. Nevertheless, if it is not possible for a man to be supremely happy without external goods, we must not think that his needs will be great and many in order to be happy; for self-sufficiency and moral action do not consist in an excess (of possessions). (1178b31–1179a22; see also, 1099a 30–32)

This repeats a refrain we encountered early on in Book I. Happiness, even construed as contemplation, cannot be had without other goods; it is not completely impervious to fortune. (To repeat, one cannot be happy on the rack.) There is, however, a difference between being impervious to fortune and being capable of bearing it nobly. Furthermore, as the quote continues, the virtuous person is capable of a happy life with far fewer external goods than one might suppose.

For she possesses a character sufficient to bear the vicissitudes of fortune nobly (1100b17–21).[9] This does not mean noble people are insensitive to misfortune or pain, but rather that they will not react as we might expect by doing what is hateful and base (1100b28–35), all of which is to say that these things have less power to control their lives than they do in the lives of others.

Here we return to a feature of happiness or of being happy which Aristotle never abandons, namely that virtuous people, happy people, are people of settled character. As such they are capable of being happy *through time,* which is the only "happiness" worth having.[10] To have a settled character means to have a history that allows one to make one's life one's own. Aristotle's comments about bad people make this plain. Unlike persons of virtue, they "do not have the element of constancy" and thus do not "remain similar even to themselves" (1159b5–8). So happiness, as lived through the virtues, involves the skills we need to be steady through the good and bad fortune of our lives so that our present (and future) is continuous with our past.

There is, then, a quite complex relation between happiness, temporality, and virtue. That we are temporal, subject not only to the storms of evil fortune but to the currents of change which sweep our characters along with them, threatens our happiness. We never outlive the threat. Yet precisely in our temporality we are given opportunity to develop virtues which set our sights on something other than our immediate comforts, making them less important, and our characters less vulnerable to change. But now, we do not gain happiness by aiming directly at it. For the activity of the virtues takes us up, not by *producing* happiness in us, not causing in us a happy temporary state, but by giving us a life comprised of the activity itself.

So it is that those who are happy cannot think of happiness as their own achievement. They must always acknowledge that they might not have been so fortunate as they have been. (They might, after all, have ended up on the rack.) Further, they have found that their virtue (if they are happy they must have virtue) isn't something they earned for themselves as one earns, say, wages for one's work. They cannot have virtue merely for the purpose of their happiness, for then they would have neither. Nor can they understand their happiness as something they have accomplished *by* being virtuous. Their happiness appears more like a gift, as Aristotle notes.

> If there is anything at all which comes to men as a gift from the gods, it is reasonable to suppose that happiness above all else is god-given; and of all things human it is the most likely to be god-given; inasmuch as it is the best. But although this subject is perhaps more appropriate to a different field of study, it is clear that happiness is one of the most divine things, even if it is not god-sent but attained through virtue and some kind of learning or training. And if it is better that happiness is acquired in this way rather than by chance, it is reasonable to assume that this is the way it is acquired. . . . To leave the greatest and noblest of things to chance would hardly be right. (1109b10–25)[11]

Perhaps now we are in a position better to understand why Aristotle insists that happiness requires completeness in virtue *and* a complete life. Happiness plausibly involves the whole duration of our life, since we know that a life can be upset, even if steered by the steady keel of virtue. Nonetheless, we cannot see happiness as some ideal final state, realizable only in the distant future. For happiness is not so much the end, but the way. Happiness comes as we acquire and live the virtues necessary to transverse the dangers and opportunities of our existence—dangers and opportunities that are intrinsic to our being essentially timeful. It is not, decidedly not, something that can be accomplished all at once, either at our life's end, middle, or beginning.

In the same vein, the question "Am I happy?" so often asked in our world (and perhaps also in Aristotle's) is frequently misguided. Requiring a sign of happiness may, in fact, demonstrate that it is not with us. For it is something we grow into, almost without recognition, like a gift so seemlessly infused into our lives that we become only vaguely aware of it in those occasional moments when we notice how disproportionately small seem the efforts of our life to its goodness. This process of growth implies, as Aristotle notes, that happiness is not possible for the young (1100a1). If, like the disciple Thomas, we persist and require a sign, it will come only as we are far enough on in life to look back over it and be glad it is ours. Of course, unless we have acquired a history, a life capable of narration, never will such retrospection be possible. Indeed, only such a life—the only sort worthy of the description "happy"—can give us the skill to look back truthfully and claim it as our own.[12]

4. On Being Happily a Christian

A fuller understanding of Aristotle's account of happiness requires a discussion of the virtues and of friendship, to which we shall shortly turn. Yet on the basis of the foregoing analysis, some tentative theological observations can be made. As we suggested at the beginning, we think Aristotle can help us understand in what way it makes sense for Christians not only to be happy, but to desire to be happy.

As we noted initially, Christians cannot overlook the profound challenge that the gospel is meant to confront, if not destroy: our presumptions about what will make us happy in this life. Christianity does not promise fulfillment but rather offers a way to live in the world truthfully and without illusion. That a people who follow a crucified God can presume life is finally about happiness seems odd at best. Christian convictions are more nearly true, not because they underwrite our assumptions about what constitutes human fulfillment, but because Christianity challenges our facile presumptions that God is primarily concerned with our happiness.

So it is that many Christian writers have suggested in critique that suffering rather than happiness is the hallmark of the Christian life. While the Christian is certainly not encouraged to seek out bad fortune, a bit of it is seen as a positive aid for learning to live as Christians. Suffering tests the genuineness of the Christian's conviction that she lives not for her own glory but for God's.

The force of this critique is enhanced when placed in a culture like our own, bent as it is on the satisfaction of every desire, no matter how shallow. In a time when the desire of many for happiness results in a desperate devaluing of all questions of significance, any challenge to the superficiality of our desires seems more likely right than wrong. By the same token, however, this devaluation of happiness for suffering is challenged by the same story of Jesus of Nazareth, whom God raised and who offers a new life that is full, victorious, *happy*.

In interacting with Aristotle we gain, perhaps, the critical tools to understand better what this happiness means. For he reminds us that happiness is not so much a goal as a way; or perhaps more accurately, "happy" names the kind of person we must be if we are to face the nature of this existence with courage and faithfulness. In this sense, Aristotle helps us appreciate why the kind of life we are called to live as Christians is better understood as a journey rather than a destination. What we are offered as Christians is not a formula for successful living but a way to go on, such that we will be able to look back happily over our lives—claiming them as ours.

Let us put it this way. One of the difficulties of taking up any significant way of life is that we never entirely understand what we are doing. Commitments are asked of us, but we are in no position to appreciate their significance when we first undertake them. Marriage is a ready example: we never know entirely what we are doing when we enter it. In twenty years, perhaps, we come closer to such an appreciation and can begin to articulate why it was good for us to marry. Ironically, it is then that we can give good reasons for our marriage, ones we could not possibly have understood at the time of our marrying. Indeed, we could not have known then what we were doing.[13]

Being a Christian is not unlike this. If we can recall a time when we became a Christian, most of us will also recall now that we did not then know what we were doing. So it steals over us that our being now Christian is more a matter of fortune than of choice. We may regret or rejoice that we are presently so identified, but there seems little we did to earn the label and, if we have been truly shaped by it, even less we can now do to shed it.

We take it that fundamental to Christian convictions is the assurance that anyone who has followed the way of life we call Christianity will be able to look back on her life and truthfully say "I would not have it otherwise." This is the one true sign of the elusive happiness Aristotle has helped us identify. It is the only true way to answer affirmatively the important question, so cheapened in our present world, "Are you happy?"[14]

The deep difference between Aristotle and Christianity is not that the one teaches us to desire happiness and the other does not. Rather, it is to be found in the differing accounts of the kind of person we must be if we are to be genuinely happy—which, of course, means what Aristotle and Christians mean by being happy is quite different. In portions of his *Nicomachean Ethics* Aristotle suggests we can be happy only if we achieve a self-sufficiency that guards us against outrageous fortune. Christians claim, on the other hand, that we are happy only to the extent that our lives are formed in reference to Jesus of Nazareth. This would strike Aristotle as the height of absurdity, not just because Jesus preached humility, but because keying happiness to a concrete historical individual makes it necessarily contingent, a piece of luck that we cannot control.

Yet to return to a point made earlier in passing, it is the Christian claim that only as we learn to have our lives determined by the God we discover in Jesus of Nazareth can we claim not only our lives but also our deaths as our own. It is by this resource that we can stand against a world whose opposing power lies in the false promise that we are capable of giving our own lives significance; of insuring their meaning and our happiness. So it is also a Christian claim, one not of this world, that our death, even if untimely, cannot be meaningless, for God has insured our life and death through the cross and the resurrection of Christ, yet present in the world in the church. Somewhat unwittingly, in our lives we were made members of this body, and we continue as such, even after our deaths.

TWO

The Virtues of Happiness

1. Why Happiness Requires the Virtues

Happiness in Aristotle is elusive. Yet we have meant to imply that this is not a fault; indeed, Aristotle does well to resist the overly simple equations to which we are all tempted in our haste to describe it. These are not just the equations Aristotle considers and dismisses early in Book I—that happiness is pleasure or honor or wealth—but those as well which identify happiness in relation to a "virtuous life" or perhaps the feeling we get while being virtuous or the position we reach at the end of a long life of virtue.

This is not to say, however, that happiness has nothing to do with virtue. On the contrary, happiness and virtue have everything to do with one another. But the relation is not simple, and the connection cannot be hurried. Nor can the description of either one be simple or hurried, for, as we shall see, neither is describable apart from the other.

So far our chief concern has been to reflect within our interactions with Aristotle's text the crucial importance of the temporal character of our lives. Yet even this emphasis upon temporality is easy to misconstrue. As we are using it, temporality is neither transitoriness nor terminality. The twin errors of associating happiness either with a transitory emotional state that is the reverse of sadness,[1] or with a terminus reached by a human life that has been both virtuous and fortunate, illustrate how different is the temporality we seek from these apparent cousins.

The intrinsic connection between the virtues and the happy life we find in Aristotle bears this out. For him, the virtues are not so much the means to happiness, as they are its form. It follows, as we have stated, that neither can be conceived independently of the other; consequently any discussion of happiness (such as the sort we have just come through) *must* lead to a discussion of the virtues.

Perhaps the framework of understanding from which we are approaching Aristotle's ethics can be better displayed by considering the difference between going on a trip and undertaking a journey. When we go on a trip, we know well where we are going, roughly how long it will take us to get there, what preparations to make, and so on. When we undertake a journey, we often have only a hazy idea of where we are going, how long it will take, or how to prepare. For either of the authors, going to India would be a journey, whereas it would be a trip back to South Bend, Indiana, where we both once lived. (This is not to say, however, that journeys must be made abroad. One of us makes regular trips to Texas, but for the other traveling the same road might well turn out to be a genuine journey.)

A contemporary metaphorical use of the word *trip* illustrates just how it is distinguished from a journey. We say of some experience that it was a real "trip," which means it was different, interesting, and a bit unusual. But as a "trip" it leaves no lasting impression and we know clearly when it is over. Thus anyone who suggests that "life is a trip" is making a claim, rather a significant one, that life is fun but nothing to be taken too seriously. We think it better, of course, to portray life as a journey; and we are suggesting that that is the way to view Aristotle's account of a life or a life span. Whatever it is, a journey is not frivolous or transitory; it is not a "trip." It is, on the other hand, essentially temporal, for it not only implies movement from place to place—which takes time—but also *development* over time of the one who journeys. (This is why the journeyer cannot know before he begins precisely where he means to end up, for he rightly expects that he will be changed by his journey to redefine its destination.)

Much of recent moral philosophy, mirroring well the working moral presumptions of our culture, has portrayed the moral life more as a series of trips than as a journey.[2] A trip back to Texas (for one of us) is always undertaken for some specific need or desire which arises occasionally in the course of life: a need to visit family, perhaps, or a desire to taste real, honest-to-god Tex-Mex food once again. Without the specific need or desire, the trip would be senseless; and so it can be judged a success or failure, and it can be pronounced over, entirely on the basis of whether or not the mission had been accomplished, the persons seen, or the lack filled. In modern philosophy, moral re-

flection is similarly done with a specific end in view, namely the solution of some problem or "moral dilemma" which has (quite incon-
veniently) interrupted our normal lives. Mind you, a given problem
(like abortion) may not be so easily solved, and its investigation may
lead to further surprises and detours, like construction on I-40. But
finding the solution is the point of the trip back to principles in the
ever-dependable motorcar of reason.

One of the deep problems, of course, with this trip-like view of the
moral life is that it simply overlooks the fact that it is not by decisions
alone that moral men live. Indeed, our decisions make sense, and the
need for them arises only within lives that already have taken a moral
form. What dilemmas we have will differ greatly depending upon
who we are. In fact, as Aristotle implies, having too many dilemmas
itself may demonstrate corruption, for one's soul can be torn in too
many ways.[3] Indeed, the good person may well find herself having to
decide with progressive infrequency, for she knows the good and does
it joyfully, with little deliberation. This is not because she is un-
schooled in its art. To the contrary, it is because she has learned over
time and partly by the practice of deliberation to recognize readily
what should be done: it has become part of her.

Modern moral philosophy is not only unable and uninterested in
giving an account of such a person, it also tends to exclude her actions
from what is moral precisely because those actions cannot be described in characteristic trip-like fashion. Since the virtues take this
form (that is, they are states of character by which one is formed to
know what is the good and to do it), not surprisingly they have received little attention in what is still the regnant mode of moral analysis. One might say that the virtues are the dispositions one acquires
on the journey that is the moral life, thus making the trips *unnecessary,*
or at least insuring that the trips undertaken by the virtuous person
will not be those of the novice, or even those of the general populus.[4]

But let us turn specifically to the virtues in Aristotle with these
metaphors in the background. In short, Aristotle's means of describing and navigating the journey to the destination of happiness (a destination understood as of a journey and not as of a trip) is the virtues.
They are for him a set of excellences by which we become capable of
making our way; they are those capacities that provide a stability of

the self such that happiness can accompany our lives. This happiness, as we have stressed, is not the *result* of our virtuous activities but is to be found within their practice, as done by the person of virtue.

While entirely indispensable to the journey, the virtues are not to be compared to the vehicle we must drive if we hope to get back to Texas, nor even the driving skill we must at sometime have acquired if we are successfully to complete the trip. For a trip one needs instruments and skills. Only a journey requires virtues. Indeed, the virtues are what they are because we do not know precisely where we are going. We do not know where we are going because the very virtues necessary to undertake the journey are crucial to its outcome—that is, they are intrinsic to the end. This is why we can only know where we have gone and what we have become retrospectively. At the same time (and as Aristotle saw, even if sometimes only dimly), we cannot know what kind of happiness we desire until we have acquired the virtues.

2. The Magnanimous Man and How to Become One

It should not be ignored that, unlike his predecessor Plato, Aristotle did not try to establish a set of central virtues corresponding to different aspects of the soul. We notice this as we read Aristotle's *Ethics*, for his relatively chaotic catalogue of one and the other virtue sometimes makes us long for Plato's more orderly account of courage, temperance, justice, and wisdom. Granted, we learn from Aristotle about each of the four so-called cardinal virtues, but they are not labeled as cardinal and his list of virtues includes not just these but also generosity, magnificence, high-mindedness, a nameless virtue between ambition and lack of ambition, gentleness, truthfulness, wittiness, friendship, and a quasi-virtue called shame. While it is plain that some virtues such as justice or courage are more important than others, Aristotle makes no explicit attempt to delineate a hierarchy of or ascribe priorities to the virtues.

This unsystematic treatment might be explained in term of Aristotle's much publicized doctrine of the mean. The various virtues he treats might be thought to serve principally as illustrations of how the mean works as it picks out just the right spot between the extremes. Yet this interpretation can be sustained only so long as some of what

Aristotle actually says about the mean is disregarded, and it is imagined (fantastically, given the characteristic incisiveness of his analysis otherwise) that he failed to notice how the mean by itself is actually quite inadequate in picking out the virtues. This is made plain enough by Aristotle's own qualification in his oft-quoted definition of virtue lying in a mean which is "relative to us" and "determined by that principle by which the man of practical wisdom would determine it" (1006a37).

In fact, the mean is no specific formula for delineating the virtues, and Aristotle does not use it as such. (If we thought he did, or meant to, we could not but become suspicious, thinking he actually abused it to justify his own predetermined and quite arbitrary choice of virtues.) Instead the doctrine of the mean serves to introduce us to the important ideas that virtues are not extremes, that there are extremes on *both* sides of a virtue which we must avoid, and that virtues govern appetites which must be felt "at the right times, with reference to the right people, with the right motive, and in the right way, which is both intermediate and best" (1106a12, Ross).

Extensive scholarly concentration upon the mean may have drawn attention away from the quite interesting (if also somewhat embarrassing) descriptions given by Aristotle of the sort of person who embodies the various virtues he recommends. For example, a generous man is characterized by giving to the right people, not by receiving from the right sources. He is especially to be praised, since excellence consists more in doing good than in having good done to one, in performing noble actions rather than in not performing base ones (1120a10–15). So a person who is good is "not one to accept good turns lightly" (1120a35). This note is held in Aristotle's praise of the high-minded man, who is worthy of honor because of his excellence and good fortune. He is the kind of person who will do good but is "ashamed to accept a good turn, because the former marks a man as superior, the latter as inferior" (1124b8–10); he is reluctant to ask for any favor but himself readily offers aid.

Aristotle's high-minded man does not appeal to our modern prejudices. We are even tempted to make fun when Aristotle tells us this man will have a slow gait, "a deep voice, and a deliberate way of speaking. For a man who takes few things seriously is unlikely to be in a hurry, and a person who regards nothing as great is not one to be excitable. But a shrill voice and a swift gait are due to hurry and excitement" (1125a12–16). We want to ask: Is this someone we would like to know?

But our judgments are premature if we have not tried to appreciate the problem Aristotle is addressing as he sketches for us this portrait of the high-minded (or magnanimous) man. For Aristotle the life of virtue to some degree must be characterized by a certain kind of sufficiency, what we might call integrity or constancy.[5] Thus, in a passage more likely to appeal to our sensibilities, Aristotle says that the high-minded man

> is not a gossip, for he will talk neither about himself nor about others, since he is not interested in hearing himself praised or others run down. Nor again is he given to praise; and for the same reason he does not speak evil of others, not even of his enemies, except to scorn them. When he encounters misfortunes that are unavoidable or insignificant, he will not lament and ask for help. That kind of attitude belongs to someone who takes such matters seriously. He is a person who will rather possess beautiful and profitless objects than objects which are profitable and useful, for they mark him more as self-sufficient. (1125a5012)

The magnanimous man is slow of gait and voice because he recognizes and lives the truth that the life of virtue demands a steadfastness of character that steels us against so many frivolous distractions. To return to our metaphor, the magnanimous man is on a journey and therefore knows he must be steadfast, since he will often be unsure where he is or where he is heading. This demands from him concentration and determination, which in turn demand that he have a center that is not easily destroyed by the good or evil fortune that he is bound to meet along the way.[6]

This point is deepened when we consider that the purpose of journey that the person of virtue undertakes is not merely to get him from here to there, not just to arrive—that would be a trip—but it is the journeying itself which is crucial. In this respect Aristotle's contrast between the arts and the virtues is illuminating. In the arts, excellence lies in the results themselves (1105a22); but in matters of virtue an act is not just or temperate unless the agent has certain characteristics as he performs it: "first of all, he must know what he is doing;

secondly, he must choose to act the way he does, and he must choose it for its own sake; and in the third place, the act must spring from a firm and unchangeable character" (1105a26–35). Or as he continues, "The just and self-controlled man is not he who performs these acts, but he who also performs them in the way just and self-controlled men do" (1105b7–9).

No doubt, knowing a canvas was painted by Van Gogh encourages us to think more highly of it. But few would maintain that there are no outward differences between Van Gogh's painting—or perhaps we should say a painting that happens to be by Van Gogh—and some other painting similar in many respects, but painted by an inferior artist. That is, in art masters are masters because they produce superior products. And their "products" are better than others' "products" not solely because they were painted (or sculpted, or composed) by a master, nor because he painted them with a certain characteristic flair, but because there is something in each, indeed many things, that is not in the others.

In important ways this is disanalogous to the relation between virtuous persons and virtuous acts. Mind you, "masters in virtue" are identified as such on the basis of their acts. Indeed, it is precisely because of their close association with their acts that we must understand masters in virtue somewhat differently than those in art. The singular fact that an act is done by a virtuous person causes us to regard it differently than some other act that resembles it in other respects but is done by another person, such as a novice in virtue. For an act cannot be considered independently from an actor (as a painting might be—or at least more nearly independently). In a related way, we can see how the life of virtue, unlike art, is not undertaken in order to produce certain character-independent virtuous acts (as if there were such things) but rather to become, as on a journey, the sort of person who performs virtuous acts as the virtuous person performs them.[7]

These points should help us interpret the following intriguing remark from Aristotle:

People may perform just acts without actually being just men, as in the case of people who do what has been laid down by the laws but do so either involuntarily or through ignorance or for an ulterior motive, and not for the sake of performing just acts. . . . [Such persons are not just men] despite the fact that they act the way they should, and perform all the actions which a morally good man ought to perform. (1144a12–16)

The complexity of the relationship between act and character creates certain difficulties. For example, it appears to suggest that we cannot know a virtuous person by any one of her acts. We recall that a (genuinely) virtuous act must proceed from a settled character, but were we to observe only one act of a man we could not know that he did it from such a character. Outwardly, in other words, his act may have been identical to some other act performed by someone with a settled character. But he may not have such character—i.e., he is performing a just act without actually being just. We cannot know until we know him.

By itself this may not be so curious; indeed, we submit it seems quite true. Yet suppose we couple it with what Aristotle otherwise tells us about acquiring virtue. We know he thinks this is done by the repeated performance of virtuous acts. But (and here's the difficulty) if we need to know characters to know acts, we shall need skill or discernment in recognizing those who are virtuous so that we can know which acts to duplicate in our training in virtue. Yet if we are only beginning on the road to virtue, how can we do this with any confidence? Discovering how to act and who to follow is a very difficult thing. We are tempted to suggest, even, that one needs the virtues to recognize them. Indeed, Aristotle sees this implication clearly enough when he puts the following objection to his own account: "Now someone may say that all men aim at the apparent good, but have no control over the appearance, *but the end appears to each man in a form answering to his character*" (1114a28, emphasis added). This is corroborated by the very strong emphasis Aristotle has placed on early moral formation when, we may suppose, children are given their first training about whom to follow; he tells us, in fact, that this early training "makes a very great difference, or rather *all* the difference" (1103b25).

It is not surprising, then, that in his response to this quite forceful objection Aristotle replies quite tentatively that we must say that each man is "somehow" responsible for his character (1114a29), for we are "*somehow* part causers of our states of character" (1114b22, emphasis added). One might read this as hopelessly circular. Yet we take the response to be interesting. Its gist is, simply, that we cannot abide the idea that we are not in some way responsible for our characters, even if we cannot say how. That is, if we affirmed that we were not responsible, we would have to give up talking about responsibility altogether. And no one, surely, wants to do that.

At this crucial juncture Aristotle has returned to the shared assumptions with which he began: to common opinion, to what we as a people are ready to consider as an adequate answer. "We" cannot accept the view that character is entirely determined as a natural gift, with us from birth, for this would wreak havoc otherwise with what "we" think: that there is such a thing as human moral responsibility for character, that good character can be acquired, and so on.

One wonders whether we modern people can count ourselves among the "we" to whom Aristotle appeals. The denial of human moral responsibility is surely more common now than (we may suppose) among Aristotle's contemporaries—or at least among those to whom the *Ethics* was likely written. For those who champion such a denial, this argument simply will not work.

We wish to make plain, however, that this is not a *mistake* on Aristotle's part. His subtle treatment of the complex relation between acquiring the virtues and virtuous acts and between virtuous acts and virtuous characters really demands a return to a "we" who share certain judgments about the moral life. This allows us to highlight the significance, once again, of the magnanimous man in Aristotle's treatment. We begin and end with a *person* whom "we" presume is virtuous. This is the man with the deep voice and the slow gait—we all know the fellow. What are his virtues? How does he act? What can we do to be more like him? These questions fan out through the *Ethics*, giving it life, subtlety, and context.

Aristotle could not anticipate that we (Pinches, Hauerwas, and many of their contemporaries) would not find his magnanimous man so attractive. But of course he should not have, for he is not writing to us; we are not his friends. Indeed, this is a feature of Aristotle's work we find all the more admirable. It is written, in a way, to his friends. (We must remember that it is the first of a two part work which culminates in the *Politics*. And friendship, as he says, is that which "holds states together" [1155a23].)

As such it should not surprise us that friendship receives such careful and extended treatment in the *Nicomachean Ethics*. This treatment is worth investigating—as we shall do in the next and final part of this extended discussion—not only for its own sake but also because it reveals how Aristotle is both eminently useful for Christians and how he cannot be used. At the least, friendship's prominence in the *Ethics*—something for which Aristotle makes no apologies; indeed, he presumes friendship must be treated at length in any serious discussion of ethics—reminds us that, unlike so many modern theorists of ethics, Aristotle does not suppose we are isolated beings who must forge from the complexities of our experience one life of virtue which is ours and ours alone. The discovery and doing of virtue is something we do together with others. Following him, we wonder if we can be virtuous only to the extent we are capable of being a friend. Or even more strongly, it may be that without friendship we are incapable of having the character necessary for acquiring virtue.

3. The Life of Christians and the Life of Virtue

But what can we say at present about how the insights concerning virtue we have so far gleaned from Aristotle might be regarded by Christians? With regard to the virtues we Christians are compelled to respond in a manner somewhat different from our response regarding happiness. While it was possible, even appropriate, to argue that Christians should care far less about happiness than pagans such as Aristotle, this will not do with virtue. Christians, we all suppose, can be no less courageous, no less just, no less temperate, no less wise or prudent than anyone else.

Yet we must be cautious. For we cannot assume that the "virtues" that help us live well are straightforward and clear. We cannot assume, that is, that we know plainly what they are. Indeed, Aristotle helps us see this point well; it is one of the principal ways in which his account of the virtues can be instructive to Christians. We cannot presume that all accounts of the virtues will come to the same thing, for the "we" who are giving the account make all the difference. To illustrate, perhaps the presumption of responsibility for our character which Aristotle assumes his audience shares is not an appropriate Christian presumption. Or even if it is, perhaps Christians cannot understand it in just the same way that Aristotle assumed his contemporaries would understand it. Maybe, indeed surely, they will not understand pride as a virtue, talking instead about humility or obedience. And if Christians agree that justice is a virtue, maybe "justice" for them will be quite different from the "justice" discussed in Aristotle.[8]

It is far from obvious to us, in other words, that those Christian theologians (such as Augustine) who have argued so adamantly that pagan virtue is nothing less than sin and is in need of a radical transformation by love before it can be of any use to Christians are so far off track. (In this regard, we wish to distance our own from other "Christian" accounts of virtue which assume that any coherent discussion of virtue must constantly be checked for correctness against what the Greeks believed.) Nor is it obvious that those theologians are patently wrong who object not only to the content of virtue talk originating with Aristotle and his culture but also to its form. For example, Luther—to choose the great pioneer of what became a Protestant tendency—is concerned to deny all attempts to establish our moral standing before the mighty God.[9] If the virtues appear as our own achievements, which might assure our righteousness, their validity must be denied. To put the point directly (as Luther might): virtue is a category Catholics use, but this only demonstrates how strong and resilient is their belief in works righteousness.

Of course we ourselves do not offer this critique, for we are among those who believe the language of virtue is of great use in displaying the Christian understanding of the moral life. Yet we wish to be extremely cautious in appropriating pagan virtues from their pagan context—particularly whole patterns of virtue such as the "cardinal virtues"—and fitting them within Christianity. (This is not to say that it cannot be done, if done warily and critically, as we attempt in subsequent chapters, particularly chapter 6.) But here again we find Aristotle more of a help than a hindrance, not the least because his account of particular virtues is so casually undertaken (in form, not content) in comparison with the more systematic work in Plato, or later, Cicero. Consequently, it is not difficult for the reader of the *Ethics* to imagine a collection of moral virtues other than those treated in Books III–V. Furthermore, as we have noted, since no easy account of the relation between the actions of the virtuous man and the virtuous man himself is offered, how we become virtuous is all the more mysterious in Aristotle. We seem powerless in ourselves even to pick out who to follow in becoming virtuous, for it seems we need the virtues to do so, and these are precisely what we lack.

Both these features of Aristotle's account—his unsystematic treatment of the virtues and the mystery surrounding how we discover and acquire the virtues—fit well, we think, with his frequent and unembarrassed reliance upon the common judgments of his contemporaries regarding happiness as our highest good or about our ultimate responsibility for our character. If there is a response imbedded in Aristotle's account to our query about who the virtuous person is, it is, simply, that if someone does not know then he cannot be one of *us*, for *we* know who our paragons of virtue are, just as we know that any view that denies responsibility for our character simply cannot do.

But now: we think that the implications of these views are surprisingly appropriate for Christians. Aristotle has undercut the idea that either virtuous acts or the virtues themselves can stand on their own apart from their display in a particular life. Which is why we think Aristotle's magnanimous man with his deep voice and slow gait needs to occupy more space than is often given it for interpreting Aristotle. As we have suggested, Aristotle conceives of the moral life as a journey which will not be successful unless undertaken with the considered care and caution of which only this man is capable. Rather than skills describable in themselves and therefore transferable from one trip to the next, depending on where we happen to wish to go, the virtues are simply those capacities that this man has.

This helps Christians in a backward sort of way. For it is far easier to suppose that Jesus was the fullest instantiation the world has ever seen of the four cardinal virtues than that he was *the* magnanimous man. (A first-century, itinerant, prophetic Jew with a low voice and slow gait?) And as we see it, imagining Jesus as the person of the highest virtue has been one of the most seductive temptations for Christian thinkers since the fourth century.

We suggest that reading Aristotle in this way makes it easier for Christians to remember that the moral life does not derive from some general conception of the good, nor even from an analysis of those skills or excellences that allegedly allow human nature to flourish. Rather, the moral life of Christians is determined by their allegiance to a historical person they believe is the decisive form of God's kingdom. After all, Jesus did not say if you are to be a follower of his you must develop those virtues that will make you a morally impressive person. Rather he said, "Come and follow me." Moreover, it seems that such a following may require nothing less than that we be willing to die for his sake.[10] The person of virtue may die rather than compromise his integrity, but here we are asked to die not for our own moral ideals but for the sake of another person.

Another way of making these points is to call attention to what one might call the emptiness at the heart of Aristotle's vision. As MacIntyre has suggested, it was no accident that Aristotle was seen by medieval thinkers to be such a fruitful source for attempts to provide a systematic presentation of the Christian life. They could supply what Aristotle's account of virtue lacked—namely, a narrative in which the development of virtues made sense. For the medieval vision, schooled as it was on the Bible, was "historical in a way that Aristotle's could not be. It situates our aiming at the good not just in specific contexts—Aristotle situates that aiming within the *polis*—but in contexts which themselves have a history. To move towards the good is to move in time and that movement may itself involve new understandings of what it is to move towards the good."[11]

With our emphasis upon journey as the governing motif for what we take to be the best of Aristotle's insights about the moral life, we have meant to suggest that his account begs for a narrative display. Mind you, the narrative in which Aristotle's list of the virtues might find a home is not the Christian narrative, just as the magnanimous man is not Jesus. Indeed, Christians must be prepared not only to see pagan virtues transformed, they must expect to see many deleted and others added, such as hope, obedience, or patience. But the difference between the narrative Christians tell and that into which Aristotle's virtues might be fit, or perhaps better put, the difference between the journey Christians are on (and therefore the virtues they believe indispensable to guide them along the way) and that which Aristotle conceives as the journey of the moral life, must be appreciated if the power and significance of either journey and either set of virtues is to be understood. The burden of our next chapter, and indeed of much of this book, is to begin to show more precisely this difference.

THREE

Companions on the Way:
The Necessity of Friendship

1. In the Beginning Was Friendship

We began by suggesting that happiness, the life of virtue, and friendship are tightly interwoven. We cannot understand the kind of happiness we should desire without understanding the life of virtue. But the life of virtue properly understood requires an account of friendship, for true virtue is not something we have or do alone.[1] Returning once again to our metaphor of the moral life as a journey, it is obvious, as Aristotle himself notes, that a journey is better undertaken with companions than alone. At the very least we need others to sustain us along the way. But further, and more strongly, traveling with others is crucial not only to relieve our boredom or to supply a hand to hold in dark and narrow places, but as well, the journey requires that we ourselves be transformed, and this cannot occur without friends.

We have used the metaphor of a journey throughout these reflections on Aristotle to convey a sense of the temporal character of our existence. We believe that any account of the moral life is inadequate if it ignores this essential feature. In Aristotle we hear it as a continual refrain, not so much that our temporality is constantly reiterated, but that Aristotle is fundamentally concerned with sustaining goodness. He recognizes well that it is time that tests our momentary flights of good intention, that not only cruel fortune but we ourselves are capable of turning us from the way, of losing our bearing as we are overwhelmed by change and flux. Constancy, a slow gait, a measured voice arising from a person of settled character whose sight is not easily turned from virtue . . . these things are required if we are to make our way in time, whose many changes, both sudden and gradual, we can never predict.

This description suggests something of a heroic quest, one in which a valiant individual conquers time by steering a steady course through

31

its hazards, as Odysseus weathered the many and varied tricks of Poseidon to come alone, finally, to the shores of Ithaca. As we shall argue, this heroic vision is never entirely expunged from Aristotle's account, for it reappears at its edges, when happiness fails. Yet his journey toward happiness, which is the moral life, cannot be understood as that of a lonely hero. Not surprisingly, his account of friendship does as much as any other section of the *Ethics* to insure that this misreading does not gain a hold.

Were we enthusiastic about the heroic picture of the moral life, our spirits could not but be dampened by the opening sentences of Book VIII:

> Continuing in a sequence, the next subject which we shall have to discuss is friendship. For it is some sort of excellence or virtue, or involves virtue, and it is, moreover, most indispensable for life. No one would choose to live without friends, even if he had all other goods. Rich men and those who hold office and power are, above all others, regarded as requiring friends. For what good would their prosperity do them if it did not provide them with the opportunity for good works? And the best works done and those which deserve the highest praise are those that are done to one's friends. (1155a1–10)

One might imagine that the challenge of climbing Half Dome in Yosemite National Park, a heroic feat in its own right, is itself sufficient to sustain the activity of climbing it. One might climb it with friends, but one does not climb it *for the sake of* one's friends. Only a fool would not see that there are other far easier and safer ways to impress one's friends. Similarly, it can hardly be said of Half Dome, as Aristotle here says of life, that no one would choose to climb it without friends.

Of course life takes a good deal longer than climbing Half Dome, a fact which relates to our earlier mention of the essentially temporal character of our existence. But that is only part of the point here. For Aristotle supposes that goods such as property or power become goods only as they can be shared. The language, interestingly, is reminiscent of what was said earlier about happiness, which is a self-sufficient end in the sense that other things are desired for it, and it is desired for nothing else but itself. If someone wishes to say that he climbs Half Dome for the sake of happiness, or for some other end, we do not wish to quarrel. Our point is rather that sharing with others seems an intrinsic part of the self-sufficient end of happiness; and this distinguishes it from other (more heroic) ends which might also appear self-sufficient. The life of virtue by its nature requires the presence and participation of others; climbing Half Dome does not. Happiness is worthy of pursuit for itself, but it cannot be pursued alone: it requires others, specifically our friends.

Now happiness, we recall, is for Aristotle fundamentally an activity, not a feeling or condition. This point he repeats in Book IX, bending it as well in the direction of friendship.

> We stated at the beginning that happiness is some kind of activity, and activity clearly is something that comes into being and not something we can take for granted like a piece of property. From the propositions: (1) being happy consists in liking and in being active, and as we stated at the beginning, the activity of a good man is in itself good and pleasant; (2) what is our own is a pleasant thing to us; (3) we are better able to observe our neighbors than ourselves, and their actions better than our own; and (4) the actions of persons who have a high moral standard are pleasant to those good men who are their friends, in that they possess both qualities which are pleasant by nature (i.e., they are good and they are their own); it follows that a supremely happy man will need friends of this kind. His moral purpose or choice is to observe actions which are good and which are his own, and such are the actions of a good man who is his friend. (1169b28–1170a3)

This quotation introduces yet another feature of the connection between friendship and happiness, or rather two features that are connected in significant ways. For like all demanding and worthwhile human activities, the activity of happiness requires learning and practice, as Aristotle has frequently pointed out. We learn virtue, which is necessary for happiness, not alone but in communities of friends. Furthermore, the activity that is happiness is a pleasant thing not only to do but to watch, not just because we can learn from watching, but because it is good in itself. We find, thinks Aristotle, that we watch others better than ourselves. It is like watching ourselves, only better, for we see the activity that is ours—both the friend's and our own—all the more clearly.

There are many reasons, then, that Aristotle gives to convince us that friendship is absolutely vital to happiness, almost too many. The belief that friendship is essential to happiness is an easy one to hold. At the very least, we have trouble quarreling with Aristotle's first assertion, that no one would choose to live without friends. But it is important to look beyond the reasons why friendship is necessary to happiness to see how friendship's inclusion in our understanding of happiness and of virtue reshapes the meaning of both. Further, it is crucial to ask what sort of friendship we have and with whom before proceeding to a more material account of just what happiness is sought and what virtues are necessary to sustain the search. As we shall see, Christian accounts of this friendship will diverge at certain crucial points from Aristotle's and so Christians find themselves in a different sort of life than that which Aristotle might have called a happy life. Likewise Christians walk on a different sort of path as they journey with their friends toward a destination they have only glimpsed but for which they together sustain the strongest hope: namely, the kingdom of God.

2. Aristotle on Friendship

We need, then, to comb a bit more carefully through Aristotle's account of friendship as it is given in Books VIII and IX of the *Nicomachean Ethics.* As many have pointed out, it is devoted in significant portion to distinguishing three kinds of friendship: the friendships of usefulness, pleasure, and virtue. In each

> the affection can be reciprocated so that the partner is aware of it, and the partners wish for each other's good in terms of the motive on which their affection is based. Now when the motive of the affection is usefulness, the partners do not feel affection for one another per-se but in terms of the good accruing to each from the other. The same is also true of those whose friendship is based on pleasure: we love witty people, not for what they are, but for the pleasure they give us. The friend is loved not because he is a friend, but because he is useful or pleasant. Thus, these two kinds are friendship only incidentally, since the object of affection is not loved for being the kind of person he is, but for providing some good or pleasure. Conse-

quently, such friendships are easily dissolved when the partners do not remain unchanged: the affection ceases as soon as one partner is no longer pleasant or useful to the other. (1156a9–20)

Useful friendships, as Aristotle goes on to say, are the shortest lived, for "the useful is not permanent but is always changing." Further, the friendship of young people seems specifically aimed at pleasure, which is why "they quickly become friends and so quickly cease to be so; their friendship changes with the object that is found pleasant, and such pleasure alters quickly" (Ross, 1156b1). Unlike these, friendship based on virtue or

> perfect friendship is the friendship of men who are good and alike in virtue; for these wish well alike to each other *qua* good, and they are good in themselves. Now those who wish well to their friends for their sake are most truly friends for they do this by reason of their own nature and not incidentally; and therefore their friendship lasts as long as they are good—and goodness is an enduring thing. (1156b4–12)

Now a good bit has been made of the difference in the object of each of the three types of friendship, the first two having a goal beyond the friend to which the friendship contributes, at least for a time. No doubt this is an important way to distinguish true friendship from these others which are related to it only by analogy. Perfect friendship wishes good to the friend for the sake of the friend. But it is also interesting, and less frequently noted, that the crucial distinguishing feature between the types of friendships, a feature which is as much empirical as it is intentional, is that perfect friendship lasts.

This point is expanded when we consider Aristotle's contention that "for the sake of pleasure or utility, even bad men can be friends of each other, or good men of bad," but they cannot share perfect friendship (Ross, 1157a18). Later on in the text he offers this explanation.

> Friendship is equality and likeness, and especially the likeness of those who are similar in virtue. Because they are steadfast in themselves, they are also steadfast toward one another; they neither request nor render any service that is base. On the contrary, one might even say that they prevent base services; for what characterizes good

men is that they neither go wrong themselves nor let their friends do
so. Bad people, on the other hand, do not have the element of constancy, for they do not remain similar even to themselves. (1159b4–12)

Bad people lack the constancy of character that is necessary for
friendships of character. Furthermore, as Aristotle notes, within true
friendship constancy is increased, for good people help keep each
other good.

The significance of this point for our own account is considerable.
For here Aristotle seems prepared to think of constancy as a communal virtue. It is not something one of us possesses alone, but something we share and into which we help each other grow. As such,
constancy taken as an integral part of the life of virtue excludes the
popular but mistaken idea that the virtuous person is self-sufficient,
entirely capable of sustaining his or her own happiness alone.[2]

The point also saves Aristotle's account of friendship from at least
two fairly substantial objections. The first is that character friendship
is so demanding that it cannot be achieved in this life, for it presumes perfect virtue, which no one possesses. If this is true, Aristotle's
ethics becomes a theoretical abstraction, and can be dismissed as
such.

Now Aristotle is quite ready to concede that character friendship is
fairly uncommon. As he says,

> To be friends with many people, in the sense of perfect friendship, is
> impossible, just as it is impossible to be in love with many at the same
> time. . . . It does not easily happen that one man finds many people
> very pleasing at the same time, nor perhaps does it easily happen that
> there are many people who are good. Also, one must have some ex-
> perience of the other person and have come to be familiar with him,
> and that is the hardest thing of all. (1158a10–16)

So it is that friendships of usefulness and pleasure are far more common, for "many are pleasant and useful, and these services take little
time" (Ross, 1158a18).

But true friendship's rarity does not imply its impossibility. Indeed,
when one considers the point just made, namely that friends grow
together in friendship and in the good, then perfect friendship be-

comes imaginable as what can and might grow from the far more common imperfect friendship, subdivided as of pleasure and of utility.

Similarly, a response suggests itself to a second substantial objection, i.e., that Aristotle's account of friendship rules out friendship among unequals because he maintains that "friendship is equality and likeness." For since friendship, even perfect friendship, *grows*, it becomes possible that unequals will be drawn by their friendship to the equality that is (indeed) necessary in complete friendship. That is to say, while equality is eventually required in perfect friendship, it is not necessary from the start, for both the friendship and the friends will grow into it over time.

To illustrate, Aristotle notes that while in most romantic relationships (which are essentially friendships of pleasure) friendship fades when the bloom of youth passes, in some others the lovers remain "constant, if familiarity has led them to love each other's characters, these being alike" (Ross, 1157a17). Consequently, Aristotle, who is not noted for holding a liberated view of women, must in principle admit that it is possible for a man and a woman, a husband and wife, perhaps, who begin for him as unequals, to come to share something closely resembling perfect friendship.[3]

Connected as they are in the point that friendship, even perfect friendship, is something that grows as do the friends within it, these responses allow us to see that the distinction between the three kinds of friendship is less marked than one might at first suppose. For while friendships of pleasure and utility are not perfect friendships, and while most will break off after a short time, there is no *a priori* reason why they cannot develop into perfect friendship, developing those within them into people capable of true friendship in the process.

This helps us to understand the connection Aristotle draws so frequently between friendship and the political. It is not that politics determines and protects friendship, as we might suppose a government protects us from unfriendly invaders who would disrupt our backyard social gatherings. Rather, for Aristotle friendship determines the political insofar as it is the purpose of good politics to make the life of virtue possible. This is why the failure of the political represents a failure in political friendship, the only recourse after the failure being a narrower friendship that begins the pursuit of virtue over again, at a much reduced level. Sadly, Aristotle casts his eye around at the city-states of his own time, observing that in most of them

> each man lives as he pleases, dealing out law to his children and his wife as the Cyclopes do. Now the best thing would be to make the correct care of these matters a common concern. But if the community neglects them, it would seem to be incumbent upon every man to help his children and friends attain virtue. This he will be capable of doing, or at least intend to do. (1180a25–31)[4]

Thus friendship becomes for Aristotle the ground of a true polity. Further, if a state fails to achieve this polity, the only available resource of virtue is, again, the association among friends who are held together even in its lack.

Virtue, then, begins and ends in friendship. For Aristotle, our task is not first to become virtuous, thus establishing the kind of equality necessary for friendship, and then to seek out friends. Rather, friendship itself is an activity by which we acquire the kind of steadfastness necessary for our being true friends. True friendship is, therefore, not some ideal that actual friendships never achieve, but rather it is a growing relation which, as it increases, makes possible our becoming virtuous in a manner that transforms ourselves and our friendship. This is why Aristotle is so tolerant of the lesser forms of friendship, for they have the potential of putting us on the road to virtue.

Likewise, equality is not so much a prerequisite to friendship, but something that comes with friendship as friends grow together toward goodness. Through friendship we are initiated into activities befitting virtue as we learn to be faithful to ourselves through being faithful to another. Social and personal inequalities can be made part of the "incidental" aspects of our existence through friendship, and good people can be made through participation in a common activity which is worthwhile in and of itself.

3. Friendship, Similarity and the Magnanimous Man

A question arises, however, as to whether equality is to be understood as similarity. In the modern world we are more ready to make these distinct; but this may be because we have lost a sense of the moral end to which any human life should tend. For us to dismiss the connection would not only mean we had failed to appreciate Aristotle's world, it would suggest we are too at home in our own. To understand the force of the question for Aristotle, we must return to the point that it is by friendship that we are formed and strengthened in virtue. By definition, furthermore, the formation is mutual; it occurs to both parties in the friendship, and especially in perfect friendship, which is between equals. Now, if virtue is one thing, a unity, it follows that friends will become ever more alike (i.e., alike in virtue) as they grow into perfect friendship.

Aristotle frequently refers to this basic similarity among friends; it is strongly implied by an argument for friendship we have mentioned, namely that a friend is a sort of mirror to the self (see 1166a31). Indeed, a strong reason to have a friend is so one's own good can better be seen.

It is not far from this point to another we find in Aristotle's discussion, namely that one should be a friend to oneself. For a friend is

> (1) a person who wishes for and does what is good or what appears to him to be good for his friend's sake; or (2) a person who wishes for the existence and life of his friend for the friend's sake. We regard as a friend also (3) a person who spends his time in our company and (4) whose desires are the same as ours, or (5) a person who shares sorrow and joy with his friend. A good man has all these feelings in relation to himself. (1166a1–10)

It is possible to put the point more strongly. If we are people of character we must be our "own best friend and should have the greatest affection for [ourselves]" (1168b9). Why is this? Let us connect the point back to our earlier theme. If we are not capable of being our own best friend we lack the constancy we need to have a happy life, extended, as it must be, over time. That is why a wicked man cannot be a friend even of himself, for evil men are characteristically on the run from themselves. "Evil men seek the company of others with whom they can spend their days, but they avoid their own company as they are incapable of remembering their past and they fear their future" (1166b10–25). In effect, they lack the means to see and live an essential continuity between what they are and what they do.

For Aristotle there is no tension between our love for others and for ourselves.[5] If we love ourselves rightly, namely as people of virtue, then we will rightly love others as they ought to be loved: as *virtuous* others. In this self-love, we are sheltered from a debased egoism that does everything for its own sake, for we, together with our friends, love the virtue which characterizes us both. Consequently we will take pleasure in time spent with ourselves. For the good man, "the memory of his achievements gives him delight, and his hopes for the future are good" (1166a24). By being a friend with another, we are in fact friends with ourselves, since our "friend really is another self" (1166a31).

Now we do not doubt there is much wisdom in Aristotle's account of the necessity that we be friends with ourselves. Yet we are uneasy with it. For it appears to imply that when we love or befriend another we are doing nothing essentially different from loving ourselves. One might ask: if this is so, does it make sense to say we are loving another as another? Granted, we are not loving them as merely an extension of ourselves, for we love them, as we love ourselves, not selfishly but for the sake of our mutually held virtue. We love them as fellow possessors of the good, both ours and theirs. But even qualified in this way the description yet fails to reflect the otherness in friendship. Indeed, when we love the friend, we love not just what we share with her, but also, and often more importantly, that in her which differs from ourselves.

The relative strength of this point as an objection to Aristotle's account of friendship cannot be determined formally. That is, there is no general account of friendship from which we can derive that friendships of the very best kind depend as much upon differences as upon similarities. At present, we mean only to suggest that Aristotle's emphasis upon similarity is not self-evident to us—and furthermore, it seems to miss something crucial about friendship as we have been privileged to know it. (Later we shall briefly suggest why differences are crucial to any Christian account of friendship.)

Perhaps Aristotle experienced friendship as likeness, but if so he had more than his experience to go on. Elements in his very understanding of goodness and virtue play into this basic perception. For example, Aristotle holds that the virtues are necessarily acquired by habit, and habit is formed by *imitation*. Moreover, he believes in the unity of the virtues—they all come together with practical wisdom. It will easily follow, then, that two friends who pass virtue between one another—imitate one another and so acquire the other's virtue—will become even more alike, culminating in a unity in which they cannot distinguish one from another.

Suppose we add to the list of Aristotle's commitments the one we have been discussing, namely his view that the virtuous character is by definition that character who is settled in time. That is to say, he is located in time, yet his feet are so firmly planted in virtue that he is able to stand steady amid its shifting currents. As such, and only as such, is he capable of genuine happiness.

Martha Nussbaum has argued that Aristotle seeks a place for the good life that is realizable yet also open, or, in Nussbaum's phrase, "vulnerable." It is realizable, for it is not trapped, as the tragedians suggest, amid the inevitable conflict of goods. It is vulnerable, for it cannot be assured, as Plato might have wished, by flight beyond the temporal to the eternal. That is to say, it is open to a world which might bring its defeat, by great suffering, an untimely death, financial ruin, or the loss of a friendship.[6]

In a similar way, we have portrayed Aristotle as open to temporality and so to the complexity and fragility of the moral life that is so often ignored. Yet we see here at the end of our account, as at the end of Nussbaum's, that certain questions arise about whether Aristotle's account is all that open after all. However, our way of posing the problem differs somewhat from Nussbaum's. For it is not *openness* itself we seek, but rather openness in friendship to the other *as another.* Aristotle rightly sees that it is crucial that friends should be able to rely on one another: as friend, I can trust you to be what we both know you should be. So constancy is necessary in virtue, in friendship, and in virtuous friends. Yet in continually reiterating the necessity of our constancy, not to the friend as he is but to the virtue in which he participates, Aristotle comes close to requiring that the constancy we share protect us from one another's difference.[7]

This is seen most directly in a fascinating series of texts in which Aristotle insists that friends will want to protect friends from their own misfortune. This is a valiant attitude, perhaps, but it confirms that for Aristotle a resilient pride is better suited to the life of virtue than an openness to the other, particularly in his suffering. It reflects as well the crucial element in magnanimity: that it is better to give than to receive.[8]

While enumerating reasons for having friends, Aristotle notes that people of virtue need friends because the "function of a friend is to do good rather than to be treated well, if the performance of good deeds is the mark of a good man and of excellence, and if it is nobler to do good to a friend than to a stranger, then a man of high moral standards will need people to whom he can do good" (1169b10–13). Or again he says that "friendship appears to consist in giving rather than in receiving affection" (1159a26). Most significantly, perhaps, he maintains that a noble man prefers friends present during good, rather than bad, fortune. He does so because it is painful to see our friends "pained by our misfortunes, for everyone tries to avoid being the cause of a friend's pain. For that reason, manly natures take scrupulous care not to let their friends share their pain" (1171b5–6). In contrast, friendship at its height is to be enjoyed in times of mutual good fortune and prosperity. In these

> the presence of friends brings with it a pleasant way of passing one's time and the pleasant thought that they are pleased by the good we are enjoying. This is the reason for thinking that we ought to be eager to invite our friends to share our good fortunes, since it is noble to do good, and to be reluctant to ask our friend to share our misfortune, since one should let others participate as little as possible in what is evil. We should invite our friends to come to our side chiefly when a little trouble on their part will mean great benefit to us. (1171b14–20)

To some this last bit will appear as a telltale sign of Western male machismo, especially since Aristotle adds that "women and womanly men enjoy sympathizers in their grief." No doubt it is that. But this also is too simple. For Aristotle does not mean to say that we should let our friends share in our good fortunes and hide from them our pain and grief in order to *impress* them. The question is not one of deceiving our friends about ourselves and our suffering. It is rather that if we are good we will want to protect our friends from the ill effects of our pain. Aristotle imagines a scene, no doubt, not unlike that in which a man is stricken with some terrible contagion. If he is good, would this man invite his friends to see him? Or suppose he suffered a devastating loss, like Job of the Old Testament. Should he not have far less to do with his friends of former days, since he can give them nothing and only cause them to reduce their bounty in assisting him or to sacrifice time in the relatively painful tasks of comfort and commiseration, time which could be far better spent in achieving excellence in virtue?

Here we are provided a remarkable window which opens onto Aristotle's vista not just of friendship and virtue but of the world that threatens both. As we have seen, virtue provides a degree of control over life that is unmatched by any other good, and this because it is constant; our characters are so firmly gripped by it that they are capable of weathering severe storms of ill fortune with relative calm. If we, by virtue, weather the storms, we can rightly be called happy. As such, we become eligible for perfect friendship, which (in less developed forms) has already sustained and encouraged us in virtue.

But if through some terrible stroke of misfortune (e.g., we fall deathly ill or lose all our financial means) we are stripped of our happiness, what then? What becomes of our friendship, nurtured in virtue and enjoyed in happiness? Here Aristotle's answer is clear. It must be surrendered, or at least suspended, to be resumed in better times. For in our misfortune the encroaching world has (at least for the moment) won the battle. And it is now our turn to bear our suffering and misfortune alone. For we must see that friendship and happiness (and to some degree the virtues) are finally to be understood in distinction from suffering and misfortune. We enjoy the best of friendship and virtue when we are in the best of positions, when our characters are firm and our coffers overflowing. Indeed, being in such a position allows us to claim with confidence the mark of perfect friendship, namely that the friend is chosen for his own sake and not for some other purpose. In contrast, if we are suffering, we are needy, like old people (1156a25); as such our friendship is better understood as one of usefulness rather than as perfect friendship.

4. Friendship in Theological Perspective

We would suggest the two points to which we have seen Aristotle's vision of friendship progress—that perfect friendship breeds not only equality but also likeness, and that friends should insulate friends from each other's suffering—are connected. Furthermore, the connection in our view is informed by the other matters we have mentioned, such as Aristotle's view that habituation is the only means by which we acquire the virtues and that the virtues are necessarily a unity. On all these points Christians need feel no compulsion to concur. In fact, insofar as they believe that the God of the universe, who has extended Himself to us in the Jewish people and in Jesus, invites us to become His friends by sharing in His suffering, Christians cannot accept a vision of friendship which excludes (or overcomes) otherness in the friend, or which shelters her from sharing our sufferings or defeats. The divergence between Aristotle and Christians on these points is not *over against* an agreement about virtue and happiness but rather *informs* and *requires* disagreement on these subjects as well.

If we turn in earnest to discover how Christians might describe perfect friendship, we cannot avoid what is likely the best known biblical passage about being friends. As Jesus nears the end of his life he speaks these words to his disciples in John:

> If you abide in me, and my words abide in you, ask whatever you will, and it shall be done for you. By this my Father is glorified, that you bear much fruit, and so prove to be my disciples. As the Father has loved me, so have I loved you; abide in my love. If you keep my commandments, you will abide in my love, just as I have kept my Father's commandments and abide in his love. These things I have spoken to you, that my joy may be in you, and that your joy may be full. This is my commandment, that you love one another as I have loved you. Greater love has no man than this, that a man lay down his life for his friends. You are my friends if you do what I command you. No longer do I call you servants, for the servant does not know what his master is doing; but I have called you friends, for all that I have heard from my Father I have made known to you. You did not choose me, but I chose you and appointed you that you should go and bear fruit and that your fruit should abide; so that whatever you ask the Father in my name, he may give it to you. This I command you, to love one another. (John 15:7–17 RSV)

It is interesting that Jesus does not *ask* but rather *commands* his disciples to be friends.[9] By doing so he does not deny the affective nature of love, but indicates the kind of friendship he has in mind is of a different order, an order just now coming into being with his disciples. So elsewhere in the discourse Jesus calls his commandment "new."

To this one might object, for have we not known all along that we should love one another? Something like love, after all, is assumed by many cultures and moral codes. Yet the new love Jesus commands is qualified: his disciples should love one another "as I have loved you." The love, apparently, is recognizably distinct from what otherwise goes by that name, for as Jesus says earlier in the same discourse, "by this all men will know that you are my disciples, if you have love for one another" (John 13:34–35).

We have here come upon the new community Jesus foresaw as the continuation of his own life in the world. The love, the friendship, in this community was to be distinct. Whether and when it has been distinct is for "all men" to judge. The nature of the supposed distinctness itself, however, requires theological display, for the love is defined by its resemblance to the love God has for us. Furthermore, the New Testament frequently claims that we can learn to love another as God has loved us only as we learn of God's love, which we do not just by seeing God's love, but by participating in it, by returning it to God.

Speaking of love in this way borders on abstraction, which is why the nature of God's love for us cannot be separated from the story of God's activity with humans. This is the story Christians learned first as Jews and continued to tell in the New Testament and in the church. Far from being condensable, this story expands as we learn and tell it. One notion, however, that is crucial to it is that God's love for us in Jesus involved the condescension or humbling of God to share our own life. This, we believe, is an important starting point for understanding Christian friendship.

A passage from Philippians registers this key theme.

So if there is any encouragement in Christ, any incentive of love, any participation in the Spirit, any affection and sympathy, complete my joy by being of the same mind, having the same love, being in full accord and of one mind. Do nothing from selfishness or conceit, but in humility count others better than yourselves. Let each of you look not only to his own interests, but also to the interests of others. Have this mind among yourselves, which you have in Christ Jesus, who, though he was in the form of God, did not count equality with God a thing to be grasped, but emptied himself, taking the form of a servant, being born in the likeness of men. And being found in human form he humbled himself and became obedient to death, even death on a cross. (Philippians 2:1–8 RSV)

The humility and "emptying," which stand out in this passage, offer stark contrast to the pride of the magnanimous man. As we have remarked elsewhere (e.g., in chapter 6), the excellence of pagan virtue assumed by Aristotle served to elevate its possessor. Likewise, the friendship of virtue, by creating equality and similarity among its participants, cannot but at the same time place distance between them and others who do not share it, or do not share their virtue.

Christians need not deny that a certain kind of friendship elevates its participants to a level of high equality. Indeed, the Philippians passage suggests this, for the humility predicated of Christ is offered as an alternative to an isolated equality and similarity, God to God, which Christ might have pursued. When pointing to this humbling, however, Christians see God in Christ as "befriending" humans. The humbling is the befriending, but described as the latter it becomes easier to point to the relationship which follows—that of human friendship with the divine. As such, it makes sense, even on Aristotelian grounds, to suppose that those who have been befriended by God might become like God. Having the mind that is in Christ Jesus simply follows, if he is our friend, for friends conform to each other's likeness. Yet this is not to say that humans are made gods. Indeed, in our friendship with God we remain distinct, different. Our connection is maintained in this: we are made participants, actors, in God's story. There is elevation in this, for humans locked only in a human story, while capable of great heroism, frequently find their efforts to control their own story futile, as our discussion of Aristotle has revealed.

Of course Aristotle recognizes this. This is why he never excludes the possibility that a life of virtue may not attain happiness for reasons beyond its control, as when that life ends upon the rack. In this feature his human story is far closer to the truth than the story most of us have come to live by, namely the story that implies individual humans as well as the corporate human community can (and must) insure their own success. Aristotle sees that this endeavor is rooted in a delusion, since through no fault of our own we might fail. Once the possibility of failure is acknowledged, Aristotle (sensibly) keeps those things which threaten happiness at a distance—and this is part of virtue's task. While not always successful, virtue can and sometimes does create an island of stability in the midst of the rushing river of time. It cannot airlift us out of the river, for this would be to become something other than human. But it can make us less easily swept away.

To extend the analogy of the island, we have learned from Aristotle's discussion of friendship that no man is one; hence, the island is rightly conceived as a *community of friends* who share happiness and virtue, and teach it to one another. Once trained the inhabitants of the island come to realize that while it is the basis of their friendship, the virtue they share is not omnipotent and so cannot guarantee that no one of them will be swept from the island bank into the swirling current. Should this occur the one who is swept away, well formed in virtue, will prefer to bear the terrors of the dark waters alone. The activities of virtue in which his friends are engaged remain on the island, apart from him as he is sucked into the cold darkness. To ask his friends to come to his aid or share in his sad fate would be to fail to see that the nature of happiness, virtue, and the community of friends is in distinction from the unhappy circumstance into which he has fallen.

Turning from Aristotle back to Philippians, we note that in that passage there are *two* humblings: God to human and, further, to suffering and death. The Christian claim, of course, is that the second is as significant as the first, or rather that the second demonstrates the meaning of the first. For by entering suffering and death Christ removes "its sting." Or, as we claimed earlier in the first chapter, by the death of Christ even our untimely deaths are rescued from meaninglessness. This is so not at all because death and suffering are any less awful to us, but rather because we are released from the terror of sustaining our own story amidst the raging flood of time. God, as it were, has written us permanently into His story by befriending us as we are, tossed and helpless amid the wildness of suffering and death, whereas, formerly the virtues and a settled character were our best refuge. And the meaning of this befriending, its depth, is displayed only as God Himself hangs limp and bleeding upon the cross.

The commandment to "love as I have loved you" must be interpreted in the light of this radical befriending. In the same Johannine discourse Jesus promises his disciples that they too will bear the weight of persecution and hate. Here it is assumed that friends will suffer with friends, indeed, that friends will suffer *because* of friends, as the disciples will suffer for Jesus' sake.

And so we have encountered a marked difference between Aristotelian and Christian friendship. For Aristotle there are a limited number of human circumstances or narrative sequences about which it makes sense for us to say that good can be found in them, or that the person who passes through them can reasonably be called happy. Virtue, of course, is necessary for happiness; moreover, it works effectively to extend the number of circumstances or narratives through which a person can live and still be properly called happy by making her more constant. But there is a limit. Part of virtue is to know when the limit is reached, especially in one's own case. There is, simply, no redemption possible of a life that has been plunged into great suffering; the sufferer does best to recognize this and let go the hand of any yet remaining on the metaphorical island of happiness. Heroically, he cuts himself loose to be carried away from his friends by the raging current.

Insofar, however, as Christians tell the story of a savior who suffered and died, they cannot acknowledge any such limit, for the same Jesus who died was raised again from the dead. (To put the difference as plainly as possible, while Aristotle maintains that no man can be happy on the rack, Christians point to a man on the cross as the model of what it means to live well; to be happy.) Suffering and death are yet great evils, but their victims are not beyond redemption. Indeed, these evils have been ultimately defeated, changed from the conquerors of goodness into its vanquished foes.

There is no question, then, but that Christians must enter into suffering for their friends. As the Johannine passage indicates, this is a sign of great love. But perhaps more importantly (and contra Aristotle), Christians must be those who are capable of sharing their suffering with others.

To be clear, the settled view that a life of virtue must be a shared life is one of the most compelling features of Aristotle's account. His quest for happiness is therefore not to be mistaken as that of a solitary hero. Nevertheless, we are alleging that something like this heroic model reappears at the edge of Aristotle's happy life where the sufferer stoically bears his suffering without friends. As the island analogue suggests, happiness, the life of virtue and friendship congeal *above* the surging waters of misfortune and suffering. It is therefore incumbent upon those upon the island to sustain its existence as such. Indeed, it is the corporate history of friends of virtue which partly holds them aloft from the currents beneath, although fortune always has something to say as well. On the island, friends may give to one another and receive gifts of friends. Indeed, friends in this condition are gifts to one another. But when fortune storms and one of the company of friends is swept from shore, friendship no more obtains and this one is most noble when carried away in silence rather than while frantically calling for assistance.

By contrast, Christians must not only see friends as gifts to one another, they must see their friendship itself as a gift. They can do this precisely because they understand themselves to be actors within a story authored not by them but by God. As Christians, our friendship is not made constant by an act of our own will, individual or corporate, or even by our own virtue, but rather because we and others find ourselves through participation in a common activity that makes us faithful both to ourselves and the other. That activity is not, as it seems to be in Aristotle, mutual enjoyment as an end in itself, but rather it is the activity of a task we have been given. That task is nothing less than to participate in a new way of life made possible by the life of the man Jesus.

That is why, as Christians, we can risk the kind of partiality required by friendship. Friendship is not just an instance of some more universal love, it is the attention and regard for another precisely as they are other, as they are different, from ourselves. We can take the risk of such love because we are called to imitate the partiality of God's love for us as shown through His Son. As Helen Oppenheimer has contended,

> "Impartiality" is not a divine virtue, but a human expedient to make up for the limits of our concern on the one hand and the corruptibility of our affections on the other. If we find ourselves neglecting,

or spoiling, or abusing, we need to be more evenhanded and partiality becomes a vice; but the august partiality of God is a taking hold of the special character of each creature as uniquely significant.[10]

In short, God is able to love each creature as a friend without His love being diminished for any other creature. It is through our friendships formed by Christ that the Christian learns to participate in that love.

Christian friendship, therefore, is dependent upon a source outside itself.[11] This may appear to diminish its importance, but it does not. Instead of being its own source of strength and constancy, it depends on the strength and constancy of the God who has first befriended humans. It is able, therefore, not only to share suffering, as we have seen, but also difference. Indeed, it requires difference.

As we have argued, for Aristotle equality and similarity in friendship are two sides of the same coin. This is so because, as Aristotle believes, the virtues unify, and so friends who grow together in virtue become ever more similar in character.[12] For their part, Christians cannot deny that friendship encourages similarity in crucial respects, for otherwise their assumption that friendship with Jesus causes likeness to him in his followers would prove groundless. Yet if Christians affirm the ultimate unity of the virtues it must be an eschatological affirmation.

Referring to the eschatological end may appear as a pious way of getting Christians off the hook of having to think about relations between the virtues now by postponing it until later. But the key to the *eschatological* affirmation is not merely that it points to the future but rather its reminder that Christians look, not for individual happiness, but for the kingdom of God. While they must always refrain from specifying the exact shape of this kingdom, they can begin to imagine it in their present life in the church. For the church, no description holds more authority than that reiterated so often in the Epistles, namely that the church is a body with many parts, each with its own beauty and difference. As gifts of the Spirit, these differences are less learned in a virtue friendship, more supplied directly from God, who is building the kingdom through the church. Yet they do not exist separate from the friendship—indeed, they inhere in it, for, as Paul sees them, they include gifts such as exhortation, wisdom, diligence,and even cheerfulness. (See Romans 12:3–8 and 1 Corinthians 12:1–10.)

The introduction of the gifts cannot but change how we will view differences among friends. While I expect to grow in wisdom as I grow in virtue, if I also suppose another might have a special gift of wisdom, I cannot suppose that my acquired wisdom need not remain open to her correction. Indeed, I must see that we need this friend's wisdom to live well together, and since (as Christians and Aristotle agree) *our* living well is *my* living well, I must see that I cannot live well without this other's guidance. So it is that I need her friendship for happiness, and for virtue. And in needing her I need something essentially different from myself.

To Aristotle this would seem extraordinary. But it is no less extraordinary than the claim that the God of the universe desires that we exist. It is this claim that undergirds not only Christian friendship but the entirety of the Christian story, which is an extraordinary story indeed.

Part II
Responses to Contemporary Revivals of Virtue

FOUR

The Renewal of Virtue
and the Peace of Christ

1. The Renewal of Virtue among Philosophers

The recent publication of William Bennett's *The Book of Virtues* is an event sufficient in itself to demonstrate that virtue is back in the public discussion of ethics. In philosophical circles this return has been on the rise for some decades, and philosophical defenses of virtue are now sufficiently plentiful and substantial.

The title of our book as well as the first section indicate that we think a reconsideration of the significance of virtue is long overdue. Insofar as we have a right to an opinion about what moral philosophers write about, it is our view that the reappearance of virtue talk among them has helped things a bit. Nevertheless, it is important for us to say that while we use them freely, the new philosophical defenses of virtue are, for the most part, of little interest to us in themselves. This is so because we have absolutely no stake in defending virtue as a thing in itself. Indeed, as we will try to show in this chapter, to defend virtue itself is a dangerous thing for Christians to do, for they may discover that the defense inevitably yields a set of virtues that are vicious—that is, vicious according to the Christian gospel.

One of the virtues of virtue language is how it works against the idea, so widespread in philosophy and theology earlier in this century, that ethics is a special realm or sphere. This idea has worked its way into the popular mind (or perhaps it began there and worked its way to the philosophers) including the minds of Christians. As one might imagine a contemporary American Christian asking: "Now that I have become a Christian, how should I express my Christian commitment in my moral life?" Here the imagined "moral life" is one of a number of life's compartments; it is a region or *realm of obligation* into which people wander when they encounter a dilemma and outside of which they can live as they like. "Morality" conceived as a special realm of obligation is what Bernard Williams, in a strong but helpful turn of words, calls "a peculiar institution."[1] As he maintains, it is an institution we are better off without, even if its presentation by Kant and others is strangely compelling. Rather, Williams would have "ethics" deal with Socrates' broad question: "How should one live?" The breadth of this question illustrates that ethics so understood cannot be assigned to a special realm into which we sometimes step.

Williams's position and his penetrating arguments illustrate how the recent philosophical defenses of virtue can be of great benefit. His use of Socrates' question to broaden the sphere of the moral life beyond the narrow realm of obligation is precisely the help we need in order to begin breaking free of the stranglehold modern moral theories have held on moral reflection. Furthermore, this breaking free is appropriately coupled with a general defense of virtue thought and talk in ethics, for virtue designations resist any easy stripping off from the character to whom they are applied. That is to say, if we imagine Joe with his virtues removed—that, for example, he is no longer kind, generous, tenacious, honest, and so on—we have lost Joe himself. The idea of a "realm of virtue" into which Joe might now and again step is simply incoherent. In this way virtue language possesses a built-in resistance to the most prevalent modern error about ethics, and that is a great benefit indeed.

No doubt, this built-in resistance can be partially explained by the fact that virtue language is old; it predates the rise of the modern world in its mode of theorizing about morality, as Williams's return to "Socrates' question" illustrates. Indeed, pre-Christian pagans spoke almost entirely in terms of virtues. Christians possessed a more diverse repertoire, inheriting from Judaism talk of obedience to Divine Law and creating their own language of discipleship. Yet quite early on they saw fit to appropriate virtue language from their pagan neighbors. At the minimum, virtue presumed character and as such forced the question regarding what sort of people we should be, a question for which Christians had the greatest passion.

The revival of virtue language, then, seems a good and prudent strategy, rhetorically and historically. Nevertheless, any reappropriation of virtue language by Christians must not lose sight of the fact that "virtue" originally described Greek virtues and not Jewish or Christian ones.[2] Hence, while we freely borrow the language of virtue from our ancient (and contemporary) pagan interlocutors, as did other Christians from Chrysostom to Aquinas and beyond, we stop short of defending virtue as a thing in itself. As just noted, Christianity is not wedded to self-expression in terms of virtue, as is borne out by the existence of alternatives such as obedience to God's law or as discipleship of Jesus. Moreover, it is apparent from its history that the mere use of virtue talk does nothing to insure what the virtues will be. (Nietzsche, for example, speaks with great power in the language of virtue, yet recommends a way of life that Christians regard as vicious.) This is a key fact for Christians, one which must always qualify their advocacy for "virtue" or for "character." If someone asserts that striving after virtue will bring one closer to God, Christians are obliged to ask: what virtues? and which God?

But the point can be made even stronger—i.e., if the language and logic of virtue tips in any direction, it is away from Christianity and toward the Greek context in which it originated. For Christians, it can be used with great reward, but it must be purified as used or else bear bad fruit.

2. Obligation and Virtue Revisited

It is not enough, then, for Christians to call for a return to an ethics of virtue. On the other hand, serious defenses of virtue can and have performed the helpful function of displacing those ideas about morality that presume the special realm of obligation, ideas that have proved immensely hard to shake. On that score, it is worth noting that even within the new philosophical defenses of virtue, the special realm of obligation has a way of reappearing. For example, some assume that virtue is best appropriated when appended to a morality of duty. They seek an ethics of virtue that can complement or supplement our duties. One way of putting this is in terms of certain minimal standards of morality—our duties or obligations—to which are added moral directives that are "supererogatory." So Philippa Foot takes the view, for example, that some things are morally required of us by justice whereas other things are, by charity, good for us to do. The good things do not preempt those that are required, for in the first order we must fulfill our obligations as specified by justice.[3]

Or, in a slightly different attempt to combine virtue and obligation, William Frankena has maintained that the realm of obligation is one in which acts are determined and stated to be objectively right or wrong, but as such it invariably ignores the importance of the subject. As he sees it, this is a deficiency of an ethics of obligation that virtue can repair. So Frankena associates virtue with the moral subject or agent who has motives, personal traits, dispositions, and the like. However, when it comes to matters of what is morally right or wrong and how this is known, Frankena quickly sets virtue aside, precisely because it is primarily (for him at least) about a subject's motives. As he says, "It does strike me that, if the only thing an ethics of virtue can tell me is to do that act which . . . I will be doing from a certain motive, then it cannot do what is needed. One can hardly go about looking to see what motive he will be acting from . . . as a way of determining what to do."[4]

Frankena and Foot are representatives, perhaps, of a generation of philosophers so thoroughly schooled in the dominant Kantian or utilitarian modes of reflection about ethics that relinquishing the special realm of obligation is simply not an option. Virtues for them will always be conceived in relation to an already well-founded notion of obligation, and so, when having recognized the need to include virtue within their systems of moral thought, these thinkers invariably fashion their "virtues" so as never directly to interfere with this basic notion.

Other philosophical proponents of virtue thinking have recently been more thoroughgoing. Yet even among them it is not uncommon for the language of obligation to intrude once again. For example, Edmund Pincoffs, who in the early part of his *Quandaries and Virtues* offers a strong critique of the standard ethical theories (i.e., utilitarianism, Kantianism, and contract theories),[5] nonetheless reintroduces the special jurisdiction of obligation when he devises a separate category among his many and various virtues called "the mandatory virtues." This is made doubly important in Pincoffs's own positive account by the fact that he otherwise offers an emaciated definition of a virtue, calling it a "dispositional property that provides grounds for preference of persons."[6] The explicit non-normativity of this definition makes the normativity of the "mandatory virtues" all the more striking, suggesting—as we think Pincoffs in fact intends—that the non-normative virtues have little to do with Socrates' question about what is the best life for humans to live. All the weight of this question, then, shifts to the mandatory virtues, which, with the exception of certain unfortunate choices such as "nonfanaticism," end up looking very much like the list of "obligations" Frankena or Foot could be expected to submit.

It is revealing that Pincoffs's "mandatory virtues" are remarkably like what one might call democratic virtues, or those which conduce to life in an "open society." Indeed, Pincoffs makes it difficult for us to resist the judgment that his mandatory/nonmandatory distinction is little more than a sophisticated version of what one hears on talk shows and virtually everywhere else in America: "You can do what you like with your life so long as you're decent in public and don't foist your virtue preferences on the rest of us." What is surprising is that Pincoffs never seems quite able to imagine that there might be other ways to live together morally than as a democratic nation-state. As such his account becomes remarkably unhistorical insofar as it fails to locate its own discourse in relation to a tradition of life and reflection which it plainly supposes is normative, namely Enlightenment liberalism.

In this respect Pincoffs is not atypical. It is tempting to speculate why modern moral philosophers so infrequently claim a tradition. Perhaps it is because so many spring from a tradition which, as Alasdair MacIntyre has suggested, is built on the supposition that it is not a tradition. Or perhaps it is because as philosophers they are uncomfortable with acknowledging that their own pursuit of truth might be limited by their bodies, which have, at the least, a specific historical location. In any case, given this predictable turn in Pincoffs's thought, we should not be surprised when he speaks as follows about "religion" and its relation to the virtue ethics he hopes will catch on:

Aside from the constitutional provisions that are designed to protect religious freedom, there are, then, good reasons not to tie moral to religious instruction. . . . [I]f it is granted that moral learning need not lean on religious belief, there is good reason to encourage its development in such a way that it not lean too heavily. Religious belief is, in an open society, a society that encourages critical reflection, a notoriously fragile structure. Many reflective persons come to disavow it. But such persons are better off if their realization that they no longer are believers is not the occasion of a moral crisis—a crisis that arises only if their motivation to be moral arises solely from religious sources.[7]

To paraphrase the last point, if you find yourself thinking that your morality rests upon a specific (religious) tradition, better start thinking again, because sooner or later you are likely to lose your belief in that tradition. Not only might you lose morality itself, you will be faced with quite a deep psychological crisis and, God knows, this is something we all should want to avoid.

This aversion to religion-based morality has nothing at all to do with Pincoffs's being a defender of virtue.[8] It has everything to do with his allegiance to Enlightenment liberalism, with which (ironically) his defense of virtue is rather at odds. The trouble in Pincoffs's case, and in Foot's and Frankena's, is that the new defense of virtue is circumscribed by the assumptions of what MacIntyre calls the Enlightenment project, creating a tension that, innocently enough, goes unnoticed and unresolved.

To some extent it appears necessary for the philosophical defenders of virtue to break free from this allegiance before a thoroughgoing and consistent defense can be offered. (This itself should not surprise us; after all, virtue talk predates talk of rights and obligations, as Socrates—with his question—predates Kant.) Which takes us to another thinker, both pre- (and post-) modern and a defender of virtue, namely Alasdair MacIntyre. In addition to the considerable debt we owe him, MacIntyre is of interest to us for another reason: he is a confessed Christian. With MacIntyre we have an anti-Enlightenment thinker who ably and consistently uses and defends virtue talk. His difficulty, we allege, arises not from the aforementioned tension between obligation and virtue, but between virtue in its Greek origins and his Christian confession, for the latter demands neither a summary acceptance nor a rejection of virtue talk, but rather its transformation.

3. Milbank on MacIntyre

In his *Theology and Social Theory: Beyond Secular Reason,* John Milbank disputes with MacIntyre about whether a universally compelling philosophical case can be made for the ascendancy of virtue.[9] Like us, on many points Milbank is sympathetic and, in fact, deeply indebted to MacIntyre. For Milbank, MacIntyre is a philosopher who has (re)discovered the importance of Christian theology, both intellectually and confessionally. This has come as he has been drawn further into his view that only traditioned inquiry is capable of sustaining coherent, rational discourse about the good life for humans. Yet MacIntyre's recently retrieved Christianity aside, when it comes time to oppose other views of ethics from within his own "tradition," MacIntyre falters. As Milbank says,

> The key point at issue is the role that must be accorded to Christianity and to Christian theology. For MacIntyre, it is true, the latter has come to matter more and more, but it remains the case that he opposes to the philosophy and practice of difference [what MacIntyre calls "genealogy" in his latest book][10] not, primarily, Christian thought and practice, but the antique understanding of virtue, the accompaniments of Socratic dialectics, and the general link of reason to tradition. Of course, for MacIntyre, one must subscribe to some *particular* tradition, some *particular* code of virtue, and here he identifies himself as "an Augustinian Christian." But all the same, the *arguments* put forward against nihilism and a philosophy of difference are made in the name of virtue, dialectics and the *notion* of tradition in general. (327)

As Milbank points out, MacIntyre recognizes that the virtues and opinions that tradition-based communities espouse are rhetorically mediated. Yet in his philosophical reflections on virtue he nonetheless bypasses any such contingent starting point, settling upon dialectical questioning as the method by which truth is to be pursued. This suggests MacIntyre believes that we can move toward universality by these dialectics. Crucial to his project is the possibility that the Christian account of the virtues can be successfully grafted onto the Greek heritage. Hence, he attempts to demonstrate how Augustine was able to resolve antinomies intrinsic to and yet unresolvable within the Greek account of virtue, and how Aquinas, revising and extending Augustine's insights, did the same, producing the most satisfactory version of morality we have had so far.[11]

This is not to say, quite, that MacIntyre believes that the Christian faith can be justified and/or accepted dialectically; it is rather to say that he believes "faith" (i.e., the traditioned account of morality offered in Christianity) can provide answers to questions that are found to be dialectically problematic given the Greek inheritance. In a way, MacIntyre is engaged in something we might in other contexts call Christian apologetics, for he wants to show that there are strong grounds for the "Greeks" (e.g., Plato and Aristotle) to accept Christianity as a way of resolving their own difficulties.

According to Milbank, a tension arises between, on the one hand, MacIntyre's philosophical perspective on Christianity, which affirms the rhetorical character of the Christian texts and beliefs but then attests to their validity by a universal method (namely, dialectics) and, on the other hand, his theological perspective, which proposes a mode of discourse involving the imaginative explication of Christian texts and beliefs that begins where dialectics leave off. In contrast to this approach, Milbank holds that we can never recommend virtue in general, but rather only Christian virtue in particular. (This point attests as well to the necessity of the rhetoric of theology.) Milbank's reasons are quite historical and concrete. He believes that Plato's and (especially) Aristotle's account of the virtues are founded on a politics of violence and exclusivity. At best, Greek views are redeemable from a Christian perspective only typologically. Speaking analogically, they can help constitute the true city only as the Old Testament allegories foreshadowed Christ.

The tension in MacIntyre's position should not be taken as a weakness in his larger position, particularly his assessment of our present moral crisis. Furthermore, as the next two chapters of this book suggest, a reappropriation of the ancient Greek accounts of virtue is a fitting strategy for moral reform, at least for non-Christians, for despite obvious differences there *is* a strong resemblance between our own world and that of the Greeks. As Milbank notes

> there is a perceived correspondence between their social-intellectual situation and our own. We find ourselves in the midst of a debased, democratic politics, frequently tending to tyranny, and at the same time struggling for responses to 'non-civic' philosophies which instill an uncompromising relativism. . . .
>
> MacIntyre's return to Plato and Aristotle belongs, therefore, in the context of a contemporary response to the problem of relativism. Plato's and Aristotle's solutions to this problem acquire a new appeal once it is seen that modern rationalist/empiricist attempts to ground ethics in universal 'natural' facts about human nature—desire for pleasure, avoidance of pain, or the freedom of human will—are untenable. Moreover, by adopting Platonic or Aristotelian solutions, one can argue that modern relativism is itself but the reflex of the falsely dogmatic claims of foundationalism.(337)[12]

MacIntyre's diagnosis of our contemporary world is not the problem. Rather, what is problematic for MacIntyre as a *Christian* is that his alternative proposal would have us return to an essentially Greek understanding of the virtues. As Milbank suggests, the deeper implications of the Greek understanding of virtue clash with the political (and essential) claims of Christianity. MacIntyre largely ignores this and so cannot see that the Christian virtues, represented (ironically) most strongly by Aquinas, actually offer an alternative which radically challenges Greek notions of virtue. For Christians, attaining virtue is not fundamentally a victory, as it is for the Greeks. In that sense, Christianity is not a continuation of the Greek understanding of the virtues, but rather the inauguration of a new tradition that sets the virtues within an entirely different telos in community.

As Milbank displays them, the fundamental points of discontinuity between the Greek and the Christian notions of virtue are to be found in the contrast between the Greek *arete* and the Christian *caritas. Arete* has meaning in relation to a fundamentally heroic image that has no telos other than conflict. The hero vanquishes his foes, and the virtues are his wherewithal, as well as those traits for which he is accorded honor in the *polis* he violently defends. By contrast, *caritas,* the very form of the virtues for Aquinas, sees the person of virtue as essentially standing in mutuality with God and with her fellow human beings.

(The pronouns qualifying the Greek and Christian accounts of the virtues are important. The "his" of the Greeks in fact rightly indicates the association of men with war. That Christians could use "her" is not an indication of early Christian egalitarianism, it rather reminds us that the telos of the Christian community was one in which male and female alike were included.)

Were Milbank discussing, say, Homer, he would face little opposition in his reading of Greek virtue as essentially built upon conflict and conquest. However, he implicates Aristotle as one who is captured by the Greek mythos of the heroic conquest. To do so he calls attention, as we have in our own treatment, to Aristotle's magnanimous man, his highest embodiment of virtue.

> Although this person [the magnanimous man] must only seek honours as rewards for a true exercise of virtue, he is still primarily motivated by this seeking for public acclaim. . . . Not only does the magnanimous man seek to be liberal, he seeks to outshine others in liberality, which implies a competition for limited economic resources. He prefers to be a benefactor rather than receive benefit, and if this sounds possibly 'Christian', one must note that he also remembers his giving rather than his receiving, and is encouraged to be 'haughty' to those above him in station, but to 'hold back' to those below. The jealousy of munificence shows that Aristotle's ideal of virtue is not perfectly separable from a heroic pursuit of honor. Excellence is still in some measure 'effectiveness', which can emerge only from engagement in an *agon*. (352)

As the magnanimous man would see it, Aquinas's *caritas* could not be a virtue. As Milbank observes,

> [u]nlike the magnanimous man, [Aquinas's] person of charity does not build up a fund of resources and then economically dispense them: instead, her very mode of being is giving, and this constant outgoing paradoxically recruits again her strength. A kind of giving can be exercised even in negative situations of poverty and weakness, and the charitable person is first and foremost the *recipient* of charity from God, and so charity begins and ends in gratitude, which the

magnanimous man prefers to keep in bounds. As friendship with God, and with fellow humans, charity always involves mutuality; Aristotle himself made this point about friendship, but he did not, like Aquinas, place friendship quite at the apex of civic achievement. Friends, for Aristotle, share a common love of the good, but this good is ultimately the fine economy of honour which is magnanimity. If friendship becomes the actual summit of virtue, then this suggests that virtue is itself relational, rather than a self-contained, internal matter. . . . In other words, a transitive giving of something to someone else is constitutive of friendship, and therefore the thing most ultimately characteristic of virtue. (Pp. 359–60)

Here we have the seeds of the contrast Milbank most wishes to emphasize: that between the *polis* and the church. As he would have it, to the degree that it bases political relation and participation on charity and not *arete*, the Christian church brings to the world the possibility of a true peace. In effect, the ancient world knew no peace, it knew only the absence of conflict in an exclusive *polis* where the virtuous life always took its meaning and direction from heroism in war. Indeed, *conquering* was pervasive, if not Athens of Sparta, then reason of the appetites, or masters of slaves. Unlike *arete*, Christian charity "generates its own field of operation, which is no longer something to be formed, dominated or inhibited, but instead liberated as a new power and a new freedom" (363). As such it transcends a model of the person whose *telos* involves the practice and perfection of the virtues of conflict, and it offers the new political possibilities of mutuality and community that previously were inconceivable.

As Milbank sums up his argument,

Because virtue presupposes justice, and justice involves a real peace, the ontological priority of peace to conflict (peace is what is most real, most secure, most guarantees human life) is an issue of yet more importance than that of virtue. Peace is not a virtue, notes Aquinas—and he does not talk about a particular virtue of peaceableness—because peace is the final end, the *principium* itself. Considerations concerning ontology, peace and conflict (the prime concern already of the pre-Socratics) have therefore, as Augustine realized, a power to unsettle one's whole conception of virtue, or of what morality is at all. And the main consideration here is that antiquity failed really to arrive at the ontological priority of peace to conflict and therefore failed—from a Christian point of view, and even from the aspirations of Plato and Aristotle—to break with the heroic conception of virtue and arrive at a genuinely ethical good. (363–64)

4. Virtue Christianly Considered

The enthusiasm among some over the current philosophical return to virtue is matched among others by a strong disquiet. While this in some cases signals nothing else but battles for turf as the hegemony of liberalism is challenged, it is not a false alarm. It is quite right to ask what sort of politics matches or is entailed by the so-called return to the virtues. Pincoffs is one thinker who tries to match it with liberalism. Strategically this involved either the privatization of the virtues, making them *personal* preferences, or the elevation of the modern quasi virtue of tolerance—which, ironically, can be championed as a virtue only within a society which was at some point "intolerant" about what could count as a virtue. Pincoffs means to leave our modern Western democratic politics intact, for it is the public right not the private good, universal obligation not individual excellence, upon which public policy about mandatory virtue would be formed. (Never mind that on MacIntyre's account it is precisely this politics that has led to the denigration of the traditions of inquiry in which virtue can make sense.)

To be sure, Pincoffs's attempt to wed a return to virtue with our current liberal polity can be bettered. Yet even when it is (as we try to show in the two subsequent chapters), virtue inevitably strains with liberalism. This suggests that the expressed disquiet among liberals about the revival of virtue is based upon an essentially correct insight, namely that a return to the (essentially Greek) virtues implies as well a return to a certain politics of war. Inasmuch as virtues spring up in a way of life of some community and tradition, and inasmuch as communities train their members to courageously defend this way of life in battle, then a return to virtue cannot but bring us as well a world of competing communities with competing notions of the good living together as did Greek city-states, all with no universal, rational referee. (The fact that this description fits the contemporary world increasingly well elucidates Milbank's earlier point that MacIntyre's return to the sages of the ancient Greek world is entirely fitting. Our world is returning, in a way, to theirs, with one frightening exception: in the 2,400 years that separate us from the Peloponnesian wars we have learned how to make much bigger weapons.)[13]

MacIntyre is the first to acknowledge that his revival of virtue leads to conflict; he means to manage this conflict, insofar as it can be managed, with dialectics.[14] But if we follow Milbank, dialectics themselves are no more than Greek philosophical presumptions writ large, from which it follows that MacIntyre's introduction of them is either a return to a (Greek) system of virtue that presumes a state of war or else a power play in the battle that already rages between opposing communities of virtue, such as those of "tradition" and of "genealogy" as portrayed in MacIntyre's *Three Rival Versions of Moral Enquiry.* Either way, MacIntyre has no means, and perhaps no desire, to stop the war, nor to confine it to discussions occurring among academics in the university.

As Milbank elsewhere points out, it is not surprising that MacIntyre overstates the case against the Enlightenment, for as primarily informed by a revived Greek notion of virtue he is not equipped to see it as a secularization of the genuinely new (to the ancients, that is) Christian vision of a community at peace.[15] In its simplest form, secularization involved the transformation of divine law into the universal rule of rationality. This secularized belief in law and obligation is now eroding, and MacIntyre is right, perhaps, to show no sympathy (as Nietzsche did not in the previous century)[16] to liberals who are finally losing their false foundation. Yet our point is that a full-scale return to Greek virtue cannot but involve a return to a pre-Enlightenment/pre-Christian world of war. Consequently, the liberal suspicion of the return to virtue is not to be dismissed. It is to some extent informed by genuine and godly worries for the relative peace and welfare of the world—worries that Christians (as opposed to Nietzscheans or Greek revivalists) are bound to credit.

What, then? Must Christians join liberals in repudiating the return to virtue? To be sure, they must acknowledge their own failings to live peaceably and pray to be delivered from the temptation to base their vision of life upon their own heroic achievements. Furthermore, as they continue in their witness to invite others to join the life of God in the world, the life of Christ in the church, they must carefully distinguish the true God from the gods of this world, including the Greek gods of virtue.

It is in the course of this distinguishing that essentially Christian notions of virtue can be recovered and made anew. As Milbank has reminded us, the ascendant Christian virtue of charity is utterly foreign to Aristotle. We cannot, then, begin with Aristotle's virtues and fill in the gaps with Christianity, nor can we, as Christians, defend virtue first and Christianity later, the strategy we find prevalent in MacIntyre.

We need not, however, leave off discussion of virtue altogether, nor need we deny the link between Greek virtue and Christian virtue, between Aristotle and Aquinas. As our first section indicates, we are convinced that the insights about virtue offered by Aristotle and other ancient Greeks are indispensable in any true and subtle treatment of Socrates' fundamental question regarding how one should live. Yet as we believe the great Christian thinkers such as Saint Paul and Saint Thomas meant to teach us, Greek accounts of the virtues are there to be *used* by Christians, not *built upon*. These name two quite different things. To use requires that one apply a thing within a framework significantly other than the one in which it originally appeared, which is precisely what Christianity requires insofar as it refounds human life on the life, death, and resurrection of Jesus Christ, God made flesh. As founded on Christ, Christian virtue cannot but be teleologically ordered to peace, just as Greek virtue cannot but be ordered to war. As Milbank has maintained, Christian virtue is wrongly construed in terms of either conquest or control; its essence is to direct us to mutuality. Characterized as Christian charity, the relation this mutuality involves is one in which love produces love, limitlessly, for it has its end in God, who is boundless love. In the end, then, Christian virtue is not so much initiated action but response to a love relation with God in Christ. This is why it makes sense for the Christian Aquinas to say that true or complete virtue is fundamentally not our own achievement but is rather infused in us by God's grace, which saves us and enables us.

Too often the notion of infusion is taken to suggest a *sudden* acquisition of the virtues. Yet as Aquinas makes plain when he considers the relation between the theological virtues whereby "faith generates hope, and hope charity,"[17] there is no reason to suppose that infusion comes all at once. Consequently, Aristotle's powerful account of how the virtues are acquired can continue to serve as a rich resource for displaying how training in the virtues might occur. Rather than the rapidity of acquisition, or even the mode, "infusion" points to the source from whence the theological virtues come, namely by a special act of God which brings us into relation with God, not only forming but utterly transforming our character.[18] As Paul says, "So whoever is in Christ is a new creation: the old things have passed away; behold, new things have come. And all this is from God, who has reconciled us to himself through Christ and given us the ministry of reconciliation" (1 Corinthians 6:17–18).

The sign and substance of this infusion of the Christian virtues is always participation in the body of Christ. This involves our reception of the sacraments of baptism and eucharist, but also includes (and entails) immersion in the daily practices of the Christian church: prayer, worship, admonition, feeding the hungry, caring for the sick, etc. By these we are transformed over time to participate in God's life. So also we become full members in a city ordered to peace. The contrast between this city and the Greek *polis* is marked, for as Christians repudiate the idea that there will always be unruly passions in the human soul which reason must police by means of the virtues, so they refuse to live on the assumption that the barbarians perpetually reign in the dark regions beyond the city wall and thus the city's heros must always be prepared to do battle. Again following Aquinas, faith leads to hope, a quite specific eschatological hope for the eventual coming of the Kingdom of God, even now present in the church. It is this hope that provides the possibility of a new politics, one that in gratitude extends friendship with God to friendship with one's fellow creatures, which is, as we have noted, the movement of *caritas,* for Aquinas the very form of the virtues.

FIVE

Friendship and Fragility

1. Introduction: Fragile Humanity

When one seriously peruses the ancient Greek sources about ethics, one finds Williams is right: Socrates' question about what is the good life is their primary focus. In her important and influential book *The Fragility of Goodness*,[1] Martha Craven Nussbaum sees this plainly enough. It is to her great credit that not only does she see that this question occupies the ancients, she sees as well that it must occupy us as we read them. As a consequence Nussbaum does far more than revive ancient Greek authors such as Pindar or Aristotle, she interprets them thematically to speak to our own questions about life. Her approach is to bring us through the first part of her book, on the tragedians, to the second, where she tells us of Plato's middle-period ethics, which she views as a response to their tragic views. Having considered each of these in turn, she brings us with certain things settled to an audience with Aristotle in the book's third and final part.

The story Nussbaum tells of Plato and the tragedians weaves around a pair of contrasting images and contrasting Greek terms: a plant and a stone, *tuche* and *techne*. For Pindar, the excellence of a good person "is like a young plant: something growing in the world, slender, fragile, in constant need of food from without" (1). This life is necessarily one susceptible to *tuche* (luck, or fortune or, in a way, the capricious world), and so those who live it are always at risk, even of losing their good characters. In contrast, Plato (at least the Plato of the middle period) proposes an entirely different conception of the good life, one which he hopes will insulate us from the impinging world and guarantee the immutability of our good character. His was an ambitious and radical proposal: by "human reason to subdue and master *tuche* through the arts and sciences. Plato took it to be the task of philosophy to become the life-saving *techne* through which this aspiration could be accomplished—through which, then, the human being could make decisive progress beyond the ordinary human condition" (237). For Plato, Socrates, that godlike man of reason, is the paragon of moral virtue. Socrates, who "refuses in every way to be affected." Socrates, who "is stone; and he also turns others to stone" (195).

Clearly Nussbaum's sympathies lie with the tragedians. But Plato's project is not, she thinks, to be dismissed lightly. We cannot live humanly without a *techne* of sorts, yet it must not turn us to stone. She hopes to discover a "non-scientific deliberation" which can help us see that and how "an epistemology of value and an account of the vulnerability of the valuable things go hand in hand" (291). With these hopes, she turns to Aristotle.

For present purposes, our interest in Nussbaum's treatment arises with her concluding chapter[2] on Aristotle entitled "The Vulnerability of the Good Human Life: Relational Goods." This chapter itself concludes with a section on *philia*—"friendship" as it is usually translated, although Nussbaum sticks faithfully with the Greek term itself. This placement in her book privileges friendship, fittingly, since Aristotle's *Nicomachean Ethics* does so as well, as we have already seen.

Perhaps it is clear from what we said earlier (in chapter 3) that we agree with Aristotle's and (presumably) Nussbaum's elevation of friendship within the moral life. This is one reason Nussbaum's account requires our careful attention. As we shall see, difficulties arise—as well as insights—when we inspect Nussbaum's treatment of Aristotle's friendship, both for how she understands Aristotle and for her view about the fragility of goodness. In our interaction with Nussbaum we mean less to dispute with her about how Aristotle is to be understood—although we shall do a bit of that—but more to further our understanding of friendship and of fragility. Furthermore, we should like to ask where a Christian understanding of friendship and fragility stands in relation to what we learn from Nussbaum and Aristotle regarding them.

2. Dividing Things Up:
External Goods, Politics and Friendship

Chapter 11 of *The Fragility of Goodness,* the chapter immediately preceding the aforementioned final chapter on "relational goods," parallels it in title: "The Vulnerability of the Good Human Life: Activity and Disaster." Both chapters have life's vulnerability as their theme, but the first displays how it is maintained (or threatened) by external circumstances such as beauty, wealth, health, enslavement, poverty, and death. For Aristotle, these are the "external goods" (or external misfortunes) whose presence in our own lives affects our *eudaimonia*. Nussbaum's burden in the chapter is to show us the "gap" between *eudaimonia* and good character that is opened by features of the world—what we call misfortunes—which we cannot insure against.

One might think that it is one of the key functions of virtue to close this gap, making happiness firm and achievable. No doubt virtue sometimes makes the good life more likely, but contrary to Plato's hopes (according to Nussbaum) it cannot insure it. In fact, as she goes on to say, the gap is sometimes *widened* by virtue.

> Certain valued excellences, particularly courage, political commit-
> ment, and love of friends, will take the good agent, far more often
> than the defective agent, into situations in which the requirements
> of character conflict with the preservation of life itself—therefore
> with the continued possibility of all excellent activity. (336)

This is an important quotation. It shows us how Nussbaum's idea of fragility is dependent upon the elevation of the "relational goods" of chapter 12 to a status beyond that of the external goods she discusses here in chapter 11. That is to say, the good life—which, as we later discover, is also the fragile life—cannot be for Nussbaum a life lived entirely in pursuit of the external goods, even if, admittedly, these goods are necessary for *eudaimonia*. To be sure, a certain kind of "openness" and "vulnerability" to the world is a feature of a life lived for wealth, bodily comfort, or sensual pleasure. He who values bodily comfort, for example, may suddenly discover himself in chronic pain, so he is cut off from his good (as he conceived it) by *tuche*. His life is thus fragile in a certain way in that it has taken aim at that which it cannot insure. Yet this is not Nussbaum's fragility, as she here displays by speaking of virtue which *widens* the gap between itself and the external goods. For it could hardly be argued that a person's pursuit of bodily comfort itself increased the probability that he not attain it. To widen the gap one must aim at something beyond the external goods themselves—and for Nussbaum this something includes, if not *is*, the "relational goods" she proceeds to discuss in her next chapter.

When we move to her subsequent discussion we find the chapter divided in two sections, built on the two "excellences" in the preceding quotation. Section one focuses on "membership and good activity in a political community" (345 ff.), section two on friends and friendship (354 ff.).

At this point, however, we must ask about the reason for such a division. Why, according to Nussbaum, must friendship and political relationships be treated separately? She says herself that what Aristotle called *philia* is a good deal broader than our term "friendship" and encompasses for Aristotle many more relations than those we today call by that name (354). Moreover, she notes in passing that political excellence is in fact perhaps best understood just in terms of friendship: "love and friendship, and the part of political excellence that is a type of friendship or love (if not, indeed, the entirety of political excellence), are in their nature relations" (343).

In fact, the division of politics and friendship is not traceable to Aristotle. He treats them together as follows:

> We may see even in our travels how near and dear every man is to every other. Friendship seems to hold states together, and lawgivers to care more for it than justice; for concord seems to be something like friendship, and this they aim at most of all, and expel faction as their worst enemy; and when men are friends they have no need of justice, while when they are just they need friendship as well, and the truest form of justice is thought to be a friendly quality.[3]

There is reason, then, to be critical of Nussbaum at this juncture. As one of us has argued elsewhere,[4] Nussbaum is a liberal, and she means to liberalize Aristotle. That she feels compelled to separate political relations from friendship, particularly when explicating Aristotle in whose works no such distinction is to be found, is evidence of this. Consider in this regard the following quote from Alasdair MacIntyre:

> E. M. Forster once remarked that if it came to a choice between betraying his country and betraying his friend, he hoped that he would have the courage to betray his country. In an Aristotelian perspective anyone who can formulate such a contrast has no country, has no *polis;* he is a citizen of nowhere, an internal exile wherever he lives.

Indeed from an Aristotelian point of view a modern liberal political society can appear only as a collection of citizens of nowhere who have banded together for their common protection.[5]

In fact Nussbaum, who is interested in arguing that the "relational goods" are the rightful foci of the fragility of goodness, is led astray by the modern distinction between politics and friendship, the result being that in her comments about fragility and politics she becomes uncharacteristically trivial. She notes that Aristotle himself had "to leave Athens twice under political pressure" and was "barred because of his resident alien status from owning property," and concludes that "he knew all too well that to attach value to the city and one's role in it was to care about something highly unstable" (345). Further she opines that despite possible disappointments, "competent and serious people [must] turn their attentions to legislation and political planning" (352), even knowing this increases the chance of further failures. This sounds like saying that by working for the Dukakis campaign we set ourselves up for the disappointment of watching Bush elected, but to do so is better than to throw up our hands in dismay and move to a lonely island in the South Pacific.[6]

To her credit, Nussbaum struggles valiantly in this section on "politics" to appropriate a comment from Aristotle, which we shall make more of directly, namely that "the human being is a political creature and naturally disposed to living-with" (1169b19). Yet the false division she has set up between friendship and political associations makes the significance of this point elusive. Ironically, we must wait until her second section on friendship before we can begin to grasp its force.

3. Beyond Instrumentality:
Nussbaum on Aristotle on Friendship

It is right to credit John Cooper with sparking a revival in the discussion of Aristotelian friendship. Indeed Nussbaum refers frequently to his seminal "Aristotle on Friendship"[7] as she develops her own view. She learns from Cooper, but in the end outstrips him in her arguments about the importance of friendship for an Aristotelian perspective on the moral life. For even as Cooper champions the importance of Aristotle's views on friendship, he says:

> It must be granted, of course, that someone who was so constituted that he could achieve these results [i.e., knowing himself and regarding his life as worth living] without forming friendships would have been given no strong reason [by Aristotle] to form them. . . . Hence anyone who thinks that, nonetheless, such a friendless person would be leading a less than fully satisfactory life will not find in Aristotle anything to support his view.[8]

In other words, Cooper does not believe that Aristotle believed that friendlessness is necessarily accompanied by unhappiness. But Nussbaum cannot agree. For on her view, in addition to defending friendship's instrumental value, Aristotle also defends it as *intrinsically valuable* for happiness.

What Nussbaum means by this is best approached by degrees. To begin, Aristotle suggests frequently that friends are useful; friends give each other pleasure and advance one another's projects. These provisions of friendship no doubt help us in our lives and facilitate our *eudaimonia*, but we cannot assume that without their help we could not achieve it.

Beyond this usefulness, Aristotle seems to imply in his "self-knowledge" argument for friendship (one which Cooper replays) that we cannot obtain self-knowledge—something essential to *eudaimonia*—from any more accurate and revealing source than from watching our friend, who is a sort of "second self." Indeed, we must have friends in order to obtain the self-knowledge necessary for *eudaimonia*. While a more ambitious argument with stronger implications, this replay of the self-knowledge argument nevertheless still falls one step short of establishing that friendship is intrinsic to *eudaimonia*. As second selves, friends might be *necessary* instruments, but they are still instruments. To be valued intrinsically in the way Nussbaum would have it, friendship must be thought to be so closely tied up with the good life that the very description of the latter cannot be given without reference to the former. In this way, friendship is not just a necessary means to the good life, it is partly constitutive of it.

This is Nussbaum's view. She lays claim to Aristotle's frequent appeal to our nature as being essentially social. Further, following arguments put forward earlier about Aristotle's appearances (i.e., that Aristotle is finally to be understood as nonreductively appealing to the way we see the world as the appropriate starting place for philosophical and moral reflection), she suggests that friendship is crucial, indeed decisive; we cannot even imagine our life without friends. So she translates an important passage as follows: "And surely it is peculiar to make the *makarios* person a solitary; for nobody would choose to have all the good things in the world all by himself. For the human being is a political creature and naturally disposed to living-with. And this is true of the *eudaimon* as well. . . . Therefore the *eudaimon* needs *philoi*" (1169b10–22; Nussbaum, 366). And she comments:

> Aristotle says that the opponent [he who supposes we can live well without friends] has a point *only* if we think of *philoi* as mere means to other solitary goods, and the solitary life which has these goods as a complete life. But in fact we do not think this way. We think that a life without them, even with all other goods, is so seriously incomplete that it is not worth living. So . . . *philoi* and *philia* will be *parts* of human *eudaimonia* and constitutive of, rather than just instrumental to, its self sufficiency. (366)

The arguments for friendship stop precisely here: we are, all of us who share the name "human being," creatures who *live-with.* In an important way, creatures who leave off living-with no longer are us, even if they resemble us in virtually all other aspects.

This point is itself an artful summation of Nussbaum's book. For she has argued that Plato's middle period ethics is an attempt to provide us a way of living self-sufficiently, alone, insulated by philosophy from the world and from our friends. In response, Nussbaum's Aristotle can answer that that philosopher, that "stone," in an important way is no longer one of us; his life, no matter how otherwise skilled or interesting, can never attain *human eudaimonia.*

> The opponent has asked us to choose a solitary life; we point out that this goes against our nature, implying in this way that no being identical to us would survive in such a life. To wish the good for oneself or for another, Aristotle has insisted, requires wishing a life in which

that sort of person will still exist: not a life which, however admirable or godlike, could be lived by someone identical with me. In asking whether this solitary life can be the object of our highest wish, the first thing to ask is, whether it can be the object of my wish at all. If it is my nature to be a social being, the happy solitary will not be identical with me; so to wish for a life lacking in the value of *philia* is to wish not for the Protagorean 'saving' of one's own life, but for a (Socratic) transformation to a different life. (366–67)

4. Parting Company:
Aristotle's Politics, Nussbaum's Fragility

In the final pages of her treatment of Aristotle, Nussbaum has offered a rich and convincing account of why friendship is crucial to Aristotle's view of the good life. She has urged that his understanding of our social nature leads him to suppose that friendships and friends are essential to *human* living well. Moreover, she thinks Aristotle is right, *philia* is absolutely essential to the moral life.

This outcome, however, is not without its price. For with so high a value placed on friendship we shall be all the more eager to know how it is to be described. Indeed, if friendship is part and parcel of *eudaimonia,* then it cannot but follow that knowing what the former involves is necessary if we are to know something of the latter. As we have argued, Nussbaum's initial descriptions of friendship are lacking, at least as interpretations of Aristotelian friendship, precisely because they sever friendship from what Nussbaum otherwise terms "political participation"; her two-part division between one and the other "relational good" is an artificial modern imposition. Indeed, more evidence for its artificiality has arisen even as Nussbaum has made the crucial argument concerning our essentially social natures. For in order to make her point that friendship pervades Aristotle's ethics such that any comprehensive understanding of it is impossible apart from friendship, she cites a passage from Book I of the *Nicomachean Ethics.* In Ross's translation that passage reads: "[T]he final good is thought to be self-sufficient. Now by self-sufficient we do not mean that which is sufficient for a man by himself, for one who lives a solitary life, but also for parents, children, wife, and in general for his friends and fellow citizens, since man is born for citizenship" (1097b14–15). When discussing another passage on friendship she parenthetically refers back to this one in an interesting way: "It is conspicuous in this case as in the political case (and in fact the two arguments are *very closely linked,* as the last citation shows), Aristotle refers throughout the argument to prevalent ordinary beliefs" (366, emphasis added). *Our* point is that it is not merely that the arguments are "very closely linked" but rather that they are one and the same. Friendship for Aristotle *is* a politics. Or as Paul Wadell has commented, "The relationship between friendship and the city-state is not friendship removed from the *polis,* not even friendship over against the *polis,* but friendship *within* the *polis.*"[9]

For Nussbaum friendship is not this, for she is a modern person, a modern liberal, and so does not conceive of political relationships in this way.

One more feature of this quotation from Aristotle should not be missed if we are to go further in exploring how Nussbaum (*not* Aristotle) connects friendship and fragility. Recall that Nussbaum has proceeded on the premise that *fragility as opposed to self-sufficiency* rightly characterizes the good human life. This is the ground on which she has rejected Plato's (middle period) views. Yet in the previous citation we find Aristotle praising self-sufficiency; for him it is, apparently, a crucial characteristic of the final good. Yet this sufficiency is not *individual* self-sufficiency, for it is not "what is sufficient for a man by himself." It is a self-sufficiency nonetheless.

To this point Nussbaum has attacked individual self-sufficiency. What does she make of this new, communal sort of self-sufficiency Aristotle assumes is descriptive of the final good? We suspect that at this point we witness a parting of the ways. Nussbaum cannot go along this path of Aristotle's. To see why we must recall that her interest in Aristotle's friendship was sparked by the fragility the "relational goods" introduced into the life of *eudaimonia.* As she mentioned, the relational goods not only introduce luck into the good life—the external goods do this already—they also themselves produce a further instability, since they often make the external goods more difficult to achieve and keep. (Loyalty to our friends can easily cost us our lives.) Yet as the quotations from Aristotle mount up, it seems increasingly clear that he believes friendship as a political relation increases the stability of the good life in the community, which, as well ordered by friendship, achieves a certain kind of communal self-sufficiency. Put simply, since it demands of them a forfeiture of the external goods, virtue may make *eudaimonia* less likely for certain individuals, yet this risk, this fragility, on their part actually increases the probability that their community will together attain *eudaimonia.*

This is a point Nussbaum cannot accept, not simply because as a modern liberal she has some difficulty thinking in communal terms (although surely this is part of it) but also because she is convinced that human relations, particularly love relations—the relations for which many of the virtues are required—are essentially *unstable.* This view of Nussbaum's can be discovered in bits throughout her book, most notably in the appendix on Euripides' *Hecuba.* It appears in a definitive way in a paper written subsequently and delivered before the American Academy of Religion in 1988 entitled "Serpents in the Soul: Love and Anger in Seneca's *Medea.*"[10] In that address Nussbaum explicitly expressed the wish to revise *Fragility*'s thesis, for she had recently become convinced that the sort of fragility offered by Aristotle is not fragile enough. Instead, the fragility she seeks is open not only to the risk of losing the external goods—as Aristotle's is—but also open to a certain evil, that born of love as it turns to jealousy. (That is to say, true love *will,* under certain circumstances, turn to jealousy, as *Medea* illustrates. That is its nature.) On Nussbaum's revised view Aristotle cheerily supposed that "we can have love and continue to be virtuous." But as Seneca suggests in *Medea,* "love is a dangerous hole in the self." Insofar as we stake our lives upon it, "love"—here quite clearly to be understood as erotic love—will (and must) always remain open to the possibility of destruction, of the love and the lovers.

We find these ideas as well in *Fragility*'s appendix on *Hecuba.* In *Medea* an erotic relationship explodes in violence; in *Hecuba* a trust relation is betrayed and, with a haunting inevitability, leads to the violent destruction of Polymestor (the betrayer), Hecuba, and the relation between them. Both treatments indicate something of the sort of fragility Nussbaum seeks; it is not the fragility of Aristotle's *philia.* As Nussbaum herself displays it (359–61), the fragility of *philia* resides in the relation's susceptibility to changes external to it, for example when one of the friends dies or is changed in some significant way or, as we discussed earlier, when one falls victim to significant suffering. All friends know their friendship can be affected by these external forces that come with time. In contrast, the loves of *Hecuba* and of *Medea* themselves create a new sort of fragility, one that transcends that already present in our lives. For it is the love itself, now inverted, that destroys the human world wherein it originated. The change in the love which swallows it is uniquely dark and violent, primarily because it is born not of the external world of caprice but from the depths of the human soul, as able to hate and seek vengeance as to love and trust.

This contrast between the loves of *philia* and (primarily) *eros* should illustrate how Aristotle can speak of the former as self-sufficient. As Nussbaum draws the contrast,

> The rhythm of *philia* in its best or highest cases seems to be steadier and less violent than that of Platonic *eros;* we do not find the element of sudden openness that is central to the *Phaedrus* lovers. . . . [N]ow is the time to admit that we do not find here [i.e., in Aristotle's *philia*], or do not, at least, find emphasized, the structure of tension and release, longing and repletion, that is so important in the *Phaedrus*'s view of true insight. (369–70)[11]

Nussbaum may believe that *philia* is intrinsic to *eudaimonia;* surely she has ably argued for the point. But it has become clear in the course of the argument that she believes something else as well. *Philia* is ultimately inadequately fragile to merit her highest praise. She reserves that for the more explosive *eros,* whose fragility arises not just from the fact that it might be cut off by death or accident but from the darkness and ferocity that ever lurks in its very soul.

5. Christianity, Friendship, and Fragility

There remains for us the matter of what Christians might say about Nussbaum and fragility, Aristotle and friendship. Any response cannot be simple. For as we have seen, Nussbaum, while giving a compelling defense of Aristotle's view of friendship, subverts it in at least one important way. Further, while initially she presents Aristotle's view of friendship as sensitive to the fragility of goodness in ways that other views, such as Plato's, are not, it becomes clear that she thinks it is not nearly fragile enough.

In ordering our response, let us consider each of the objections, ours about Nussbaum's liberal subversion of Aristotle's politics, and Nussbaum's about Aristotle's lack of fragility, to see how a Christian vision of friendship and fragility might address each. To do this we do not need a complete account of Christian friendship—something neither of us is prepared to offer. We need only consider if Christian friendship is political, if it is fragile, and, if fragile, to what degree.

To begin with Nussbaum's depoliticizing of Aristotle's friendship, rather than focusing our concern on how accurate Nussbaum is about Aristotle, let us instead consider whether in fact her liberal (re)vision of Aristotelian friendship is not better suited to a modern world shaped by the Enlightenment—a world peopled with MacIntyre's "citizens of nowhere, internal exiles wherever they live."

In the opening paragraph of this chapter we commented that Nussbaum comes to Aristotle not merely to interpret but also to appropriate many of his insights about the moral life. She wants to find what he has said that will help us think about our own lives. Given this concern, we should not be surprised that she depoliticizes his friendship. Her division of "friendship" from "political participation" is better suited to our present vision of the moral life than the more integrated political friendship in Aristotle. Modern friendship is "personal" not "political," so if Aristotle is to be helpful in thinking about personal friendship he must be reworked.

In one sense, then, Nussbaum does the right thing with Aristotle, given the shape of the modern world to which she speaks. But the question arises: is it the right thing for Christians to do? No doubt what the modern world is impinges on us Christians as well, but we can hardly take it as the only or even most pressing reality.

As Christians of all ages have maintained, the Christian is a Christian in the church; she cannot know what being a Christian entails apart from the community of friends who together form one another into selves who reflect the image of their God. In this way Christians (and other groups who have something similar to what Christians call an ecclesiology) should be in a position to appropriate Aristotle's insights about *philia* as Nussbaum cannot, particularly those who assume friendship is a kind of politics.

Nussbaum herself has opened up a way for this appropriation to begin. Aristotle, she has shown us, could think friendship of *intrinsic* worth because he also thought humans were by nature beings who live-with. Friendship is therefore not to be primarily thought of as a relation we might benefit from, or into which we might decide to enter. For apart from friendship, there *is* no "I."

By and large this point has been neglected among post-Enlightenment theologians. Christian thinkers from Kierkegaard to Outka have struggled with the *"tension"* they presume exists between friendship and "Christian love," usually called *agape*. Behind this tension stands a presumption: there is some solitary Christian self who alternatively enters into (chooses to enter into) relations which are *philia* or relations which are *agape*. But if we follow Nussbaum's reading of Aristotle, this presumption must be denied.

This is not to say the Christian notion of *agape* should be abandoned. Rather it reorients how *agape* might be described. Aristotle's notion of a human person as one who "lives-with"—when appropriated within a Christian ecclesiology—requires that distinctively Christian love be communally given; it is a love in which individual persons share, rather than a love one of them possesses or even gives by himself. Or, to place *agape* in relation to the *philia* we have been discussing, one might say that *philia* in the Christian church forms Christians to embody the love theologians have described as *agape*. Yet in saying so we must hold tight to the Aristotelian insight. For it is not that we Christians are formed by *philia* to become individuals who can individually practice *agape*. Rather it is that we are formed by *philia* in the church to become a community which in its corporate life in the world loves the world in the manner of *agape,* whose practice it has learned in seeking to conform itself to the God who is in Christ.[12] (In an important way the church is never a *friend* to the world, and so there is good reason to keep alive both the terms *agape* and *philia* in our vocabulary.) As Paul Wadell says, "To pledge oneself to Christian love is to place oneself within a history of love, to become part of the drama of salvation which one's own love hopes to continue. Agape is the community of those who share this common memory and pledge to keep it alive . . . community formed from a historical event, the revelation of God in Jesus."[13]

Turning to Nussbaum's criticism that Aristotle's account of friendship ultimately lacks fragility, and what Christians might make of it, we have suggested already that her quest for fragility takes her beyond what Aristotle calls friendship. (We have also meant to imply that Christians also should think his account inadequate—perhaps inadequately fragile—since he thinks friends should not share in one another's grief.) To draw out her point, Nussbaum paraphrases a criticism originally lodged by Bernard Williams, namely that Aristotle's friendship is "cozy and insular: that by concentrating on the love of people *similar* in character it removes the element of risk and surprise that can be a high value in an encounter with another soul" (368).[14] This is to be linked with Aristotle's "sort of cozy defense of the status quo" and his "notoriously crude and hasty investigation of the potential of women for excellence" (371), for which he is so frequently indicted.

Of course Nussbaum has otherwise praised Aristotle, so she tempers her criticism by noting that his blindness on these points arose not from his "appearance method" but from his own failure to follow it consistently. Yet we are inclined to believe that there is stronger substance to the charge, for as Nussbaum has helped us see, Aristotle appeals continually to the commonly held "way we see things," and in fact the "we" in his time wrongly and falsely saw women as inferiors. Aristotle's appearances cannot save him from this. Happy slaves, light-minded women—these *were* his appearances.

Insularity is in fact a serious and important charge to be considered by defenders of friendship, Aristotelian or otherwise, precisely because friendship is so often built upon likeness, shared projects or shared judgments.[15] Indeed, if the Christian church is a community of friends, invariably it will turn strangers into friends by calling them to share in a set of judgments they could not have had before entering the community. Formally this is as true of friends in the church as friends in Athens, or in the academy.

Mention of the stranger, however, provides the chance to recall an important Christian commitment, one learned from Jews. This is that the Christian community is continually required to offer hospitality to the stranger. As Thomas Ogletree has written

> To offer hospitality to a stranger is to welcome something new, unfamiliar and unknown into our life-world. . . . Hospitality designates occasions of potential discovery which can open up our narrow, provincial worlds. Strangers have stories to tell which we have never

heard before, stories which can redirect our seeing and stimulate our imaginations. The stories invite us to view the world from a novel perspective. They display the finitude and relativity of our own orientation of meaning. . . . The stranger does not simply challenge or subvert our assumed world of meaning; she may enrich, even transform that world.[16]

This commitment is difficult to maintain properly, as the Old Testament story of Ezra and the returned exiles displays. However, the ideal suggests the possibility of a fundamentally different politics of friendship not to be found in Aristotle. Somewhat ironically, Nussbaum hits upon it when, as an aside, she describes a theology whose political implications are unlike the communal self-sufficiency of Aristotle's city of friends. Speaking of Dionysus, she says:

he is the god who dies. He undergoes, each year, a ritual death and rebirth, a cutting back and a resurgence, like a plant, like desire itself. Among the gods he alone is not self-sufficient, he alone can be acted on by the world. He is the god who would be of no use for teaching young citizens the "god's eye" point of view. And yet, miraculously, despite his fragility, he restores himself and burgeons. This suggests that an unstable city, an unstable passion, might grow and flourish in a way truly appropriate to a god—a thought that has no place in the theology of the ideal city. (194–95)

The God of Abraham, Moses, and Jesus is not the dying and rising Dionysus, but Christians will recognize in Nussbaum's description something of the character they attribute to the God who in Jesus comes to share our fragile humanity. As they worship this fragile God, Christians will be challenged to sustain and nourish their friendships in the midst of a community that does not protect them from the stranger. At the very least, they have learned their friendship from Christ, who welcomed children, prostitutes, and Samaritans, and who commands them to do likewise.

6. Conclusion: Nussbaum and Christians on Tragedy

Earlier we stated parenthetically that the world can never be thought of by Christians as friend. Ogletree's comments qualify this in an important way. Although "the world" is rightly thought of as an enemy to whom Christians offer themselves in *agape,* they must be guarded in their designation of just what "the world" is. Frequently we discover in what we are wont to call "the world" strangers who speak to us as friends.

Christians can find such in Nussbaum. Like Ogletree's stranger, she tells a story that "redirects our seeing" and "stimulates our imaginations." Nevertheless, as we have attempted to display, Nussbaum's desire for fragility within friendship is not and cannot be shared by Christians. We can share with her the concern that Aristotle's friendship lacks fragility precisely because it lacks openness to the significantly other, as the material consequence of a body politic based on that friendship makes plain. Christian friendship must exceed the openness and fragility of Aristotle's; nevertheless, it cannot attain the fragility Nussbaum apparently seeks. Hers, ultimately, is a fragility based on tragedy, one which supposes our greatest loves and passions, exposed to the naked world of luck, can just as easily destroy us as exalt us. In reply, Christians must say that love, true love, is not like that. Put another way, the story Christians tell of God, the world and human life is not ultimately a tragedy—or, if it is a tragedy, someone else besides Christians must tell it.[17]

The pattern we have tried to display in Nussbaum's thought has involved a steady drift from Aristotle's stable friendship to Hecuba's violent passion. This is not to say that Nussbaum herself embraces the violence; she calls it evil throughout. Rather, she seems to have reached the conclusion that it is love's nature to have a dark side, one which can rise up explosively if the time and circumstances are ripe. When it does, as with Hecuba, the narrative it controls turns tragic, and the transformation of the lovers is ultimately an annihilation.

Aristotle kept his distance from this love, embracing instead the steadier and safer relationship he called friendship. Christians must also eschew such "love," not in order to remain immune to contingency and risk, but rather because they know of another love they call true love. Its specific name is "God." God's love in its manifold forms never annihilates; it always frees and offers new life.[18]

The fundamental claim that God's love frees and creates rather than tragically destroys is layered throughout the Christian story in many forms. In light of its implications, Christians can discover the places where they must part ways with Nussbaum's fragility, of which we here note three. First, with Jews, Christians affirm that "the earth is the Lord's and the fullness thereof, the world and all those who dwell within it" (Psalms 24:1). Moreover, they claim to know something of the character of this Lord, of His promises and His will for the world He created. When Nussbaum speaks of "openness to the world" and understands this in the light of tragedy, she is making the point that we cannot and should not insulate ourselves against the possibility of utter meaninglessness. We must be open even to the possibility that not only our meanings but any meaning at all may be tragically wrenched from us by the world and destroyed before our eyes. By contrast, Christians think they know that this finally *cannot* be the character of the world, for it is a creation of a gracious God. Or, put succinctly, Christians' affirmations of the fragility of goodness must always be qualified by their eschatological convictions.

Second, as Nussbaum (building upon Aristotle) notes, one of the tragic emotions, pity, cannot be felt by Christians: "In the *Rhetoric* he [Aristotle] makes the interesting observation that the person who is too pessimistic about human nature will not feel pity at all—for he will believe that everyone deserves the bad things that happen to them (a remark pregnant with implications for the question of Christian tragedy)" (384). Here Nussbaum is correct in her inference that Christians cannot feel pity, but she is wrong about the reason. As she goes on to say, pity arises when we see that only luck stands between us and the sufferer, the victim of the tragedy. Christians cannot allow luck of this sort to stand and, so she implies, they replace it with blame.

It is correct to say that Christians cannot speak of luck as others might. As one of us has elsewhere put it, Christians "rage against fortune."[19] Yet contrary to Nussbaum's implications, Christians do not replace luck (and therefore pity) with blame, but with compassion, with "suffering-with."[20] This is what they have been taught to do by God, who does not stand apart from His human creatures, pitying them, but enters into their fragile world, ultimately to be killed for them, as well as at their hands. As Reinhold Niebuhr has put it, "Christianity is a religion which transcends tragedy. Tears, with death, are swallowed up in victory. The cross is not tragic but the resolution of tragedy. Here suffering is carried into the very life of God and overcome. It becomes the very basis of salvation."[21]

Thirdly and finally, as Nussbaum's treatment of *Hecuba* reveals, the possibility of tragedy arises from the strong loves and commitments upon which Hecuba stakes her life, for she has bonded herself in trust relations with others which they might betray. Betrayal, in fact, shadows love; more than any other eventuality, it gives rise to the evil that, for Nussbaum, lurks in the very structure of love itself. This is a feature of human love Christians can readily admit. Invariably we will fall short of the trust others who love us place in us, just as the children of Israel fell short of God's trust as they journeyed from Egypt and beyond. Of course as Jews and Christians tell the story, God is entirely trustworthy, even when His covenant companions are not. As this story also affirms, while a breach in trust can and must bring damage to love (its rightful fruit is anger, as we suggest in our next chapter), it need not give birth to revenge, as in Hecuba's case. As Nussbaum tells that story, when Hecuba discovers Polymestor has betrayed her trust and murdered her child Polydorus, she decides between only two available options:

> Now confronted with the failure of *nomos*, she seems to have two choices only. She can blind herself to these events, finding some way to distance the knowledge or confine it. . . . Or she can accept the knowledge, touch it, take it as something true of nomos, of social bonds in general. But then it seems impossible, in these rending circumstances, to escape the corrosion of that openness on which good character rests. She cannot escape being caught up in a questioning and suspicion. . . .
>
> From now on the *nomos* of trust, and Hecuba's trust in *nomos*, will be replaced by something new from these new events: "O child, child / now I begin my mourning, / the wild newly-learned melody (*nomos*) / from the spirit of revenge." (*Hecuba*, 684–87; Nussbaum, 409)

Aristotelian friendship lacks this violent, vengeful underside. And so for Nussbaum it is not finally open and fragile enough; it is not capable of the depths, so neither is it capable of the heights. It lacks the fragility that is open to tragedy.

Christian friendship also lacks this fragility. But this is because it breaks the connection Nussbaum sees here as inseparable. In the face of betrayal, it refuses her either/or of blindness or revenge by offering another way: forgiveness, reconciliation, restoration.

Can Polymestor be forgiven? Can he be reconciled to Hecuba? Can their friendship be restored? Christians must always claim that the final dissolution in their lives and loves after tragedy is not inevitable. These things—forgiveness, reconciliation, restoration—are real possibilities for fragile humans like Hecuba and Polymestor because, and only because, they have already become actual in the God who was in Christ reconciling the world to himself.[22]

SIX

Pagan Virtue
and Christian Prudence

1. Introduction: John Casey on Pagan Virtue

Martha Nussbaum means to revive certain of Aristotle's and the tragedians' insights on ethics. One might ask, in doing so does she mean to revive as well the paganism which stood as the backdrop to their reflection? As we have suggested, backdrop makes a good deal of difference for what sort of conversations can be had about ethics. Within the context of the Enlightenment, discussions of virtue are difficult; within the context of paganism they are much easier. This itself may serve as an argument for the revival of paganism or at least certain of its features, such as, for Nussbaum, the ascendancy of luck and of tragedy. Yet neither Nussbaum nor MacIntyre really works toward any such revival.[1]

In his recent *Pagan Virtue* [2] John Casey is on this point more bold. He sets about to write out an account of pagan virtue which is cognizant of the political life-world it presumed. While this is the life-world of the ancient pagans, it is also to some degree our own, since, as Casey alleges, pagan assumptions and ways of life have continued to exist and thrive alongside Christian ones in Western societies.

Casey begins by embedding pagan virtue in a foundation of what he calls the "active emotions," such as anger and jealousy, which on his account encourage a direct engagement with another person. By contrast, passive emotions form in us a limpness with respect to another person, for they ignore her particulars and allow us to remain distant, regarding her as one of a class we hate, or perhaps pity. Unlike the active anger which confronts a person, rebuking her on some specific point, the passive hate shrouds its object, often classing her within a group which shares an objectifiable characteristic, such as racial descent.

Casey suggests that the active emotions in general, and anger in particular, issue from a demand for respect at the same time that they echo respect for the one to whom they are directed. Tactically, this is an important point for him, since he hopes for the support of Kantians in his subsequent discussion of pagan virtues. Immanuel Kant, he thinks, was right to urge respect for persons, yet Kant's notion of person as rational being remains an abstraction. In contrast, Casey's idea of a person is "someone who essentially has a history. We cannot get at the idea of a person unless we think of his life as a history. . . . The life of a man is the story of a man . . . and this means also that every life has a significance, a meaning, offers itself for interpretation and assessment" (89). It is these persons who are angered and are themselves the worthy objects of anger.

Kantians are, according to Casey, representatives of a tradition of moral reflection which owes much to Christianity. This "Christian" tradition is on many points the antithesis of the pagan tradition that Casey favors, yet it is too much with us to defeat. Evidently he hopes for some degree of complementarity between the two traditions, as he shows when he attempts to refurbish Kantian respect for persons with what he seems to suppose is a pagan view of the self. But combining the traditions is not Casey's explicit undertaking in this book. Rather, he seeks to "modestly recover" the pagan ethical traditions, not just because they have been overshadowed by its Christian rival but also because they "make sense of our experience" (ix).

Without dwelling on the tension between paganism and Christianity, Casey at various points acknowledges it. For instance, he notes that "[p]ride, a desire for worldly glory, a sense that one can be 'a principle to oneself', a lack of any apprehension that there might be some order of values in comparison with which those of the world are as nothing—all these are included in what Christianity has called 'paganism'" (208). Casey imagines that Christianity not only disparages these values of paganism but also replaces them with a universalism—understood in a Kantian fashion—and advocates sympathy and pity (212), which lead to more passive responses to wrong or insult than does the active anger that he, following paganism, praises. So in his concluding discussion of *King Lear*, Casey supposes Lear embodies certain central tendencies of Christianity, as his pride is too easily broken and he "is never touched by noble anger" (219). Lear's character is finally disturbing to Casey, for he sees him as lost in love and fantasy—giving us reason to suspect that Casey views Christianity similarly.

Unfortunately, the question of whether Christianity is fantasy does not arise in the book. From a pragmatic point of view, Casey sees Christianity as a powerful moral force that has marked our history deeply. Like it or not, it must be reckoned with. Perhaps this should be soothing to us Christians, although frankly we'd rather be refuted than reckoned with in this way. Moreover, it is a bit of an affront to see one's Christian convictions conflated with Kant's. At the least one might have hoped for some equal recognition that Aquinas, whom Casey uses constructively throughout, was a Christian and that his (non-Kantian) Christian convictions had something to do with what he said about virtue.

Yet the question of whether Casey gets Christianity right will not concern us in this chapter. Rather, we should like to consider Casey's intriguing attempt to present pagan virtue as a coherent way of describing and living the good human life. As we shall argue, Casey's account, while engaging, falls short on certain important points. These points are independently interesting. In the first place they display how different kinds of paganism are importantly at odds. Furthermore, they provide a way to show how Christianity is at odds both with ancient paganism and with Casey's modernized variety and so open a way to consider how Christians might understand prudence, friendship, and anger differently from either of them.

In considering Casey's contribution to the discussion we have already begun in this book, it is a signal that his suggestions about the life of virtue are more programmatic, concrete, and "traditioned" than either MacIntyre's or Nussbaum's in that he writes a chapter on each of the four cardinal virtues. It is beyond our scope to treat each of these in its turn; instead we shall attempt to display what we regard as the basic pagan pattern by which his four cardinal virtues are organized and unified: the aforementioned active emotions (and especially anger) are directed by courage and prudence to a culmination in the bond of pagan friendship, which is nothing less than the embodiment of justice.

Once this pattern is noted, a significant question arises, one which Casey well recognizes. He knows that he cannot repristinate ancient pagan virtue; he is, after all, a modern writer with modern readers. How, then, can he revise the pagan tradition to fit the modern world? And further, in any such revision can the force of the ancient pagan pattern be preserved? On this second question we will argue that its force is significantly diminished precisely because Casey backs away from the *particularity* of pagan virtue in favor of a modern formalized account of friendship. Friendship, we allege, must be particular to be worth its salt, by which we mean that friendship must form us in certain particular virtues. What virtues those are, their difference, is the measure between one friendship and another, a point which can be applied to the difference between pagan and Christian friendship, particularly as the latter culminates in prudence rather than in the virtues of justice as defined by the friendship itself.

2. Anger, Pride, and Courage

In his book Casey sets out to give anger its due. Paraphrasing Aristotle, Casey contends that, while "it is possible to hate a universal class, or under a universal description, we can be angry only with individuals" (10). On the schema of the active and passive emotions already mentioned, anger is clearly active, calling us out of ourselves to confront the other. As Casey comments, "anger is in the nature of self-assertion. As I have suggested, anger involves a readiness to confront another person, to rebuke, punish, seek justice or revenge, and consequently requires self-esteem" (56). Or to reverse the thought, if people cower in the face of offense against them, if they believe themselves worthless specks in relation to others, neither will they be angered (although they may hate), nor will they possess what they need to endeavor to live a life of virtue.

Casey's point may at first appear to be another bit of psycho-babble about the need to assert oneself. Yet it is preserved from this by the fact that his self is not the kind of formal self so often identified with Kantianism, but, as mentioned above, a storied self. The story is not everyone's, rather, it is *particular*. An account of the moral life should be particular as well; it should meet specifically with the life of, say, Odysseus, adventurer, rightful ruler of Ithaca, son of Laertes, conqueror of Troy. This Odysseus cannot leave the newly blinded Polyphemos without giving his name and story. Anger, rightly had, cannot remain anonymous, it confronts and identifies, precisely in these specific and particular terms.

For Casey, it is in paganism that these connections are best recognized and carried through. For paganism, unlike Christianity, rests upon a *pride* in a self that is no abstraction but is rather embedded in a story that relates him to his family, his city, his past deeds, his reputation, and so on. It is precisely this thick connectedness of the self to his particular social world and personal history which makes a compelling account of the virtues possible.

Of course pride is not uncommonly called a virtue. Aristotle sees it so, offering it high praise: "Now the proud man, since he deserves most, must be good in the highest degree; for the better man always deserves more, and the best man most. Therefore the truly proud man must be good. . . . Pride, then, seems to be a sort of crown of the virtues; for it makes them greater, and it is not found without them."[3] Since Aristotle is less concerned than others to delineate a clear set of cardinal virtues, one might wonder whether an account like Casey's which has this delineation in mind should count pride among the cardinal virtues. Instead, Casey's strategy, not unlike Aristotle's, is to make pride a necessary companion of the cardinal virtues. He does this not so much by placing pride atop the virtues but by writing it together with anger into the nature of courage, the first of the four traditional cardinal virtues he treats.

Courage typically has been understood to involve the control of fear. For Casey, "[t]he control of fear is related to capacities such as anger, and hence to the 'spirited' part of the soul and to courage" (57). Yet courage is intelligible only in relation to what one is courageous *for*. (No one thinks it is courageous to give one's life for one's toys, for example.) Thus, a person is not courageous unless she seeks a noble end. Indeed, courage connects us directly to questions regarding what nobility involves and what, therefore, is rightly called noble.

Here is a place to mix Friedrich Nietzsche into the brew. Casey reminds us of Nietzsche's noble soul, who is rightly prideful, rightly egoistic. "Nietzsche's man of noble soul is an *egoist*, . . . not in the sense that he is 'selfish', but in the sense that he feels himself to be a standard and creator of values" (81). Yet once mixed in, Casey must prevent Nietzsche from having too positive a place in his account. In response to Kant, Casey has already proposed a view of a person as essentially storied. It is a short step to affirm what should be plain: This story is not one a person tells to herself of herself; rather, her story fits within and gains meaning from a larger "political" context. Nietzsche, for all his brilliance, seems to miss this point. As Casey puts it, "Nietzsche also rejects any picture of man as a social being. His ideal types (such as they are) can only be thought of as solitary creative geniuses. Or, as MacIntyre [*After Virtue*, 122] puts it: 'Nietzsche replaces the fictions of the Enlightenment individualism, of which he is so contemptuous, with a set of individualistic fictions of his own'" (82).

Nobility and pride might be essential for courage—and for the whole life of virtue—yet they cannot, on Casey's account, stand apart from the communities and stories which ground them. Any discussion of nobility, pride, and courage makes far better sense when placed in this political context, a point grasped more clearly in previous ages than in our own. "It was a characteristic vision of the ancient world, and again of the Renaissance, that a human being was not just the sum total of his thoughts and feelings, but the whole pattern of his life, his reputation, the true assessment of his deeds, his glory after death, his inheritance of a particular form of life, his citizenship of a particular city" (89). Indeed, courage is best understood precisely in these *political* terms. For courage leads "us naturally to think of those ways in which men attach themselves to a larger world, to their deepest loyalties, their pride, and sense of honor. And one way in which men can become consciously courageous is precisely in coming to see themselves as political beings" (90).

If Nietzsche's pride is purely individualistic it cannot support this political courage. Could Nietzsche call death for one's city on the battlefield courageous? In contrast, this is plainly the definitive act for pagan political courage. To good pagans, the noblest end is, simply, the good of one's noble city—not just the good of its people but of its life in story, which its people carry. As a man without a city, perhaps Nietzsche can have no courage.[4]

Yet this judgment of Nietzsche may be premature. Pagan courage assumes a social setting that, as he saw, no longer exists. Political courage, like Peter Berger's honor, may be obsolescent.[5] And if this is so in Nietzsche's time, it seems doubly so in ours and Casey's. As he candidly observes,

My account does indeed contain unresolved contradictions. 'Political' courage includes both patriotism, or loyalty to the state *and* the emphasis on 'noble egoism' of Nietzsche. . . . For modern man . . . the State cannot be seen as entirely stable, the object of an unproblematic loyalty. Our experience makes such a vision only something we can entertain with a certain ironic detachment. This may mean that courage, for us, strives toward a form it cannot attain. (103)

Unfortunately for Casey, pointing out these "unresolved contradictions" does little to lessen their impact on the argument so far. As the premier example of the active emotions upon which Casey's virtues will be built, anger is rightly linked to a confidence in the self. Contra Kant—and now Nietzsche—we have found that this self is necessarily storied, and that the stories are communal. Courage flows not merely from self-assertion but from pride in one's city and the stories for which and through which one lives. Yet today (and here is the difficulty for us) where is the city? Where are the stories that sustain the self and its virtues? Indeed, what Casey calls our modern ironic detachment from the state cannot but be deeply destructive of any revival of the ancient pagan account of courage.

3. The Primacy of Justice/Friendship in Pagan Virtue

We are suggesting that Casey has put himself in a tight spot, one shared by most modern people, especially those who aspire to courage. His defense of pagan virtue has worked to undo our modern formalistic and universalistic presumptions about morality so we can see, with him, that persons are not private consciousnesses, suspended, as it were, in midair. Yet the recovery of virtue requires more than relinquishing these formalistic and universalistic presuppositions, for as modern people we find ourselves, as Casey puts it, "ironically detached" from any particular state or city. At the very least, this modern status deprives us of the storied context that is the condition of courageous action.

Perhaps Casey should simply discard courage and look instead to recover other pagan virtues. As we discussed in chapter 4, this would be similar to Pincoffs's attempt to privatize virtue, subsuming it under a liberal ideology. Casey toys with this strategy when he suggests, with Machiavelli, that there may in fact be a strong distinction between virtue in public and in private, temperance being one cardinal virtue better suited to the latter (143). In the end, however, he resists any full turn toward private virtue—wisely, in our view, since privatization would forfeit not only courage but the storied and communal sense of the self which has made Casey's attempt to reclaim pagan virtue credible and his reworking of Kantian respect for persons a genuine revision. Courageously, Casey looks in earnest to find another political home for courage. On his way, he raises the stakes. For, as we discover, practical wisdom (or prudence) also requires such a political home if it is to be developed and passed on. An ongoing community is essential if a tradition of reflection about what is good and true (the province of prudence) is to be sustained. As Casey says,

> The man of practical wisdom cannot be imagined to exist outside of a tradition. He may be radical, but then he criticizes the tradition. Or in criticizing the tradition he may be "traditionalist"—i.e., he may call for the tradition to be revivified. . . . Intelligent goodness does not spring fully disarmed from nowhere, but requires the support of a tradition of human life. (170)

These comments suggest that the acquisition and practice of practical wisdom require not just that one be prepared to give oneself for the community (as in courage) but that one actually live within it. That is to say, one might imagine a modified, modern courage by which an individual could die for an abstracted form of a state, one in which he could not live but which, nonetheless, stood in his mind as an idea or representation of the good state. Yet no mere *idea* of a state can teach practical wisdom as Casey here describes it.

Casey's treatment of courage, and now practical wisdom, has created in his readers considerable anticipation. Courage and practical wisdom require a community.[6] Courage needs to discover a set of noble ends to which it is rightly offered, such as those provided in ancient paganism by the *polis* for which one was courageous. Practical wisdom cannot be had without a cross-generational community in which a tradition of practices is passed on, sustained, and modified. Both direct our attention to some well-ordered community and to the virtue or virtues that sustain it. Where can it be found?

Traditionally *justice* is the virtue which orders and sustains the community of virtue. Fittingly, Casey reserves his discussion of it until last. As we plunge in, we are initially surprised. Rather than treating us to a delineation of the "rules of justice," Casey sets about to describe the sort of community in which justice is possible. It is, essentially, a community of friendship.

> If we are to look for the category that best fits the virtues that underlie friendship, can we do better than call it justice? Friends treat each other justly. The moral relationship between them is, as it were, an informal version of the justice, in the form of law, that holds states together. And the justice, in the form of law, that holds states together, requires as its basis a 'civic friendship' between citizens. If we can envisage a relationship between individuals which has no further purpose than to achieve the good which is inherent in virtuous mutual love, then we can also envisage an analogous relation amongst men in the public sphere. (193)

Casey speaks here of envisaging. One cannot but wonder if envisaging is quite enough; not unjustifiably, we have been looking for something more concrete. Nonetheless, we must recall that Casey means in this book to rediscover a tradition of virtue which existed once in relation to actual communities and which might exist again. Pagan communities might yet take new forms; perhaps Casey and his friends have begun one. Indeed a book like this is an appropriate starting place, for it revives the wisdom of a certain past, re-presenting sage voices to which new generations once again might listen and learn.

We believe, actually, that Casey's movement from courage and practical wisdom to justice is completely appropriate, especially for the purpose of rediscovering paganism. Moreover, identifying justice in terms of friendship rather than, say, Rawlsian principles of justice, seems the right next step. But there are more steps to take. For we will want to know more about the specific character of the friendship Casey recommends as the basis of justice—and therefore of all the virtues. Around what is it formed? To what is it dedicated?

Precisely at this point Casey's book delivers its greatest disappointment. He appropriates the views of Michael Oakeshott concerning the best civil condition. It is one, namely, that aims at no "extrinsic substantive purpose." Oakeshott's treatment of this condition illumines as well what Casey has in mind for friendship. Following Oakeshott's understanding of Aristotle's views on friendship, Casey holds that

> [f]riendship does not achieve a good extrinsic to itself. Analogously, we can think of the civil condition not as achieving a good for man that can be independently specified, but as fulfilling man's nature. The 'end' of the *polis* is the same as that of human conduct in general—the good life, or human excellence. But this end cannot be understood apart from the activities which characterize it. The good to be achieved is the good of man *qua* 'political animal'. (191)

Oakeshott's views encourage Casey to adopt a highly formal notion not only of friendship, but of the good and of any community which lives by it. Oakeshott believes that the

> pursuit of happiness is a 'formal' description of human conduct, and does not attribute to men the desire for a 'substantive' end. Analogously, civil association does not aim at such substantive ends as prosperity, 'social justice', or the kingdom of Christ upon earth, even though some of these ends may in fact help to make possible and preserve the association. . . . He [Oakeshott] suggests that in those states where people are disposed to cultivate the freedom inherent in human agency, the understanding of the state will be that of the 'civil association' which he has described. States which set themselves substantive purposes . . . fall away from the condition of civil association into that of 'enterprise associations'. The modern state engaged in war is perhaps the prime example of an enterprise association. (192–93)[7]

It is worth noting that just when Casey denies that a civil association serves another end, this quotation suggests one, namely, a world of nation-states at peace. Perhaps this bespeaks a modern utopian sentiment: if each nation would tend to its own civility, the world would be freed of war. Yet quite aside from this modern utopian intrusion, Casey's appropriation of Oakeshott's ideas is problematic. First, Oakeshott adopts a strong reading of Aristotle's friendship as having no extrinsic good[8] *and then* "analogously" supposes the civil condition also has no such extrinsic good. However, we have been taught by Casey to see friendship as that which sustains (even *is*) the civil condition. We have, then, formalism piled on top of formalism—

a sort of vicious circle of intrinsic goods—and so are left with no-where to turn for help in specifying what "the virtues of friendship" (that is, justice) are.

This puts Casey's account in double jeopardy. First, insofar as we have been led from his prior treatment of courage and practical wisdom to expect a concrete display of the kind of community for which we might be prepared to be courageous or in which we might live with wisdom, we are disappointed. Secondly, and connectedly, the particularism of paganism by which Casey has resisted Kantian formalism about persons seems entirely lost.

As Nietzsche rightly saw, paganism's resistance to formalism is one of its greatest strengths.[9] A pagan is angry, loyal, courageous, honorable, not as he is formally committed to pursuing his own happiness in the context of a community of friends but as he is an Achaian, a conqueror of Troy, a son of Laertes. Only when we take these more specific parameters into account can we understand the high severity of pagan friendship, which Casey has uncovered by emphasizing the place of anger in the life of virtue. A friendship rooted in the Achaian traditions of hospitality and storytelling, or in the adventure, carnage, and sorrow of the Trojan War, demands loyalty to, as well as imitation of, the nobility of those who have gone before, those whose names fill our best-loved stories and whose memory we honor. Friendship of this sort demands accountability. The friend is unfaithful not merely if he treats his friend improperly (if, for example, he insults his dignity) but also if he fails to uphold the high standards of virtue upon which the friendship rests. These standards fundamentally are not the invention of these two friends but the gift (or the good fortune) they have both received from the political community and its past—which is why the betrayal of pagan friendship is also the betrayal of the "civil condition."[10] Indeed, an insult to a friend's dignity or pride is an affront to this community as much as to the individual friend. This is why it is so serious an offense in pagan friendship and why it is the rightful object of the hottest anger. Anger, like courage, requires a vision of the good, the noble, to which it is directed. Paganism provides this with its particular *poleis* in which particular friendships are nurtured and lived. Casey might have given us some equivalent modern context in which his concept of friendship could be given concrete form. (Cambridge dons, perhaps?) But as we have seen, he lapses instead into formal (and empty) notions of happiness and of "civil associations."

One might suitably ask: Is this, then, our modern fate? Is there nowhere in particular for us to turn to contextualize the virtues, pagan or otherwise? And so, does our courage or wisdom, or our anger, become arbitrary or merely general, calling us and our friends to a friendship of no particular sort?

There is another resource upon which some of us might call. The Christian Aquinas insisted, for example, that anger be governed by "reason." Indeed, his view that anger and justice have the same object—which Casey cites (10, 173)—assumes an "order" by which anger is checked. "[T]o wish evil to someone under the aspect of justice, may be according to the virtue of justice, if it be in conformity with the order of reason; and anger fails only in this, that it does not obey the precept of reason in taking vengeance." That is why Aquinas can say it is sometimes good to be angry. "[I]f one is angry in accordance with right reason, one's anger is deserving of praise."[11]

"Reason" may connote for many nothing more than the formalism Casey tries unsuccessfully to avoid. But there are good reasons to think a Christian account of it, rooted in Aquinas, is not formalistic. To see how, we will need to say more about prudence.

4. On Christian Prudence

In our treatment of Casey's notion of courage, we have suggested that courage (or fortitude) needs an anchor. The point is an old one. Ambrose, for instance, once said: "fortitude must not trust to itself."[12] Or as Casey might put it, for fortitude to be fortitude, it must seek a noble end. In effect, our traverse of his book has been a search for this end, one which has turned out unsuccessful.

Joseph Pieper speaks clearly about where the end of fortitude is to be discovered. "In truth, fortitude becomes fortitude only through being 'informed' by prudence."[13] This link to prudence parallels that just mentioned between anger and reason. For prudence is, for Aquinas, "the right reason about things to be done."[14]

It is important to resist the temptation—so great in a world wherein a "rationalistic conception of rationality"[15] has dominated reflection about morality—to see Aquinas's "reason" as akin to the skepticism of Descartes and his successors. As Pieper reminds us, "for the classical theology of the Church, reason always and only means the 'passage' to reality. We must avoid the temptation of transferring our justifiably contemptuous lack of confidence in the dictatorial 'reason' of the idealist philosopher of the nineteenth century to the *ratio* of scholasticism, always closely related to reality."[16]

Insofar as prudence affords a passage to reality about what is to be done, it cannot but expose truths of the greatest variety, for acts are particular and therefore various, as are the human beings who do them. As Pieper says,

> Now, the realities which surround man's concrete activity are of an almost infinite variety, *quasi infinitae diversitatis.* And above all man himself—in this distinguishing himself from the animals—is "a being of manifold and diverse activities; precisely by virtue of its rank in the order of being is the soul of man directed toward infinite variety."
>
> Since this is so, "the good of man changes in manifold fashion, according to the various condition of men and the times and places, and similar factors."[17]

The use Pieper makes of Aquinas on these points must contend with Aquinas's other well-known claim in the *Summa* that prudence sets only the *means* of moral virtue, while reason as *synderesis* sets the ends.[18] By way of response to this apparent difficulty, it is worth noting that Jean Porter has argued that while *synderesis* provides the first principle that the good of the human soul is to be in accord with reason, "this principle does not take on substantive content apart from an account of what the concrete specific good of the human creature is."[19] The discovery of this substantive content is in the domain of prudence. As Porter continues,

> Prudence, which takes account of the specifics of an individual's own character and circumstances, determines what, concretely, it means for this individual to be in accordance with reason; prudence does this in and through determining the mean of the virtues relative to the individual and to the demands of equality and the common good.[20]

On the reading suggested by Pieper and Porter, prudence does its work within the mix of specific relations and goods that give the moral life of any person its texture. Prudence as such is *political* in a way similar to courage: it makes sense only within the context of a concrete human life as that life is located within its community(ies).

To be sure, Aquinas reserves a space for "political courage," and clearly this is not exactly the same thing as the prudence he discusses prior to its introduction. Yet a closer reading of his questions on political prudence actually supports the understanding of prudence *simpliciter* we have been defending. Following Aristotle, Aquinas divides political prudence in two according as its possessor is either governor or governed in a particular society. The counsels of prudence will differ accordingly, hence prudence responds specifically to the concrete particularities of one's life, including where one finds oneself within the body politic. Furthermore, as Porter points out, what specific way political prudence is expressed "will depend upon the form of political life in a particular community."[21] Thus, the specific determinations of justice in that community will depend on prudence.

In shortest form the point is this: Prudence is wisdom about the (political) realities of a life lived within a specific and communal history, wisdom which proceeds to act. As such it is the basis for justice, the virtue by which the community is ordered and sustained. Happily, this essential connection between prudence and justice opens for us a way to return to some of Casey's best insights. To recall, Casey forges a similar link between prudence and justice by suggesting that prudence is available only in a community in which the passage of wisdom from one generation to the next is not only possible but also encouraged in those who would learn of it. Casey actually uses Aquinas to make his case, seizing upon the latter's view that *docilitas,* that is, a kind of humility that makes us teachable, is one of the essential parts of prudence.[22] He quotes Aquinas's point that *docilitas* requires that we "carefully, frequently and respectfully attend to the teaching of men of weight" and adds this commentary:

> It would be easy to interpret this as meaning that the man of *docilitas* is traditional, conservative, respectful of authority, and—well—*docile*. But we do not have to understand teachability in this way. Indeed, docility and ductility may actually war against the true virtue of *docilitas*.

We notice that Aristotle says that the reason why the unproved assertions of old and sagacious people deserve attention is that 'they grasp principles through experience.' Grasping principles through experience is essential to those arts and skills which form a context in which we understand practical wisdom. A teacher is needed who, through his personal influence and example, passes on a tradition of practice. (166–67)

For both Aquinas and Casey, then, the possession of prudence requires location within a community which hands on its wisdom about how to live.

Of course, on our argument, Casey's great error lies in his unwillingness to specify precisely what practices he, *qua* pagan, wishes to pass on, and in what specific community. This follows from his unfortunate capitulation to modernity as he conceives of friendship, and so of justice, in purely formal terms.[23] Nevertheless, even as it stands we believe Casey's treatment of pagan virtue opens a helpful pathway into the differences between pagan and Christian virtue. This is to be seen in the very arrangement of the cardinal virtues. Casey, we recall, holds justice till the end, and throughout his treatment points forward to it. It is his capstone virtue.

This is not true of Aquinas's ordering of the cardinal virtues, which culminates in prudence. The significance of this fact can be understood as follows: Christians mark the difference between themselves and paganism by insisting that the teaching of their tradition is about something other than the tradition itself. This, quite simply, reorients how Christians conceive of prudence. As MacIntyre notes, it is an identifying feature of Aquinas's prudence over against the pagan Aristotle's.

> There is a dimension to Aquinas' discussion of *prudentia* which is not Aristotelian. *Prudentia* is exercised with a view to the ultimate end of human beings, and it is the counterpart in human beings to that ordering of creatures to their ultimate end which is God's providence. God creates and orders particulars and knows them precisely as what he has made and is making. We, if we act rightly, reproduce that ordering.[24]

As we have emphasized, Casey follows Oakeshott in asserting that "happiness" is nothing but a formal designation; this leads him to affirm as well that the end of human friendship is nothing but human friendship. The Christian Aquinas, by contrast, believes there is an ultimate end for human beings to which prudence is attuned. What is that end? We may need to suppress common knowledge of Aquinas's account of the virtues to appreciate the surprise. It is not, as one might expect, a natural life well ordered by reason, but rather *caritas,* or a "certain friendship with God."[25]

5. The Theological Virtues and Pagan Virtue

To insist that we get prudence from our tradition, that it is passed to us by our friends, is not equivalent to insisting that prudence is about nothing other than our friendship. However, since Casey follows Oakeshott in believing that the political community should have no substantive ends, this conclusion does follow for him, for there simply is nothing beyond the community to which prudence (or practical wisdom) might point.

To be sure, genuine pagan sentiment need not (it cannot) follow Casey in his formalism; a pagan community must have substantive ends if it is to be particular—that is, if it is not to be just an undesignated *polis* but Athens, Sparta, or even Rome. In this it calls its citizens (its friends) to sustain and perhaps spread its particular history by living in its memory and stories, and passing them on, even if this requires of them the sacrifice of their very lives. Nevertheless, there remains another sense in which Casey's appropriation of Oakeshott's reading of Aristotle on friendship—that it achieves no good extrinsic to itself—is instructive of a certain crucial feature of pagan virtue and pagan friendship. Athenian friendship (pagan friendship, now particularized) exists for Athenian friendship. That is, pagan virtue, which Casey rightly sees culminating in justice/friendship rather than in prudence, is built on the supposition that Athens exists for Athens, Rome exists for Rome . . . or perhaps even the world exists for Rome.[26] By contrast, Christians are bound to say that the church is not its own end. For friendship in the Christian church fundamentally calls these friends (and their enemies) to a reality through which it exists: the reality of God made known in Jesus Christ.

Recall that Pieper thinks of prudence as opening a passage to reality. In Aquinas's schema, this passage widens dramatically (indeed it becomes a new sort of prudence entirely, namely *infused* prudence) with the introduction of the theological virtues. The first of these are faith and hope, which direct us to charity and our final end. Both faith and hope look forward in this way to a completion beyond themselves. A community which lives by them, one that lives eschatologically, must look forward as well. That is to say, its members must think that their friendship, or even their community of friends, has some other end besides itself. For they look forward to a world that is not yet. This is in contrast, of course, to ancient paganism and to Casey's updated version of it.

As we have seen, Aquinas describes charity as a sort of friendship with God, who is our last end. Of course the language of friendship with God does not originate with Aquinas; John the evangelist uses it when he speaks of Jesus' disciples becoming his friends: "You are my friends if you do as I command you. No longer do I call you servants, for a servant does not know what his master is doing; but I have called you friends, for all I have heard from my Father I have made known to you" (John 15:14–15). No doubt a danger in the Johannine account lies in its tendency to understand the knowledge of God as a kind of apprehension: one sees a sign, looks behind to see Jesus, looks behind again and sees God. Indeed prudence itself might be understood in a similar way. One might suppose that we *investigate* the reality of God, and the world as well, thereby possessing knowledge to be used in action. Yet Aquinas takes pains to close this path to error by asserting the excellence of charity over faith. "[F]aith and hope attain God indeed in so far as we derive from Him the knowledge of truth or the acquisition of good, whereas charity attains God Himself that it may rest in Him, but not that something may accrue to us from Him."[27] Or again, in response to an objection that since faith is in the intellect it surpasses charity in greatness, Aquinas argues that "in things above man [most clearly God], to love them is more excellent than to know them. Because knowledge is perfected by the known being in the knower: whereas love is perfected by the lover being drawn to the beloved."[28] Knowledge grasped solely by intellect (as Aquinas understands it in faith) is susceptible of a certain objectification, as here with God. By contrast, charity demands participation with what is known.

One of Casey's concerns in requiring that friendship have no end but itself is that it would otherwise turn into a mere instrument, thereby violating its very character. Were prudence the highest of the virtues, this could very easily follow: one might value one's friend, even think her indispensable, but for the greater purpose of attaining the knowledge of the good by means of which to live. However, for Christians prudence is not the highest virtue; rather, charity is. Indeed, it is charity that transforms prudence, not only adding more "realities" to know, but by redirecting us from the proximate end known by natural prudence to our true last end. This is why we receive a new (infused) prudence with charity. "Now for prudence to proceed aright, it is much more necessary that man be well disposed towards his ultimate end, which is the effect of charity, than that he be well disposed in respect of other ends, which is the effect of moral virtue. . . . It is therefore evident that neither can infused prudence be without charity; nor, consequently, the other moral virtues, since they cannot be without prudence."[29] Moreover, since we receive full knowledge of God in the communion of charity rather than in the intellectual apprehension of faith,[30] it follows that infused prudence is the result not so much of apprehending but of communing. In short, we know God and God's world in communion, in friendship.

For Christians this has at least two important consequences. First, they need not view a friendship with another human being either as having no other end but itself or as being solely a means to friendship with God. God is known in communion, but of course communion, the eucharist, is not passed between God and the individual alone, but shared among the community of God's friends. Friendship with God, our true end, *necessarily* includes friendship with others. Second, since Christians claim God is best known in communion, in charity, they must see that what they acquire in the relation is not so much accumulated knowledge about living, but rather transformed lives.[31] Human beings can be remade to live in the world in fellowship, with both friend and enemy. To live in such a way is prudent, that is, according to a prudence transformed by charity.

All this is clearer in Aquinas than in John. On the other hand, John (with the other gospel writers) may provide a corrective to Aquinas insofar as the friendship to which he refers is with Jesus, through whom God is known. Aquinas affirms that our last end is in the God who befriends us, to which it must be emphatically added that this God is present to us in the story of the Jews and in Jesus, whom we now call friend. The God who befriends us, therefore, is not just any god, but this one. Only in relation to the specific God they know in Jesus can Christians go on to say anything specific about the life of Christian virtue.

6. Anger, Forgiveness, and Christian Friendship

Friendship of any sort (even with God) is a producer of appropriate anger, for it presumes standards of treatment or achievement. Friends can fall short; they can disappoint. This fact itself is rooted in a significant moral good, for it presumes not only love—love, that is, of the specific other, the friend—but also genuine community, for friends must share a vision of what is worthy. As Casey has rightly pointed out, pagan pride is a proper context for this anger, for the high expectations of love and of community rely upon a marked distinction between its recipients and all others. The loved one is noble, and as such, worthy of love and admiration. Conversely, he is worthy of anger when he fails to uphold the high standards which the friendship sets. Both love and anger are proud pagan privileges, sustained together in pagan friendship.

A connection between anger and love can also be found within the stories Jews and Christians tell. Deep within the Pentateuch, we find the commandment to which Jesus so frequently referred, here prefaced in an intriguing way. "Thou shalt not hate thy brother in thine heart: thou shalt in anywise rebuke thy neighbor, and not suffer sin upon him. Thou shalt not avenge nor bear any grudge against the children of thy people, but thou shalt love thy neighbor as thyself: I am the Lord" (Leviticus 19:17–18).

In contrast to hate, which in this passage is unequivocally prohibited, rebuke, carrying with it the sharpness of anger, is commanded. The simple implication is that people can do or say things which call for reprimand, and rebuking them is in fact closely connected to loving them. It is hate, born perhaps of resentment and envy as it is in its first biblical representation by Cain towards his brother Abel, that God's people are to shun. In that story, of course, Cain announces that he is not his brother's keeper (Genesis 4:9). Rebuke makes sense only if one thinks otherwise; hence, its connection to love.

But the passage carries another point. Anger must not only never change to hate; it must not avenge itself. This is a point we find neither in Casey's book nor in the pagan wisdom he hopes to renew. The difference is to be found in the fact that Christians, following Jews, cannot locate their anger in proper pride. For while Jews (and Christians) understand themselves to be an exceptional people, this special election is not of their own doing but of God's choosing. They offer no other reasons for this choice than that the God who loves them loves the world. Pride in being exceptional and the distance from others (that is, the world) which it encourages is therefore inappropriate. Indeed, pride is among the greatest sins for Christians, since it is based on overblown and fundamentally false ideas either about one's own merit or about the ultimate significance of the communal history in which the pride (i.e., pagan pride) is rooted.[32]

In addition to recognizing that God's choice of them rests on nothing other than God's grace, Christians acknowledge that the sustenance of the community which carries the memory of Jesus and of the saints, while a work accomplished in them, is nonetheless God's work. The betrayal of this memory is cause for rebuke; yet Christians do not believe that the friend's friendship itself ultimately sustains the memory. So if the betrayal is not arrested by rebuke and the friendship is lost, this is not something to avenge but rather a source of perpetual sorrow, now for the lost friend as well as the lost friendship. Hate is no option, nor is vengeance, but sorrow replaces the anger whose rebuke goes unheard.

In a similar way, forgiveness, which is commanded of Christians as friends of Jesus, qualifies anger. For instance, in a passage that rehearses the command in Leviticus, Jesus instructs his disciples that "if your brother sins against you, go to him and tell him his fault" (Matthew 18:15). In the text, this is followed immediately by Peter's query about how many times he must forgive his brother, to which Jesus replies "not seven times, but seventy times seven" (18:22). Here, then, rebuke and forgiveness are locked together. It is not pride but forgiveness that provides the context for the love to which Christians are called and by which they rebuke. Of course Christians are capable of forgiveness and the friendship it supports only because they have been forgiven by the God made manifest in the person Jesus, who here in Matthew admonishes his disciples to practice forgiveness with their sisters and brothers.

Forgiveness plays little role in Casey's discussion of pagan virtues or of friendship; its absence is filled by pagan pride. As Nietzsche well recognized, pride is severe. What Casey sees more clearly than Nietzsche is the power of pride to create community: the "we" more than the "me" is the natural unit of pride. Yet communal pride must resist forgiveness, for forgiveness represents another avenue into the community than mastery of the self by means of the community's practices and traditions. Pride and a properly severe anger are the keepers of excellence and, concomitantly, the guarantors of the perpetuity of the pagan community.

By contrast, Christians require nothing more (nor less) of those who join them in the church than that they recognize they are forgiven. There is risk in this for the community, for wolves may creep in unawares. Yet as friends of God, Christians cannot think, as pagans might, of the preservation of their friendships in community as the end to which all other ends lead. God, they believe, will preserve God's people; their calling is simply to be that people in the world, living and acting by a prudence transformed by charity.

Part III

Christian Virtues Exemplified

SEVEN

On Developing Hopeful Virtues

*Therefore, since we are justified by faith, we have peace with God through our
Lord Jesus Christ. Through him we have obtained access to this grace in which
we stand, and we rejoice in our hope of sharing the glory of God. More than
that, we rejoice in our sufferings, knowing that suffering produces endurance,
and endurance produces character, and character produces hope, and hope
does not disappoint us, because God's love has been poured into our hearts
through the Holy Spirit which has been given to us.*

Romans 5:1–5 RSV

1. Virtue Talk and the Bible

It is a fair question to ask whether virtue language fits with what the
New Testament tells us. As our colleague and teacher John Yoder has
often reminded us, the New Testament seems to speak more about
what we can and cannot do than it does about the virtues we ought
to have. Even in texts like Galatians 5 where Paul speaks of virtues
such as love, joy, peace, patience, kindness, goodness, faithfulness,
gentleness, and self-control, he does so only after forbidding the works
of the flesh, namely, immorality, impurity, licentiousness, idolatry,
sorcery, enmity, strife, jealousy, anger, selfishness, dissension, party
spirit, envy, drunkenness, carousing, and the like. The force of this
second list, its length, and its ordinal priority to the list of the virtues
(not to mention what it implies about the human condition) may suggest that instead of dwelling on the more affirming—and less specific—virtues we ought to attend to rules and law. This point can be
made more forcefully when one considers the fact that when Christians read and study the New Testament as a guide to their lives, they
discover therein both the admonition and the stories to support loyalty to a concrete person rather than to a set of abstract dispositions,
such as the virtues may appear to be.

It is in this light that we will consider at some length in this chapter
the opening quotation from Romans 5. In its shadow we will argue

that the virtues do in fact express central aspects of the Christian life. It also suggests to us possible answers to certain questions about the distinctiveness of the Christian virtues and how that distinctiveness might relate to the peculiarity of the Christian story. As we offer these suggestions, we intend as well to reflect on more general questions of "human nature" and how an understanding of it might relate to the story Christians tell.[1]

On the first matter, that regarding the Bible and virtue, the text from Romans is intriguing, since virtue talk lies so close to its surface. Suffering is not a virtue in itself, but it is related to virtue, and endurance, character, and hope seem to name dispositions that most of us would think of as virtues. Taken by itself, then, the text seems to give virtue a boost. But, as Yoder might remind us, no biblical text stands by itself. Glancing around (the text's surroundings are in fact quite well known), we see that this little bit of virtue talk is settled comfortably in the middle of some of the most profound and forceful reflections ever written about justification by faith.

This proves very interesting. For fidelity to justification by faith has been one of the strongest reasons why many in the Christian tradition have objected to the primacy of virtue language for displaying the nature of the Christian life. The objection has been put in two related ways. First, justification implies that the new life of grace comes to us as a free gift of God. Talk of virtue, on the other hand, seems to assume that the moral life is a kind of human achievement. Indeed, the forgiveness that is so crucial to the Christian understanding of justification seems to strike at the very heart of an ethic of virtue. Consider, for example, Aristotle's man of virtue. As we have suggested, his whole purpose seems to be to live in such a way that he need not be forgiven of anything. By giving favors rather than receiving them he insures his invulnerability to a love that might render him dependent. In contrast, unearned justification of the sort Paul expounds cannot but make those who receive it dependent upon the one who offers it as a free gift.

Second, an emphasis on justification seems to make reference to growth and development in the moral life suspect; by contrast, any virtue account seems required to highlight it. To build on the previous point, emphasis upon growth appears to imply achievement, even *self*-justification. When we set about to acquire virtue and when we believe we can and do make progress, we are inevitably tempted to believe in our own power to know and do what is right. Yielded to, this temptation cannot but deafen us to the true command of God.

It is hardly surprising that Karl Barth has put the point at issue in its starkest form. As he says,

> the relation between God and man is not that of a parallelism and harmony of the divine and human wills, but of an explosive encounter, contradiction and reconciliation, and which it is the part of the divine will to precede and the human to follow, of the former to control and the latter to submit. Neither as a whole nor in detail can our action mean our justification before God. . . . Our sanctification is God's work, not our own. It is very necessary, therefore, that there should be the encounter, the confrontation of our existence with the command of God.[2]

Barth is well known for his emphasis upon the command of God. (As we suggest in the next chapter, commands are indeed crucial to the Christian life, although we receive them best when our obedience is constitutive of our virtues.) Command language fits well with a certain understanding of justification. From such a perspective the Christian life appears as a series of responses to particular commands, without the response implying a lasting effect in those who are commanded. There is continuity in the commands, but it is provided by the character of the commander, not the commanded. For Barth, therefore, the fundamental image for the Christian life is not growth, but repetition. Only God's command is capable of such repetition, for the

> repetition and confirmation of all other commands is limited: partly because, so far as content is concerned, they aim only at individual temporally limited achievements; partly because they aim at attitudes and therefore at usages which once they are established need no new decision. But the necessity as well as the possibility of repetition and confirmation of the command of God is without limit. Even if it aims at definite achievements and attitudes and actions and usages it always aims beyond them at our decision for Jesus, and just in this substance the decision demanded by God's command is of such a kind that it can and must be repeated and confirmed.[3]

Gilbert Meilaender has characterized this construal of the Christian life as essentially dialogical. The Christian life has a distinctive nature but no clear progression. It is a "going back and forth, back and forth. That is to say, the Christian is simply caught within the dialogue between the two voices with which God speaks: the accusing voice of the law and the accepting voice of gospel. Hearing the law, we flee to the gospel. Life is experienced as a dialogue between these two divine verdicts, and within human history one cannot escape that dialogue or progress beyond it."[4]

"Going back and forth, back and forth" implies movement, but not necessarily growth, which is the point at stake. Movement in a journey, however, does imply growth—although what kind remains open for specification. (For example, as we discussed earlier, a journey's destination is not fixed so clearly as a trip's. On a trip, we know where we are headed, and so how far we are from reaching it, something the very character of a journey precludes.) Since we have emphasized the metaphor "journey" for the moral life, we are committed to the genuine possibility of growth and development—as we suppose anyone who uses the metaphor must be.

Meilaender himself speaks of journey, although with qualification. "Righteousness . . . consists not in right relation with God but in becoming (throughout the whole of one's character) the sort of person God wills us to be and commits himself to making of us. Picturing the Christian life as such a journey, we can confess our sin without thinking that the standard of which we fell short, in its accusation of us, must lead us to doubt the gracious acceptance by which God empowers us to journey toward his goal for our lives."[5] Meilaender proposes journey only after proposing dialogue and then recommends that we hold both together, despite their obvious differences, purposely refusing to resolve them. "The tension between these two pictures of the Christian life cannot be overcome, nor should we try to overcome it."[6] This outcome fits well within Meilaender's faithful Lutheranism; less faithfully, we no doubt appear to leave justification behind in emphasizing sanctification and the virtues it makes available.

This is an appearance we hope to dispel. To begin, it is important to distinguish genuinely Christian notions of growth in the moral life from the view (to which Christians have often been tempted) that our moral development "unfolds" from what is in us naturally as potential. Growth in Christian virtue is hardly an inevitable movement to the higher and better, nor are the virtues the result of the development of a teleology intrinsic to human nature. This is not to say our growth has nothing to do with our "nature"; with Aquinas we hold that the kind of individual nature each of us has must inform how our virtues are determined. Rather, the view we wish most to reject is that suggested by Edmund Pincoffs when he states what to him seems obvious, that "a just man is a just man. He needs no imprimatur to show forth what he is. Courage is no more a Catholic than it is a Buddhist virtue; honesty commends itself to Presbyterian and Coptic Christian alike."[7] To the contrary, we hold that just as a Calvinist unbeliever is different from a Catholic unbeliever, the courage of a Christian is different from that of a Buddhist. No appeal to human nature is sufficient to insure the commonality of all human virtue. Instead, as Alasdair MacIntyre has emphasized, any account of the virtues requires a teleological understanding of human existence articulated through a community's narrative.[8] For our purposes, the significance of this point is that an account of growth in Christian virtue cannot be generic. If, contra Pincoffs, all virtues are not the same, that the "just person" is *not* everywhere and always recognizable as the "just person," then the account of how someone came to be virtuous or just will need to be placed in relation to the particular sort of virtues she has come to have.

What has this to do with our text from Romans and Paul's long discussion of justification in which it is placed? Suppose we fix on what is perhaps the most rudimentary notion of justification imaginable: by justification we are made just before God. As Paul makes plain, something decisive has occurred in Jesus that has changed our status as God sees us. Put this way, we can see that "justification" begs for narrative display: what were we before, what are we now, and where is this change taking us?

Reference to narrative gives us room to note briefly that recent scholarship has done much to recover the centrality of apocalyptic eschatology in Paul's theology, or, to put it contentiously, to rescue him from the Lutherans. As J. Christiaan Beker notes,

Paul's proclamation of Jesus Christ (= the Messiah) is centered in a specific view of God and in a salvation-historical scheme. What does this mean? It expresses the conviction that, in the death and resur-rection of Jesus Christ, the Covenant-God of Israel has confirmed and renewed his promises of salvation to Israel and to the nations as first recorded in the Hebrew Bible. These promises pertain to the expec-tation of the public manifestation of the reign of God, the visible pres-ence of God among his people, the defeat of all his enemies and the vindication of Israel in the gospel. In other words, the death and res-urrection of Jesus Christ manifests the inauguration of the righteous-ness of God.[9]

As we hold, Paul's emphasis upon justification, and virtually all else he says, is incomprehensible apart from his eschatology. Eschatology names the narrative of God's salvation appropriated by hope—the key term in Romans 5:1–5. It is true, crucially true, that justification is a gift, a point that reminds us that the hope by which we journey is not of our own making. Far from arising from our own worthiness, our hope comes as an open invitation to locate our lives in a new history that is made present in the life, death, and resurrection of Jesus Christ.

2. Hope, Forgiveness, and Suffering

It is an important and largely unexplored question as to what the relation may be between Paul's eschatology and the teleology insisted upon by MacIntyre. Put abstractly, the question concerns the relation of nature (teleology) to history (eschatology) and would require con-sideration of the relation of happiness to suffering. In lieu of a full inquiry we will say what we suspect: as formed in Aristotle, MacIn-tyre's teleology, while explored (of necessity) in a tradition and there-fore in relation to a community, need not end in community. In con-trast, this is a requirement of Christian eschatology, which looks toward the communion of all the saints. Only within this eschatologi-cal framework can the Christian virtues receive full display.

Aristotle's teleology is necessarily based in some form of natural-ism. That is, it will suppose that there is some common human nature which can be fulfilled or frustrated. This provides an important benchmark for the virtues. Insofar as we share a nature we will share virtues, that is, if we live a fully human life. This need not be all the virtues, for flourishing occurs in a concrete life, and the circumstances and environments of our various lives will differ. But *qua* humans we cannot have completely different sets of virtues, as one might suppose there would be an entirely different set of virtues for some nonhuman species of being with different capacities and a different telos.

Christian eschatology is less clearly bound by this requirement of nature, not the least because Christianity imagines a new world in which we all will be changed. It remains an open question, then, whether and how Christian virtues compare to the virtues others will claim.

At the very least, the comparison is tricky, as Robert Roberts has helpfully noted. In an attempt to find some commonality between virtues irrespective of their communal and traditioned context, Roberts suggests that the virtues have a grammar, a set of rules embodying a system of relation. For example, the structure of gratitude requires the reception of a nonobligatory good from another person; this is true of gratitude wherever it is found.[10] If this is true, and it surely seems plausible, some formal parallel might reasonably be drawn between the various historic virtue traditions.

As to the material implications of this formal point, however, we remain somewhat agnostic. No doubt there are some things we all share as humans: we all are embodied beings and as such have certain common material needs, most if not all of us live with a knowledge of our death, and so on. From this it likely follows that there is something like eternal questions for humankind which arise out of a "human condition" that is, at the very least, a condition of neediness. However, registering this point must not blind us to the crucial importance of the way in which these questions are put. For instance, while it is true that "naturally" we share a weak, needy, or fallible nature, from the perspective of the Christian gospel this is not the deepest truth about our human nature. We are, rather, fundamentally sinners for whom Christ died. And, contrary to Reinhold Niebuhr, sin is by no means self-evident; Christians and Jews know of it only by the story given in their peculiar history.

We do not think it is accidental that the diagnosis of our sinful condition is the burden of much of what Paul writes in Romans prior to chapter 5. "All have sinned and fall short of the glory of God" (3:23), he says, a point that melds in the next verse with the assertion that justification comes to all "by God's grace as a free gift, through the redemption that is in Christ Jesus."

If one should wish to say that Paul is implying that sinfulness is "natural," since it is universal, we have no reason to quarrel. *Knowledge* of sin, and of God's forgiveness of it is, however, another matter. Indeed, as Paul goes on to claim, Jews are advantaged over others precisely because their law, which arose as God came to share their history, allows them to tell their story, and the story of the world, as one of sinfulness. Sin and redemption, while universal, are imbedded in a particular history, one we must come to share if we are to know our true state.

Roberts perceives this point as he considers how a grammar might be discovered among the Christian virtues. As he says, it may seem improbable that a virtue's grammar, as a formal notion, could be built on a historical belief. Nevertheless,

> the doctrine of righteousness through Christ's atoning death for sinners is the hub of the Christian view of the world, the axis upon which everything else turns. And the virtue of forgiveness is especially close to the hub. So in this case, like it or not, a particular historical belief is essential to the grammar of a virtue, and every exposition of Christian forgiveness must give a central place to this belief, just as every instance of distinctively Christian forgiveness involves envisioning the offender in the light of the cross. To put this in the terms of the Christian virtues-system, the historical fact that Christ died for sinners became an essential feature of human nature.[11]

Roberts's comments help us make an important epistemological point about the nature of Christian claims about "our natures." As he notes, there is an essential feature about our nature—a natural fact—that Christians claim is disclosed in a particular history. (Whether it might also be disclosed in *another* particular history is something Christians need not initially address, although by no means must they, nor should they, eliminate the possibility.) This feature about us comes in the Christian story with our need for justification—we learn of both together. It follows, then, that our instruction in our sin and in our redemption of necessity brings us within the narrative that sustains the Christian virtues. For example, the closeness of forgiveness to the hub of the Christian virtues depends upon the importance of the part of the story that tells us of our sin, and of our justification through the gift of God's son. This story, as we allege, is upheld by a Christian eschatology which itself implies the centrality of hope.

With this in mind, we see no reason to hold that there is an unresolvable tension between justification and the virtues of hope. Indeed, Christian hope, like sin, is something we must learn of as we come to share in a story which teaches us both why hope is essential and why it can be had at all. Furthermore, that the answer to our sin is the free gift of redemption in Christ focuses our hope: its source is in the God who forgives us, and its object is this forgiveness, which responds to our deepest need, of which we have lately learned. All hope relates to a felt need; if we have attained all that we might, there is nothing to hope in. Therefore, our knowledge of what we lack cannot but affect that for which we hope. If we return again to the question about our "nature," the knowledge that we are weak, dependent, or fallible is easily attained—as easily as the knowledge that we suffer. A "natural" or generic hope can arise in relation to this knowledge, namely that we will be cared for and loved. This hope may prove a seed of new life, not only because it is grounded in a truth about our need for love but because, rather than attempting to deny or transcend fragility by grasping at power, it looks beyond itself for help from another. Yet defined merely in this way, "naturally" we hope more for acceptance than for forgiveness. No doubt we are accepted by God as He forgives us, but precisely because it is an acceptance of forgiveness it is truthful in a way that mere acceptance without forgiveness is not—and the reason for this is that we are, in fact, sinners. Concomitantly, as Roberts notes, the gratefulness that can be found in certain other grammars of virtue is subtly changed within the Christian grammar. Phenomenologically, gratefulness is appropriately offered to someone stronger on whom we depend, or to someone who loves us despite our weaknesses. Yet this gratefulness will not be the same as that offered by those who have been forgiven, precisely because the gift of forgiveness is given to us when we are the least deserving. "While we were yet sinners, Christ died for us" (Romans 5:6).

When we begin to explore the specific character of Christian hope, dependent as it is upon the undeserved gift of our forgiveness, we discover an essentially receptive element within it. As Aquinas notes, the theological virtue of hope is related to fear, both because by fear we shrink from that which is evil (i.e., our sins) and because we stand in need of strengthening with respect to what is arduous. The cardinal virtue of fortitude as that which strengthens us to do what is difficult bears a certain similarity to the theological virtue of hope, yet the strength we receive in Christian hope does not arise within ourselves; it is received of God. The appropriate description given for this gift of strength in hope is that it is something we "lean upon."[12] Here hope speaks less to our difficulty in actively doing something than in bearing or suffering or enduring something.

This is borne out in the text from Romans. We rejoice, says Paul, in our hope, which comes to us as gift. But further, we rejoice in our *sufferings*. On the face of it, this is an extremely odd thing to say— unless of course one is a masochist.[13] Suffering is no fun, as Paul knew. Why, then, should we rejoice in it? We do so only when the sufferings come to us as gift. And we are only able to receive them as such when we hope. Christian hope puts a spin on our suffering, but it is a different spin than that for which it is commonly mistaken, namely the spin of explanation. Hope does not explain to us why we suffer; indeed, precisely because we hope, we recognize that our suffering lies beyond present explanation. Instead, hope places us squarely in a narrative in which our suffering can be endured and accordingly made part of our life. As we enter this narrative we are given the grace to see our suffering as leading somewhere; as a part of a journey that stretches before us toward a destination that includes sharing in the glory of God. Put abstractly this destination sounds fanciful. But Paul does not mean it abstractly. Our sufferings are not so much something that will someday (in the great beyond) bear fruit. Rather they are a form of our participation in Christ.[14]

Mention of Christ's suffering has a double meaning in this context, for we have come round to speak of our own suffering in the light of Christ's, all in a discussion which began with the sacrifice of Christ by which we are justified to God. In short, Christ's suffering brackets ours. Lest we forget the nature of this suffering, Paul reminds us in verse 7 that while suffering and death might be endured for a righteous man, Christ's suffering was endured for us, who are sinners. If, then, we participate in Christ's suffering, we learn the endurance of Christ, which in turn can produce in us the character of Christ.

It is easy to associate endurance with passivity toward evil. Yet we must recall that evil, particularly evil as sin, is something we must learn to see. Conceived as misfortune, evil is rightly passively received, since nothing can be done about it. Raging against fortune, while possessed of a certain nobility, is deceived.[15] The reception of evil as the result of sin, on the other hand, is a positive act in the sense that another avenue is open, namely punishment, or even revenge. Fortune is impermeable to our retaliation; we cannot harm her. Persons who harm us, however, can be harmed in return; they can be made to pay the price of their injustice.

God's response to our sin was to forgive us, doing so by enduring suffering and death at the hands of those He came to redeem. We may be tempted by this description to suppose that our suffering in a similar way arises entirely out of injustice done to us. But of course the analogy does not hold, for as Paul constantly reminds us, we are sinners. No doubt we do suffer injustices, and we are called to forgive them as Christ forgave us. We do so, however, not because we are righteous but because we are forgiven. More generally, however, whether deserved or undeserved, when drawn within the narrative of God's presence in human history in the Jews and in Jesus, our suffering produces an endurance which can turn our fate into calling. For in the narrative, we are given the means to turn our past, which is a history of sin, into love capable of being of service to the neighbor.

More often than not the term "sin" is used to point to an act or set of acts that do not measure up. We need not call this a misuse of the term to offer another and deeper sense, namely that sin is a state in which we stand. Some call this state "natural"; we hold, however, that it is better described as a history, one that holds us captive. The gift of hope which comes with the forgiveness offered in Christ's sacrifice frees us from this captivity, not so much extracting us from sin's history but by placing it in relation to a new future. As Paul elsewhere develops in Romans, this is a future life made possible by Christ's victory over sin and its principal effect, namely death. Indeed, Christians can endure because through Christ they have been given power over death and all forms of victimization that trade on it. The ultimate power of Christ is the victory over death that makes possible the endurance of suffering; we can endure because we have confidence that though our enemies may kill us they cannot determine the meaning of our death. Christians have been given the power to overcome oppression, not by retaliation, but by the stalwart refusal to be defined as victims by the oppressor. We endure because no matter what may be done to us we know that those who threaten our death are powerless to determine the meaning of our lives by killing us. Likewise, our decisive service to our neighbor is to open to her a place where she is no longer a victim, of others or of herself. If we can relieve her suffering, we should, but more importantly we offer her the endurance to live with her suffering, now no longer meaningless, since it is carried by an eschatological hope that is confident in what it has already witnessed, namely Christ's victory over death.

3. Endurance, Character, and Hope

Endurance that allows us to rejoice in our suffering can never be described by Christians as an individual achievement, not only because it follows from a gift, but also because it is the endurance of a *whole people* committed to remembering the saints. From the saints we learn how to be steadfast in the face of adversity. By remembering them we become members of a community and history that gives us the power to prevail. Of course, the saints make no sense apart from the life and death of Jesus of Nazareth. The memory of them, therefore, derives its power from the memory of Him, whom we celebrate in a meal, a meal that offers us the opportunity to share together in His calling. The saints' faithfulness to this calling is concrete demonstration that by Jesus' resurrection a people is formed who can sustain the virtues necessary to remember His death.[16] As we sustain that memory, Christians receive the power to make our deaths our own by learning to endure.

Like suffering, endurance is not an end in itself, but produces character. On the other hand, neither is endurance merely the means to character. We do not suffer *so that* we may endure and we do not endure *so that* we may have character. Rather, in our suffering we learn endurance and in our endurance we learn of our character. For "character" names the history we have been given through the endurance of our suffering. As such, our character is indeed an achievement, but one that comes as a gift.[17] Moreover, we attain character not by our constant effort to reach an ideal but by discovery, as we look back on our lives and, by God's forgiveness, claim them as our own. Character, in other words, names the continuity of our lives, the recognition of which is made possible by the retrospective affirmation that our lives are not just the sum of what we have done but rather are constituted by what God has done for us. In short, character is recognized in the discovery of those narratives that live through us, making us more than we could have hoped.

This is one reason Christian ethics is so at odds with other accounts of the moral life that assume ethical reflection and behavior are primarily matters of prospective judgments about moral dilemmas. These accounts are built on rationalistic self-deceptions about the power each individual has autonomously to determine his "choices." In contrast Christian ethics, at least the kind we are willing to defend, is not concerned so much with decisions and choices but with the character of a person, who is as much the choices he did not make as those he made. While we are related to our choices, we are never entirely captured by them, since we know our character by discovery, as if a gift bestowed on us.

Finally, for Paul character (re)produces hope, this time a hope "that does not disappoint" (v. 5). How are we to understand this relation? As we have been arguing, character is something we discover, a sort of epiphenomenon that arises with the endurance produced by suffering. But as we have tried to make plain, this is not just any suffering nor any endurance. Rather, the character that is capable of producing hope is that formed within the story of God's redemption in the person of Jesus Christ. Put simply, the character of Christians is possible only if Jesus has in fact been raised from the dead.

To review the series of points we have been making in a slightly different vein, who we are and what we do has everything to do with what story we are in. This is so because stories form worlds. As Wittgenstein reminded us, the world of the happy person is not the same as the world of the unhappy. Or, as MacIntyre has argued regarding human action, we

> place the agent's intentions . . . in causal and temporal order with reference to their role in his or her history; and we also place them with reference to their role in the history of the setting or settings to which they belong. In doing this, in determining what causal efficacy the agent's intentions had in one or more directions, and how his short-

term intentions succeeded or failed to be constitutive of long-term intentions, we ourselves write a further part of these histories. Narrative history of a certain kind turns out to be the basic and essential genre for the characterization of human actions.[18]

More than endurance or other virtues, character is a designation that marks the continuity present throughout the changes that constitute a complete human life. Remarkably, character in this context arises as we respond to our suffering by placing it within the narrative of God's redemptive activity for us. As we receive this narrative we discover it provides us the resources of character to make our past intelligible, including a past (and present) of suffering. Or in other words, as we endure our suffering as the suffering of Christ we discover that God gives us a character capable of sustaining a hope that does not disappoint. Of course we began this road with hope. The hope our journey has produced is not different from that with which it began except in this: as we began to hope, we could not anticipate where it would lead.

The character we have come to have through suffering and endurance is able to produce hope because by it we learn to inhabit the narrative of God's work in Jesus Christ and so to see all existence as trustworthy. Viewed otherwise, "existence" does not warrant this assessment, but in the story that now shapes our character we grow to see all that is as a reflection of the glory of the God who made it. Hope, then, is not merely sustained but grows as we are taught to ask more and more of God's creation. In the language of the Scholastics, God's grace rewards itself by increasing in us the ability to enjoy God forever.

The Scholastics called this process "merit," perhaps an unfortunate choice of a word since it encourages the assumption that men and women might be able to place God's grace under necessity—i.e., by their efforts cause it to come about. Yet Aquinas insists that "man is justified by faith not as though man, by believing, were to merit justification, but that he believes whilst he is being justified."[19] We are ordained by God to an eternal life of friendship with God, not by our own strength but by the help of grace.[20] In this sense, "merit" but names the process by which God's grace becomes ours because of God's unwillingness to leave us alone. To return to the text in Romans, merit is nothing other than love "poured into our hearts through the Holy Spirit." Our hope begins in love as God justifies us even in our sin. Now, as the text demonstrates, hope also ends in love, one that is able to rejoice in all it has created. Love echoes love, yet it grows within us as we hope, suffer, and endure. Indeed, to deny love's growth is to deny the power of God's grace.

Like "merit," one might prefer another term for the virtues we receive as we enter into the story of God's redemption in Christ than "infused," the term Aquinas picks. Nonetheless, the point behind the designation is essential. The infused cardinal virtues—infused temperance, fortitude, justice, and prudence—come together with love, or Aquinas's theological virtue of *caritas*. While resembling the acquired cardinal virtues, they are different in species since they lead us to act in relation to our life with God.

Especially since, as we have been maintaining, the character produced by the endurance of suffering involves a certain unity of the self, it is important to consider a difficulty Aquinas's notion of infused virtue has occasioned. As Robert Sokolowski has put it, when the idea of infused virtues is introduced "we seem to have not only a contrast between moral and theological virtues but also a contrast between two levels of moral virtues, the natural and the infused. In what sense does one remain a single agent in such differences? . . . [C]ould a person who is weak in self-control as regards natural virtue be, at the same time, temperate and courageous through his infused virtue? Does he acquire such temperance and courage simply by infusion, without actual performance?"[21] The difficulty is that we appear to be divided within ourselves by grace. The set of infused virtues, as unified in love, seems to threaten the intactness of the person of virtue who has acquired his character by repeated acts.

One way to solve the apparent puzzle is to propose, as does Sokolowski, that finally there is no difference between what the good person and the Christian should do in the concrete—i.e., to tell the truth, to be honest, to be temperate and courageous, to defend one's home and country.[22] This solution is unsatisfactory, especially when we remember that the life of virtue is a matter not only of action but also of passion and perception. Indeed, Aquinas is rightly struggling with the fact that the person whose life is lived in love and peace with God simply does not live in the same world as the person whose is not.

As we might say, they inhabit different narrative contexts. Translating Sokolowski's problem into this idiom, the problem of the divided self arising from the distinction between the infused and acquired virtues is a problem of divided narratives.[23]

This point opens a way to return to Barth and Meilaender, and ultimately to sin. One need not deny that growth occurs to affirm that, as wayfarers, our present selves are yet constituted by two narratives. We are not yet what we will be; to suppose that we are is a temptation not only to self-deception and hubris, but also to a falsification of the world through which we travel.

Yet the reality of this world (the world of sin) and the dividedness of our selves should strengthen rather than diminish our resolve that this world should not determine our growth in hope. No sin is more damning than to fail to hope in the power of God's love to release us from our sin. Likewise, our growth in grace is not a denial of our sinfulness but rather the basis for our knowledge and acknowledgment of our sin. Indeed, it is the common testimony of the saints that as they draw closer to God, they are increasingly overwhelmed by the knowledge of their sin. As we have emphasized, without God's grace we cannot even know we are sinners. Precisely because God has invited us to be part of His kingdom, the truth of our sin can be known and confessed without that knowledge destroying us.

We can grow in Christian virtue, yet it is best to describe this as growth in grace, whose hallmark is forgiveness. (That is, if we do not forgive—and perhaps even more—if we refuse to be forgiven, we grow neither in virtue nor in grace.) We forgive not as a people who by their own perfection can do so gratuitously, but rather as those who have themselves been forgiven. The test of that forgiveness is, in fact, our own willingness to receive it from others, a test, as we have argued before, that most "men of virtue" (such as Aristotle's) would fail, with clear and haughty intent. Our acceptance of forgiveness is the means by which our souls are expanded so that we can hope. Through hope we learn to endure suffering, confident that God has given us the character faithfully to inhabit the story of the redemption of all creation, of which we are part. While we inevitably live divided lives, we can grow in the unity of the story so that our virtues might finally be unified. That is why all virtues for Christians cannot but be hopeful ones.[24]

EIGHT

Is Obedience a Virtue?

1. Some Linguistic Considerations

If someone said, "Bob is obedient," would we suppose she meant to praise Bob? The phrase surely does not carry the negative connotations of "Bob is spineless," even if someone might, on some cleverly contrived moral theory, suppose obedience is a kind of spinelessness. That link has not yet been made in the development of our language, despite so much recent emphasis upon "independence" and "choice." Nevertheless, to say Bob is obedient is more equivocal morally than saying he is courageous or honest.

Suppose we don't know Bob at all and so ask, "Who's Bob?"—and get the response, "He's my dog." It might puzzle us that someone would start up like that talking about her dog, but our other uncertainty would be cleared up—the one about whether she meant to praise Bob for his obedience. Obedient dogs are good dogs, at least as we usually talk.

We are concerned here with the question of whether obedience is a virtue. Of course, Christians cannot base their conviction that it is (or is not) entirely on linguistic conventions. Yet the term "obedience" has a home in a language Christians share with others (in a way, for example, the term "atonement" does not), so we should be interested in understanding this. What we have discovered thus far leads to a suggestion: Perhaps "obedience" is a virtue for some kinds of beings (e.g., for dogs) who are both like and unlike humans, the unlikeness being marked enough for us to stop short of calling it a human virtue—hence the linguistic ambivalence. And this suggestion leads quickly to another: Perhaps obedience could be called a virtue for human beings at an early stage in their development—when they're children—but becomes less true as they grow older. So, if we find out that Bob is a child, things clear up as they did when we learned he was a dog. Our speaker *does* mean to praise Bob (the child) when she calls him obedient.

This line of reasoning leads us into the moral universe of Aristotle, who held that we become virtuous by repeated acts, to which we are at first directed by our parents or other wise people.[1] "Do that," they might tell us as children. Only if we obeyed, and did it, could we begin on the road to virtue.

Perhaps it would be most faithful to Aristotle to classify obedience with *shame* as a "quasi-virtue." About it he says, "(t)he passion [shame] is not becoming to every age, but only to youth. For we think young people should be prone to shame because they live by passion and therefore commit many errors, but are restrained by shame; and we praise young people who are prone to this passion, but an older person no one would praise for being prone to the sense of disgrace, since we think he should not do anything that need cause this sense."[2] "Obedience" could be read into this passage in place of "shame" without much difficulty.

Patrick Nowell-Smith takes up this slant on things with a vengeance, turning it on Christians, whose morality he finds "infantile." Adopting Jean Piaget's well-known scheme of moral development, Nowell-Smith finds Christians "fixated" at the second stage which Piaget calls "heteronomous." This can be clearly seen, he argues, in Christians' "deontological" attitude towards rules. This is the attitude that rules are to be obeyed without questioning what the rules are for. Questioning the purpose of the rules is essential to Piaget's third and final stage, where an autonomous attitude towards them emerges, namely "that the rules are no longer regarded as sacred, i.e., as worthy of obedience simply because they are what they are, but as rules serving a purpose, as rules for playing a game that [one] wants to play."[3]

Of course Nowell-Smith's own positive position about morality, what he calls "humanism," predisposes him to reject obedience out of hand. Here is how he begins his treatment of it: "I shall simply start with the idea that a morality is a set of habits of choice ultimately determined by the question 'What life is most satisfactory to me as a whole?' and I start with this because I simply do not understand the suggestion that I ought to do anything that does not fit into this conception."[4]

This reflects the familiar vision of morality we referred to earlier, a kind of liberalism particularly strong on "choice" and "independence of mind." In fact, Nowell-Smith's attacks on Christian morality are just not very interesting, expressing as they do this ubiquitous spirit. There is something interesting, however, about the form the attack takes in this case. Because he builds on Piaget's scheme, Nowell-Smith draws attention to matters concerning moral development. As such, he is not so much alleging that the problem with Christians is that they *at some time* obeyed. As we were reconstructing Aristotle, obedience seems at some point essential to our becoming virtuous (or "moral" as Nowell-Smith might prefer), and surely Piaget and Nowell-Smith would agree. The problem with Christians, rather, is that they do not have the good sense to *stop* obeying when the right time comes.

It is worth noting that an incoherence may well arise for someone like Nowell-Smith when he employs developmental arguments such as these outside an Aristotelian political context. For developmental accounts of morality assume that there is something to be trained up into. For Aristotle it was the virtues. What could it be for Nowell-Smith? Morality, after all, is for him the habits that he chooses, those which are satisfactory to him as a whole. What sort of training does one need for this? Human beings, as Augustine saw as clearly as anyone, *begin* with desires; it requires training to shape our desires, but no training is required merely to have them. An untrained, desirous human surely could choose some habits and have a notion of what is satisfactory to him. What's to develop?

In fact, of course, Nowell-Smith believes training is necessary. All the talk about choice notwithstanding, he believes in "virtues" like autonomy, independence, and self-sufficiency. If he has had children, likely he has trained them to be like this; and we can see how this *would* require training since we are hardly independent by nature. But note: Nowell-Smith's virtues will function as the control that tells him when obedience should stop. That is, if we change the question from whether we should obey to when we should stop obeying (if ever), that question cannot be answered in any other way than in relation to the kind of character, and the concomitant virtues, we take to be worthy. Now it is not surprising that Nowell-Smith's (and Piaget's) answer to the "when" question will be "as soon as possible," for his worthy virtues are ones that by definition exclude obedience. For others who aspire to quite different kinds of virtue, the answer will likely be different.

To put this series of points another way, if someone has the least bit of concern about the virtues, they must also have a concern about how we develop them. Once manifest, this developmental concern will have great difficulty eschewing obedience altogether. Instead, those who feel the concern will need to develop an account of if and why and when obedience needs to cease in the life of virtue. This account, though, is not one that can be given generally, for it will depend on what particular sort of life of virtue is presented. Someone like Nowell-Smith will be hastier than most to stop obeying, for he seems to believe that the virtues are essentially defined by their exclusion of obedience. If one believes what Nowell-Smith believes, then there is little else to say. But Christians do not believe that way, so for them there is a good deal more thinking to do, thinking that will involve their substantive convictions, not merely the linguistic conventions surrounding the term "obedience."

However, we have not yet exhausted what the language can tell us, and so we return once again to our opening discussion. What is it about dogs and children that so readily cleared the initial fog about whether Bob's obedience was good? We had said, rather quickly, that an obedient dog is a good dog; but why do we think that? (Some may object, finding this a sort of affront to dogs. To be sure, it could be, if one took it to imply that dogs were for nothing else than to obey. But we need not attribute that attitude to our speaker. Rather, let us suppose she is saying that among the admirable traits possessed of Bob the dog is obedience.)

We suspect the reason the clarification that Bob is a dog is so helpful has not just to do with it putting him in a certain category of creature, but also with the fact that it implies quite clearly to whom Bob, the dog, is obedient. In context, we infer it is the speaker herself, but that is not to say that we judge the goodness of Bob's obedience on what we know of the speaker (we may know almost nothing) but rather on the fact that the speaker is a human being. We assume it is good for dogs to be obedient to their human masters. (If the human master uses the dog's obedience to mistreat the dog, we blame the human master, and perhaps praise the dog's obedience all the more.)

Something like this also applies to children. Children's obedience has an assumed target: their parents, teachers, or other adults who care for them. This obedience might be abused by these adults, but that does not change the fact that we think it is generally good for children to obey adults.

In contrast, when we consider the obedience of adult human beings, things change. At the very least, if someone says Bob is obedient and we find out that he (Bob) is an adult, we will rightly want to know to whom he is obedient before we can go any further in discovering whether it is good for him to obey.

Nowell-Smith seems to think that no adult human owes obedience to anyone, ever. So he won't need to inquire further. But this is not true for Christians, for they will think that obedience is owed to some persons in some cases and not to other persons in other cases. So, for example, when Peter says "We must obey God rather than men" (Acts 5:29), he implies that obedience offered to God is right and good, while obedience offered to "men"—in this case members of the Sanhedrin who have forbidden Peter and the apostles to preach—is not.

As we argued earlier and will develop at length below, a virtue such as courage requires a context. In determining its praiseworthiness, we will want to know what someone is being courageous for. This seems to be even truer with obedience. For even if we disagree with someone that the end for which he is courageous is noble, we can nevertheless recognize his courage as courage and admire him for it. With respect to obedience, our concern will be all the greater, for we think obedience offered to the wrong person is not virtuous in the least and may even be vicious.

2. Obeying an Authority

Suppose we introduce a new term into our discussion: "blind obedience." It is intriguing to note that this term can be used of dogs only in a sort of protracted sense. For if someone says that the dog obeyed blindly, we will want to know what "blindly" has added. Is there a difference between the behavior of a dog who obeys, and one who obeys blindly? Similarly, the sort of behavior we often expect of children is not unlike what in other contexts might be called blind obedience. "Never mind the reason," parents sometimes say to their children, "just obey me!" Issued to an adult this would sound like a command to blind obedience; issued to a child we do not think of calling it that.

In fact it is of adult humans that we predicate blind obedience and whom we suppose ought not blindly to obey, for the term is pejorative. To be sure, sometimes we do think circumstances call for a sort

of blind obedience from adults, such as a rescue attempt where time
is of the essence. But even in these cases the obedience is not blind,
for we assume that the one who obeys without question will perceive
that there is a reason for him to do so in this case. "Blind obedience"
suggests that the one who obeys refuses to ask for a reason why he
should obey, he just obeys. The term is pejorative for that reason.

E. D. Watt has suggested that having a reason to obey is the distinctive feature of the sort of obedience we attribute to human beings.

> Material objects, animals and human beings may all be said to follow,
> to conform, or to obey, but not in the same sense. Projectiles are said
> to obey the laws of motion; but it would make no sense to speak of
> their disobeying the laws of motion, and animals, which are some-
> times said to disobey as well as to obey, can hardly be said to have a
> reason for their disobedience, or to pretend to obey, as human beings
> can. The difference lies in the capacity of human beings to know what
> it is to act for some reason, to follow a rule or to obey a command.[5]

When a person obeys for a reason he adds an ingredient that is absent
from the obedience of dogs: consent. This point can be illustrated by
contrasting "obedience" with "compliance." We can comply with a
rule or a command without obeying it; so too we can "pretend to
obey," which would mean something like that we feign consent to
some ruler's commands while merely complying with them. As Watt
maintains, dogs and children (of a certain age) cannot comply without obeying (their obedience is their compliance) nor pretend to obey,
so neither can they obey in this "reasoned" sense.

This new difference between compliance and obedience is interesting when we consider those cases where adult humans comply but
do not obey. (When one obeys one could also be said to comply, but
we are interested here in those cases where compliance applies but
obedience does not.) In his discussion, Watt draws our attention to a
related contrast between *power* and *authority*. Power can be used to
coerce compliance, but it is powerless to coerce obedience, since obedience depends on the consent of the one who obeys, while mere
compliance does not. If we obey someone, in effect we grant him
authority, which is not to say simply that we treat him as if an authority, but rather that we concur that he is rightfully an authority to
us. Put another way, obedience requires that we believe the one we

obey is worthy of our obedience; we cannot be said to obey someone unless we believe he or she is rightfully an authority.

Two things follow from this, both having to do with the one who obeys. First, it gives him considerable force in the relation, for it is his obedience that in a certain sense determines the authority of the authority. Second, it gives him a certain responsibility, for he must ask whether the one he obeys is, in fact, a rightful authority.

To consider the first point, obedience and authority are correlative concepts. If someone obeys he necessarily obeys an "authority" in the sense that his obedience by definition requires that he believe that the one he obeys is an authority. Put in terms of the relation between the two persons, we can say that it is an interdependent relation, for authority cannot be exercised without obedience and obedience cannot be offered unless to an authority. Interestingly, however, the power in the relation as a relation is weighted to the side of the one who obeys. As we have said, an authority can be thought to have authority either because she is in fact obeyed or because she is a rightful authority. Someone might be a rightful authority but go unrecognized, and so not be obeyed. Yet if a *relation* of authority holds, it will depend on the consent of the one who obeys. If it is withheld, the authority, even if rightful, can be only a power in the relation. Furthermore, since humans beings are distinctively capable of pretending to obey, it becomes possible for the one who "obeys" to gain a certain power over the authority by deceiving her in this pretense. (There is, in this sense, a sort of vulnerability in being in a position of authority, which exacerbates an already strong temptation to make the relation more secure by turning it into one of naked power, something which is always possible for an authority to do—even if it means that in so doing her rightful authority is lost.)

Second, the responsibility that is held by the one who obeys relates to his duty to obey only rightful authorities. To speak of a power sightly different from that just discussed, those who obey can create authorities by offering their obedience. This is a remarkable power, for it can give birth to a whole "moral" universe—which is to say, a complex of beliefs and practices regarding what is owed to whom. The abuse of this power has devastating effects on everyone, including the one who offers obedience.[6] Put simply, the one who obeys must ask himself if the one he obeys is worthy of his obedience. If he does not ask, or if he hides the answer from himself, the correct way to describe his obedience is "blind obedience."

In what many consider an unfortunate turn of phrase, John Paul II has suggested that the first political duty of any age, and particularly our own, is to offer "obedience to truth."

> *Obedience to truth* about God and humankind is the first condition of freedom, making it possible for a person to order his needs and desires and to choose the means of satisfying them according to a correct scale of values, so that the ownership of things may become an occasion of personal growth. This growth can be hindered as a result of manipulation by the means of mass communication, which impose fashions and trends on opinion through carefully orchestrated repetition, without it being possible to subject to critical scrutiny the premises on which these fashions and trends are based.[7]

John Paul II is suggesting, in effect, that in our present cultural condition we are encouraged to obey fashions and trends blindly, something obedience to truth necessarily opposes. The implication is that blind obedience is not just a personal misstep, in fact whole cultures foster it, our present culture as much by its cynicism about truth (on John Paul II's analysis) as by its manipulation of media technologies.

Unfortunately, John Paul II is less clear about the alternative to this modern form of blind obedience. Concerned to respond equally strongly to what he perceives as the other political threat in the modern world, totalitarianism, he says

> In the totalitarian regimes . . . [a] person was compelled to submit to a conception of reality imposed on him by coercion, and not reached by virtue of his own reason and the exercise of his own freedom. This principle must be overturned and total recognition must be given to the *rights of human conscience,* which is bound only to the truth, both natural and revealed.[8]

The difficulty is that the notions of both freedom and conscience as they are presented here are profoundly individualized. As such, the alternative John Paul II presents against the totalitarianism he so strongly rejects ends up being colored by the liberalism he otherwise attacks when approaching from the other side.

Of course it is not our concern here to criticize John Paul II's political philosophy. We bring him into our discussion to consider one final linguistic point. John Paul II's appeal, while it begins as political, in its turn to conscience may suggest that obedience is finally offered alone, in one's heart. This seems inaccurate, at the very least because we obey most frequently in a role, and roles make sense only within a polity. Furthermore, if obedience is a virtue, we must be trained in it; it must be capable of development and growth within us rather than just being there, in the depths of our untrained hearts. At the very least it will require *practices,* actions. As Jesus noted in his parable of the two brothers, one who says he will work in the vineyard but doesn't and one who says he won't but does (Matthew 21:28–31), we obey as we act, not as we think or say.

If a virtue, obedience is surely political. All virtues, in a way, are political since they are learned in a community. Obedience, however, has a different relation to this community than other virtues, whatever their name. To illustrate, if we consider the notion of *character* in relation to the virtues, we see that it directs us not to any particular virtues, but rather to the integrity of the self over time.

Now the self can be integrated around different ends. Hence character in its broad usage is a formal notion. That is, to say someone has character does not tell us what *sort* of character she has. This is not to say character is an empty notion; at the least having character eliminates widely erratic behavior. Indeed, character is related to integrity in that the person who has it will behave in a *characteristic* way. Erraticism, in other words, is symptomatic of a lack of integrity, and so a lack of character (or even of self). Likewise, having integrity requires a certain faithfulness to one's story, a commitment to living it out through time. Yet—and this is our point—"integrity" or even "character" require nothing with regard to the sort of story it is. (Both Saint Francis and Nietzsche, for instance, had integrity.)

Analyzing character in terms of integrity of the self puts us in a position to see how the justification for obedience as a virtue requires a certain material—and also political—content to the character we aspire to. An easy and commonplace justification of the possession of a given virtue or the doing of a certain action is the "I must do it (be honest, have hope, leave a marriage, float the Amazon) to be true to myself." This is an appeal to integrity; something about my character requires that I do a specified thing, or develop in a specified way. Whatever one thinks of this appeal in a particular case, it cannot be made to work with obedience. One cannot say with much sense: "I must obey to be true to myself." If and when we obey we place the "truth of myself" beyond the self; we obey the other *as opposed* to ourselves. (This is not far from what John Paul II is pressing in his use of the contested "obedience to truth.")

In this way, the presence of obedience among the virtues functions as a clear sign that the other virtues cannot have complete self-sufficiency as their final end. From this it follows that obedience fits only with *some* lives of virtue, it is incompatible with others. Whoever believes he should obey can never suppose he is not a member of a community, numbering two at the least. This explains why the eradication of obedience from the virtues is for some such a pressing matter. Nowell-Smith is a good example. He simply cannot understand the suggestion that he ought to be anything other than what is satisfactory to himself.

In this way we might say that rather than presuming a political context, as do other virtues, obedience requires that the politics be named. And the answer to the question, Whom do you obey? is the answer to the question, To what (if any) community do you belong?

3. Obedience as a Virtue

The title of this chapter asks if obedience is a virtue. Initially we treated that question as if it meant: Is obedience praiseworthy? Is it a good thing? Some, like Nowell-Smith, have suggested that it is not, so we have tried to deal in the first section with some of their objections by looking more closely at what "obedience" involves. Yet the question can be taken in another way. One could hold that obedience is indeed a good thing; under the right circumstances we ought to obey. Yet, they might add, the term "virtue" is not the right way to describe what we do when we obey.

For Christian thinkers this line of argument has been indirectly pursued by those who maintain that morality is better understood as the specification of actions done in application of a set of correct moral principles rather than as the elucidation of the set of virtues a good person has. The difference between these general views spreads throughout contemporary writing about morality, as we noted earlier, particularly in chapter 4. The way it applies at this point in our discussion, however, is quite direct. In a certain sense, for those who see morality in the first light there is nothing but obedience to it. That is to say, one comes to know the correct moral principles (by whatever means), and then obeys them.

We stress, however, that this is obedience "in a certain sense." For while the term "obey" fits in this description of morality, it is subtly different from the obedience we have been discussing. It has been *flattened* and now can be replaced with terms like "follow" or "apply" without significant loss.[9] One could say, in other words, that on the first description morality involves the discovery of correct moral principles and their *application,* rather than obedience to them.

To observe the nature of the change, Kant's picture of morality serves well. He urges us—or rather argues that we are required—to obey the universal moral law. Yet we discover, of course, that this is no law other than rationality itself. As such it is impersonal and also self-referential, in that we give the law to ourselves as rational beings. Or, as MacIntyre has put it, "[a]ccording to Kant, the rational being utters the commands of morality to himself. He obeys no one but himself."[10]

It has been frequently observed that Kant removed from God any direct influence over the content of the moral law. What is less frequently noticed is that the form of our obedience either to "rationality" or to ourselves as legislators in the kingdom of ends cannot but be different from that offered to God. On Kant's proposal there is no person to whom obedience is offered; there is no active second will to whom we, in our obedience, must conform our will. In Kant's scheme, we obey, but our obedience is not offered to another.[11]

Obedience to an abstract law and obedience to a person are, we think, quite different. For example, could we be said to pretend to obey the categorical imperative? At whom would we aim our pretense? Iago, for example, pretends to obey Othello, all the while plotting his downfall. If Othello suddenly became impersonal, or an expression of Iago *qua* rational being, we could make little sense of the pretense. Indeed, we'd quickly redescribe Iago's plotting as delusional.

Moreover, consider our earlier distinction between compliance and obedience. Compliance describes behavioral conformity to a command, but leaves room for dissent. Often someone complies because he knows he must, not because he wants to; indeed, as he complies he may think all the while that were he free from the power of the commander, he would do quite otherwise. Obedience, on the other hand, implies an acquiescence which is possible only when the one who obeys places his trust in his lord. It includes a surrendering of what he wants, as does Kant's acting "from duty," but the surrender is offered willingly, not just because he knows he has a duty to obey but because he trusts the one he obeys. Kant's obedience to the moral law cannot include this crucial subtlety, since it is not offered to a person, God, who can be loved or hated, trusted or scorned, but rather to a formula, whose formulators are none other than ourselves. It is a *flattened* sort of obedience.

Ironically, many contemporary Christian theologians and philosophers have rushed to recombine an essentially Kantian view of morality and with the idea that it is not impersonal rationality but rather God who issues the commands of morality. These are the so-called divine command theorists.[12] Their connection to Kant is not in all cases so clear, especially since William of Occam is the thinker they more frequently invoke. Occam, however, did not have so much the formulation of a theory of morality in mind as the defense of God's sovereignty and so came to assert that whatever God commands is right, by definition. That Occam's scattered comments can be turned in our time into a "theory of morality" is, we would suggest, more our own problem than his.

The ironic result of these efforts has been the production of a commanding God who is impersonal, entirely lacking a history. For the God who commands could have commanded anything; it only so happens that God somehow decided to command us to refrain from murder and theft, a coincidence that provides divine command theorists with considerable relief from what might have been a quite embarrassing situation. In their relief the divine command theorists generally fail to note that trusting and worshipping a god who might have commanded us to do anything at all seems to have lost its point and so, for that matter, has obeying him.[13]

Alasdair MacIntyre has taken up the case of the divine command theorists in a related way. As he argues, the God of the divine command theories runs into the difficulties of Blake's Nobodaddy, who might command anything at all. As he formulates his complaint, divine command theorists begin with a meager set of resources and so lose any check on what sort of god should be obeyed.

> [M]oral theories of the type advanced by Occam and Adams are unlikely to be able to distinguish adequately between the claims to human allegiance made in the name of a variety of different gods who allegedly issue commands to us, because they approach these claims with too meager a set of resources, conceptual and otherwise, with which to evaluate such claims. And the meagerness is itself surely due to the attempt to make divine commands in some way foundational to morality.[14]

In other words, the god whom one obeys on a divine command theory of morality might be any god. It doesn't matter that it is *this particular god,* for example, the God of Israel and of Jesus.

MacIntyre goes on to argue that it is not "rational" to obey such a god. As we have tried to point out by maintaining that Kant's morality requires nothing but obedience (which turns of necessity into a flattened sort), MacIntyre holds that since "there is nothing to the good other than obedience *qua* obedience," we are left with "no conception of goodness in terms of which to justify obedience to the commands of any one god rather than of any other."[15]

While there are difficulties in his way of putting it, MacIntyre's point is helpful. When Christians obey God, they obey the *Christian* God. As they tell the story, God is a person, whom one might attempt to deceive (ultimately unsuccessfully, mind you) by pretending to obey, as did Ananias and Sapphira, or to whom one might offer one's obedience precisely because he had learned in God's history to count God trustworthy, as did Abraham. Obeying this God has the context of a historical and personal relation. Within it, God issues commands which Christians must obey. But the relation is not constituted entirely by the commands and the obedience. Christians, for example, come to trust God, or hope in God's promises as they learn of God in the stories of God's faithfulness in preserving Israel or sacrifice in offering up His son Jesus. Learning these things, they can speak of "trusting" or "hoping" as part of their obedience, now understood in an expanded sense. But their obedience, either in this expanded sense in which they obey God as they trust, or in the narrower sense in which they obey God's commands because they have come to trust in God's promises,[16] is different from what a Kantian might offer to the categorical imperative precisely because it does not stand alone; it arises within a particular story that gives it sense (MacIntyre would say "rationality") and by which it is carried to others who might also come to trust and obey this particular God.

Within this context, it is easier to see what it might mean for obedience to be a virtue. Ironically, by elevating obedience to constitute morality Kant and the divine command theorists diminish the meaning and significance of actually obeying someone in a relationship. Since for them obedience is equivalent to acting morally, there can be no other virtue than obedience. But of course this can mean nothing other than that the virtues disappear, including, ultimately, the virtue of obedience, since it can no longer be understood alongside other virtues.

When we return it to its place among the virtues, we can recover some of its particular features. To recall our earlier discussion, there we noted that obedience in relation requires the existence of two wills: the will of the authority and the will of the one who obeys. This can be extended, now, to include specifications about the sort of relation the wills must be in. At the very least, obedience requires that the one who obeys must perceive his will as potentially at odds with the will of his lord. This distinguishes obedience as a virtue from a related but more rudimentary form we discussed initially, i.e., that of dogs or small children. Dogs can be reasonably said to have wills, but it is quite unclear that a dog can perceive its will as different from the will of its master. This is why the ingredient we called "consent" is absent from the form of obedience we attribute to them and from the compliance discussed earlier.

In obedience consent is offered in the face of the possibility that the two wills will be at odds, and this tells us something important about the reason for the obedience. The will of the authority is generally (although not always) made known to the one who obeys in the form of a command. We can see now, though, that the reason for obedience to the command does not arise from within the content of the command itself. Rather, the consent in obedience attaches to the relation, making it possible that if the command turns out to be at odds with the will of the one who receives it, he will still obey. The wills need not *actually* be at odds, just potentially. Hence, some actual command from an authority might fit with what the one who obeys would have done in any case, for other reasons. (Here *pretending* to obey is especially tempting.) However, he obeys if he follows the command because he has been commanded by the authority rather than exclusively for these other reasons.

Thought of in this way, obedience is easily connected to other developed dispositions we generally call virtues. One obvious virtue is temperance, which seems a necessary condition for obedience, since without it we are given over to the concupiscible appetites and cannot entertain anything other than what we desire at a particular moment. (I.e., in our actions we cannot even consider a will that is other than our own.) Humility is the specific virtue Aquinas picks as that which not only tempers the appetite (it is a virtue of temperance for him) but also "moderates and restrains moral virtue" from "tending to high things immoderately."[17] Humility on Aquinas's view is due more to God than to our fellow human beings, a point that distinguishes it for him from obedience, which he calls a virtue of justice, since it demands a specific active response to a command from someone, divine or human, to whom we owe it. Yet insofar as Aquinas believes we owe obedience to God, there is a clear connection between our capacity to humble ourselves before God and our capacity to receive and follow God's commands. Indeed, as Aquinas's point suggests, we need restraining not only in our appetites but also in our developed sense of the coherence and intactness of our own moral selves, which can easily become overblown.

In another passage Aquinas gives us a further nuance regarding the actual practice of obedience and the skills it demands. "Wherefore obedience is a special virtue, and its specific object is a command tacit or express, because the superior's will, however it become known, is a tacit precept, and a man's obedience seems to be all the more prompt, forasmuch as by obeying he forestalls the express command as soon as he understands his superior's will."[18] If we think of obedience as grounded in the relation between the authority and the one who obeys and, further, that its specific point of contact is in the submission of one will to another, then there can be variance in the quality of obedience. For example, some are more ready to obey than others. Or, some are better than others at discerning the will of the authority. Jesus' parable about the two brothers demonstrates that at a bare minimum obedience requires action; we cannot obey by merely planning to. However, this does not imply that the brother who at first refused to go to the vineyard but later went obeyed *well*. When we speak of someone as *more* obedient than someone else we need not understand this to imply that the first one obeys more frequently or with a greater ratio to the number of times he is commanded, as if obedience were only doing the act specified in the command. People obey better if they obey promptly (as Aquinas says) or more intelligently. "Intelligent obedience" is suggested by Aquinas's idea that a command can be tacit as well as expressed. Since obedience relates to the will of the authority, the one who obeys may be able to anticipate what that will is without receiving an explicit command. This will make him better able to understand it when it comes and so to do it more quickly and thoroughly, or perhaps even to obey it before it is issued.

Obedience offered in relation, then, can be easily placed alongside other apparent virtues. We cannot obey, let alone obey well, unless we have come to embody in our lives a range of concomitant skills that make us capable of offering obedience to someone.

4. Obeying the Christian God

We have tried to prepare the ground for an affirmative answer to the question borne in this chapter's title. But it cannot yet be given. For as we noted earlier, the question "should I obey?" cannot be answered until we know who is to be obeyed. We have argued that obedience implies a relationship, but that makes the nature of a particular relation all the more significant. Should the relationship remain the same? Should this person subject her will to that one? We cannot know until we know who each one is.

It is no accident that MacIntyre moves to a form of this same question: whether obedience to a particular person is "justified." However, he has put the point in an unfortunate way when he asks what makes obedience to a particular god "rational," which can suggest that the obedience religious people offer to their god must seek grounding in rational principle. This returns us to the rather unhelpful terms of the *Euthyphro* regarding whether a thing is pious (or just) because it is loved by the gods, or loved by the gods because it is pious, roughly the way the divine command theorists, following the assumptions of Kant and Nowell-Smith, continue to insist on formulating their questions.

While Christians are better off putting it in another form, they need not nor cannot avoid the issue. They begin to answer it with a story that tells of who God is and who it is that obeys. In its full form this story will include accounts of others such as Abraham, who obeyed when it counted, or still others, like Peter, whose obedience to God entailed disobedience to men. Such a full account exceeds our limits of space as well as our capacities; instead, we will conclude this chapter with a brief sketch of the possible implications of a crucial peculiarity of the God Christians claim worthy of our obedience.

Richard Mouw is the rare defender of divine command morality who has considered the peculiarities of the God Christians obey. Rather than treat God abstractly, merely as the source of certain commands, Mouw notices that Christians must attend to the fact that God is the "triune commander." For Mouw's own purposes, this entails a recognition that Christians obey God as Holy Spirit, whose "sanctifying work is the provision of the *charismata* for our moral lives,"[19] an observation that makes the commander much more intimate and involved in the formation of the lives of those who obey than the divine commander of most of the divine command theories.

Following Mouw's example we should like briefly to consider how the triune character of the Christian God affects the form of Christian obedience. The claim that God is triune is a peculiar one, and yields, we suspect, a peculiar obedience. The peculiarity begins with the fact that Christians call the first person of the Trinity "Father" and not merely "creator." As Athanasius pointed out, "If one predicates the words 'maker,' 'creator' and 'unoriginate' of God, one plainly has the created and originated order in mind. But if one calls God 'Father,' then the Son is immediately brought into view."[20]

It has sometimes been noted by divine command theorists that God has the right to command us in whatever way God might like, for, after all, God created us.[21] As Athanasius intuits, however, the relation between creator and creature is hardly the same as that between father and child. The former is characterized merely by sheer power, something, as Athanasius goes on to say, even the Greeks attribute to God. As we have argued, however, the relation between an authority and the one who obeys is not secured by such power. That someone has power over us is a reason to comply with that person's commands, not a reason to obey.

Calling God Father, then, places God in an office primarily characterized by authority, not by power. Furthermore, in the biblical record "father" is more frequently associated with one who cares for his children than one who wields power over them. As a place to begin knowing God, the parental role, even as imperfectly filled by human parents, is one of love and care. This care is perfected in the love offered us by God the Father, as emphasized by Jesus in the Sermon on the Mount.

> Is there anyone among you who, if your child asks for bread, will give a stone? Or if the child asks for a fish, will give a snake? If you then, who are evil, know how to give good gifts to your children, how much more will your Father in heaven give good things to those who ask him! (Matthew 7:9–11)[22]

God's provision for His people as father is the seat of His authority. Christians are bound to obey God the Father not because He created them, but because He created them in love, and has continued to strengthen and sustain them.

Of course the prime corollary of "Father" for Athanasius is not we children of God but the Son, whom Christians call Jesus Christ, the second person of the Godhead. Considering the Son, we discover that the story Christians tell of him speaks as much or more of his obedience to the Father than of our obedience to him. Indeed, if we follow out the full implications of calling God triune, we must admit that the Christian God is as much the "God who obeys" as the "God who commands."

An oddity that marks the triune conception of God carried by Christians is that God can be thought to include persons with distinct wills. As we noted earlier, the notion of obedience requires this distinctness of will; it is therefore doubly interesting that the relation between wills in the Godhead is described as a kind of perfect obedience. So Jesus in the garden asks the Father for relief from his suffering, but concludes his prayer with "yet not my will but yours be done" (Luke 22:42). Later we are told more in Philippians about what lay behind this obedience, namely, that Christ Jesus did not consider equality with God, which was rightly his, "something to be grasped, but made himself nothing taking the very nature of a servant, being made in human likeness." Humbling himself, "he became obedient to death—even death on a cross" (Philippians 2:5–8).

As the passage goes on to say, the obedience here described of Christ serves as a model for Christians who are "to work out their salvation with fear and trembling" (2:12). As offered to the Father, the Son's obedience has the unique feature of not being required by office. The Son does not so much owe obedience to the Father, for he is himself in the very nature of God, but he nonetheless offers it. As such, its offering is rightly described as sacrifice. The reason it is offered is that the Son has come to share entirely in the purpose of the Father; he knows his mind and conforms to it willingly. (Part of the perfection of Christ's obedience is his knowledge of the will of the Father. As Aquinas noted earlier, such knowledge provides for the possibility of a promptness in obedience that need not wait for an explicit command, since it knows the mind of its lord so well.)

John Locke discusses the parental relation at some length in *The Second Treatise* in a chapter entitled (revealingly) "Of Paternal Power." There he says the following:

> Children, I confess, are not born in this full state of equality, though they are born to it. Their parents have a sort of rule and jurisdiction over them, when they come into the world, and for some time after; but it is a temporary one. The bonds of this subjection are like the swaddling clothes they art wrapt in, and supported by, in the weakness of their infancy: age and reason as they grow up, loosen them, till at length they drop off, and leave a man at his own free disposal.[23]

Locke's justification of parental "power" turns on the weakness or irrationality of the child, which will in time disappear. Children are bound to obey their parents, then, only in this weakness; it is a temporary relation of authority lasting only until full equality is reached. The description in Philippians is fruitfully juxtaposed with this idea. There the Son does not count equality a thing to be grasped. His obedience, in other words, is not out of weakness but out of his desire to join his will to that of his Father. (There is here the provocative idea that the Son might have become a second God, with purposes independent of God the Father.)

This obedience offered freely by one who has reached the full extent of his powers is in distinct contrast to that presumed by Nowell-Smith, and now Locke, who mark it as something the moral life, grounded in the twin emphases of equal rights and independence, requires that we move beyond. Indeed, the Christian can never conceive of herself as having moved beyond obedience, since she, like Christ, does not will independence but rather radical dependence, by which her own purposes meld with God's as she comes to share God's mind.

This obedience makes sense only in the light of Christ's obedience, which transformed creation precisely because it opened up the possibility of a community of diverse persons who come willingly to share in one another's purposes. On earth, this is the work of the Spirit who enables us to submit ourselves one to the other and to God. The Spirit trains us up into the obedience of Christ. As obedient to Christ and like Christ, Christians obey one another in what John Yoder has termed "radical subordination" which the New Testament writers require of all members of the community to one another, not merely of the weaker party to the stronger.[24] The politics of obedience to truth, then, is radical not because it is attuned to private conscience rather than the dictates of the culture, but because it creates and signifies a community whose members do not lord it over one another as do the rulers of the gentiles. "Not so with you. Instead, whoever wants to become great among you must be your servant, and whoever wants to be first must be slave of all. For even the Son of Man did not come to be served, but to serve, and to give his life as a ransom for many" (Mark 10: 43–44).

NINE

Courage Exemplified

1. The Arming of Virtue

The newfound enthusiasm for a recovery of an ethic of virtue which has concerned us in this book might be thought to be a "good thing" for religious communities in the United States. Widespread enthusiasm for virtue may provide the churches, who have become increasingly irrelevant to the public discussion of the issues before the American polity, a way to contribute to that polity by producing people of virtue. Or so some hope. In this chapter we want to suggest that, even if enticing, this is a false hope, one Christians must eschew.

To be clear, we do not mean to deny that issues concerning virtue are important for political practice and/or theory. Indeed we have argued against the predominant forms of moral theory produced by liberal society precisely because they have been based on a lawlike paradigm that ignores the significance of the virtues. In short, it has been the project of liberal political and ethical theory to create just societies without just people, primarily by attempting to set in place social institutions and/or discover moral principles that insure cooperation between people who share no common goods or virtues. Examples of this project are legion, although none is better than John Rawls's *A Theory of Justice*,[1] where the art of argument is elegantly displayed. Mind you, Rawls does not exclude considerations of virtue, but he follows the standard theories we have already investigated in assuming that any account of virtue is secondary to "principles of justice" and institutions based upon them.

Without systematically engaging Rawls at this point,[2] we hope it is sufficiently plain that we think the liberal project he represents has failed, as it was bound to. But now, one might interject, with this failure behind us, isn't the public recovery of virtue all the more pressing? And isn't it irresponsible not to work to further it? For if liberalism cannot create a just society without just people, must we not return with renewed vigor to creating just people so a just society can remain within our sights?

While not unfamiliar in the more distant past, this is a new and interesting challenge for our age, one we must take seriously. To begin to respond, we would like to draw attention to a series of comments made by Jean Bethke Elshtain written in answer to the call for a return to civic virtue made by the authors of *Habits of the Heart*. As she notes, "the problem with the tradition of civic virtue can be stated succinctly: that virtue is *armed*."[3] As we emphasized in chapter 4, "virtue" is of Greek origin, and not accidentally so. As Elshtain observes, for the Greeks war was a natural state of affairs and the basis of society. Moreover, the presumption of war was continued by the great civil republicans such as Machiavelli and Rousseau. Thus the first duty of Machiavelli's prince is to be a soldier and create an army of citizens, that is, not simply to create an army to protect citizens, but to make citizens an army. Napoleon in this respect is but the full realization of Machiavelli, and democratic order itself is based on the idea that all citizens should be armed.[4]

In fact, according to Elshtain, Rousseau is the great prophet of armed civic virtue, because he saw most clearly that for modern societies a vision of total civic virtue is required. The chief process that draws people out of their provincial loyalties and makes them conscious of belonging to a wider community—a national community— is military conscription. Elshtain comments, "[the] *national* identity that we assume, or yearn for, is historically inseparable from war. The nation-state, including our own, rests on mounds of bodies."[5] Indeed, the United States is a society that is especially constituted by war. As Elshtain observes, a nation-state can exist on paper long before it exists in fact. Accordingly "a *united* United States is a historical construction that most visibly comes into being as cause and consequence of American involvement in the Great War. Prior to the nationalistic enthusiasm of that era, America was a loosely united federation with strong and regional identities."[6]

Within this context the virtue of courage assumes great importance, for at root courage is a virtue of war that is best exemplified by soldiers facing death in battle. This fits well with the common notion that courage involves a disposition toward death that pervades many aspects of our life, but for all of these aspects the courage of soldiers in battle is the paradigm. However, we want to suggest that for Christians "courage" cannot start with these assumptions nor this paradigm. In fact, from a Christian point of view such "courage" is not courage at all but only its semblance, which when wrongly used can turn demonic.[7]

If, then, the trumpeted return to civic virtue involves the arming of virtue with the courage of the soldier (as Elshtain has suggested) and if Christians are committed to another sort of courage not formed on war, there is good reason to think that the Christian churches cannot nor should not underwrite a program of return to civic virtue, at least not in all of its aspects.

2. Aristotle on Courage

To see how accounts of courage might differ, we propose to look, once again, to the two great proponents of virtue around whom much of this book has revolved: Aristotle and Aquinas. The latter, of course, depends significantly on the former, yet with great insight deviates on an especially important point: for Aquinas it is the martyr and not the soldier who exemplifies true courage.

To see the significance of this difference, we must begin with Aristotle's account of courage. It is offered in Book III of the *Nicomachean Ethics*,[8] where it is coupled with an analysis of temperance. Although Aristotle says little about this explicitly, we may suppose that he followed others in believing that this pair of virtues, courage and temperance, controls our desires, rendering us capable of the habits which make possible the lifelong process of formation of our characters to the good.

For Aristotle, and Aquinas as well, any account of the virtues requires that they be exemplified in concrete lives; after all, we become virtuous people by copying the deeds of virtuous people. Here to "copy" is not to imitate mechanically, though that may not be a bad way to start, but it involves having the same feelings, emotions, desires, and so on that the virtuous person has when she acts. As Aristotle observes, it is a hard task to be good, and it requires growth in knowledge: "not everyone can find the middle of a circle, but only a man who has the proper knowledge. Similarly, anyone can get angry—that is easy—or can give away money or spend it; but to do all this to the right person, to the right extent, at the right time, for the right reason, and in the right way is no longer something easy that anyone can do. It is for this reason that good conduct is rare, praiseworthy, and noble" (1109a25–30).

The point, then, is that being virtuous involves not only having dispositions for appropriate action, but also a right "attitude" that includes having the appropriate emotions and desires. This is one of the reasons virtue requires such training, for we become what we are only through the gradual buildup of the appropriate characteristics. It also helps us see why and how courage needs to be carefully distinguished from its counterfeit: recklessness.

Courage and temperance are the virtues that form what Aristotle assumed were our most basic appetites—fear and pleasure. Their purpose is not to repress these appetites but to form them to function rightly. Hence courage does not eliminate fear—that would be recklessness. Rather courage forms us to have fear in the right amount, at the right time, about the right things, and so on. Granted, a reckless person may appear to do just what a courageous person does but he is not acting courageously as he does, for he is not being properly affected by fear.[9]

It follows that courage is not only difficult to practice, it is difficult to recognize. To decipher it we must consider the various possible objects of fear, and which of these is most fearful. So Aristotle comments:

it is true that we fear all evils, e.g., disrepute, poverty, disease, friendlessness, death. But it does not seem that a courageous man is concerned with all of these. There are some evils, such as disrepute, which are proper and right for him to fear and wrong not to fear: a man who fears disrepute is decent and has a sense of shame, a man who does not fear it is shameless. Still, some people describe a man who fears no disrepute as courageous in a metaphorical sense, for he resembles a courageous man in that a courageous man, too, is fearless. Perhaps one should not fear poverty or disease or generally any evil that does not spring from vice or is not due to oneself. However, it is not the man who has no fear of these things who is courageous. But we call him so because of his resemblance to the courageous man. For some people who are cowards on the battlefield are generous and face the loss of money cheerfully. On the other hand, a man is not a coward if he fears insult to his wife and children, or if he fears envy or the like; nor is he courageous if he is of good cheer when he is about to be flogged. (1115a10–24)

The great variety of circumstances in which we are faced with fear calls for a paradigm case. What fears put courage to the test? What circumstances plainly distinguish the truly courageous person from those who display its counterfeits like recklessness, or even from those who display courage, but only now and then? The paradigm must involve death, for it is the most fearful thing. Yet not all deaths allow for the display of courage.

> For example, death by drowning or by disease does not. What kind of death, then, does bring out courage? Doubtless the noblest kind, and that is death in battle, for in battle a man is faced by the greatest and most noble of dangers. This is corroborated by the honors which states as well as monarchs bestow upon courage. Properly speaking, therefore, we might define as courageous a man who fearlessly faces a noble death and in situations that bring a sudden death. Such eventualities are usually brought about by war. But of course a courageous man is also fearless at sea and in illness, though not in the same way as sailors are. Because of their experience, the sailors are optimistic, while the courageous man has given up hope of saving his life but finds the thought of such an (inglorious) death revolting. Furthermore, circumstances which bring out courage are those in which a man can show his prowess or where he can die a noble death, neither of which is true of death by drowning or illness. (1115a 28–1115b5)

It should not surprise us that the paradigm for courage for Aristotle is facing death in battle, for we know that his ethics is but the preface to his politics.[10] All virtues are in a sense political virtues, since they reflect the common good as well as provide it with specific content. They are, therefore, inescapably conventional, as they depend on practices that are generally agreed to be good. To call them conventional is not to call them into question but rather to indicate that any account of the virtues for any community requires the display of behavior that is commonly held to be good.

It is important to see that this behavior is more than an example of virtue in the way chess is an example of a board game, for the virtues have no sense unless there are practices that hold them in place in the arena of everyday human exchange. To take an example from another culture than our own, Lee Yearley has noted that propriety was a virtue central to Chinese culture in the time of Mencius. It covered such activities as solemn religious activities, like funerals, as well as what we call etiquette, including not just which fork to use when but also common rituals such as saying "excuse me" after a sneeze. Mencius links the solemn activities with the more mundane because he assumes they both foster a behavior that manifests distinctly human activities rather than instinctive reactions. As Yearly comments:

> Mencius believes these emotional reactions require conventional rules for their expression; they can find expression only through the ritual forms a society possesses. The rules or forms, in fact, are what allows people to achieve the good found in expressing and cultivating these reactions. For example, I cannot easily, or even adequately, show my respect for a cook, a host, or an elderly person unless social forms exist that allow me to express such attitudes. Furthermore, both I and others must know what those forms are and what they express. I need to know, for instance, that a slight bow and somewhat servile smile express respect, not irony or rancor. The attitude of respect toward others, Mencius thinks, must express itself in a disposition to follow the conventional rules of propriety. A person observes these rules as an expression of reverence for people, their roles, and even the social-organism that they embody and help preserve.[11]

The point we can derive from this is that virtues such as "respect" or "courage" are more than the attitudes a person might hold within himself, bringing them to expression now and then in some activity. No doubt respect or courage include certain attitudes, as we have noted, but they require display as well. Indeed, we cannot know their shape unless we see them in particular behaviors that we together identify as good. As the central paradigm of courage, facing death in battle is like this for Aristotle. It not merely an example of courage, it is rather the rightful *exemplification* of what true courage entails. It follows that without war courage could not be fully known.

All this is not to say that Aristotle thinks the courageous person is by necessity warlike. As we noted in chapter 6, courage cannot stand on its own; at the very least it requires the guidance of prudence regarding how much fear to have, about what, and so on. Soldiers may lack fear in battle, but that does not by itself mean they are courageous. For example, Aquinas notes that some soldiers "through skill and practice in the use of arms, think little of the dangers of battle, as they reckon themselves capable of defending themselves against them; thus Vegetius says 'no man fears to do what he is confident of having learned to do well.' "[12]

Likely this is true of a certain General Skobeleff, whose comments are reproduced by Yearley, although there is something more than mere familiarity with danger or with arms at work in his self-appraisal. Says he:

> I believe that my bravery is simply the passion for and at the same time the contempt of danger. The risk of life fills me with an exaggerated rapture. The fewer there are to share it, the more I like it. The participation of my body in the event is required to furnish me an adequate excitement. Everything intellectual appears to me to be reflex; but a meeting of man to man, a duel, a danger into which I can throw myself headforemost, attracts me, moves me, intoxicates me. I am crazy for it, I love it, I adore it. I run after danger as one runs after women; I wish it never to stop.[13]

From Aristotle's perspective, General Skobeleff is not a courageous man, not only because he is untouched by appropriate fear, but also because he lacks the wisdom to subject his daring to the appropriate purposes. Nevertheless, who would doubt that Skobeleff is in one sense an excellent soldier, perhaps even better because he lacks true courage? Indeed, at one point Aristotle muses that the very best soldier are not courageous but rather those who are ready to face danger because "they have no other good" (1117b–17).

The General Skobeleffs of the world notwithstanding, the battlefield is still the true test of courage for Aristotle. As opposed to men like Skobeleff, the courageous person, because he has the other virtues (he is "happy"), knows that his life is a true good, rightly prized, and its loss is rightly feared. Nevertheless, this man stands and fights knowing full well what this might bring. "Death and wounds will be painful for a courageous man, and he will suffer them unwillingly, but he will endure them because it is noble to do so or base to do otherwise. And the closer a man is to having virtue or excellence in its entirety and the happier he is, the more pain will death bring to him. Life is more worth living for such a man than for anyone else, and he stands to lose the greatest goods, and realizes that fact, and it is painful. But he is no less courageous for that and perhaps rather more so, since he chooses noble deeds in war in return for suffering pain. Accordingly, only insofar as it attains its end is it true to say of every virtue that it is pleasant when practiced" (1117b7–15).

Death on the battlefield, therefore, stands as the paradigm of courage for Aristotle precisely because it gives the genuinely courageous person the chance to offer the one great good which unifies all other particular goods, that is, his life, for an even higher good, namely the common good of the state. Moreover, he can do this in a noble manner—in what Aristotle calls the "noble deeds of war"—with full knowledge of what is at stake. This is the height of courage, by which all other acts of courage take their bearing.

3. Aquinas on Courage

Many of us are prone to a certain suspicion of Aquinas's intellectual originality when we discover how frequently he borrows from Aristotle.[14] This suspicion can arise particularly when Aquinas moves from the natural to the theological virtues, for at first glance the latter appear as no more than a fluffy topping spread over the natural virtues—which virtues depend substantially on Aristotle for their clearest articulation. Yet this perspective cannot jibe with the role Aquinas ascribes to the theological virtues, and particularly to charity. As he says,

> In morals the form of an act is taken chiefly from the end. The reason for this is that the principle of moral acts is the will, whose object and form, so to speak, are the end. Now the form of an act always follows from a form of the agent. Now it is evident that it is charity which directs the acts of all other virtues to the last end, and which, consequently, also gives the form to all other acts of virtue; and it is precisely in this sense that charity is called the form of the virtues, for these are called virtues in relation to 'formed' acts. (II-II, 23, 8)

If we take Aquinas at his word, no true virtue is possible without charity. Yet, as he specifies, apart from the true virtues formed by charity, there exist semblances of the virtues which have their particular orderings, generally corresponding to the ordering of the true virtues. Indeed, as Yearly points out, these semblances themselves have semblances according as we move closer or further from a given true virtue.

> For instance, acquired virtues are semblances of virtue if we use infused virtues as the standard of measurement. But any specific, acquired virtue will resemble more or less closely the integral form of that virtue. Acquired courage always is a semblance of infused courage and yet a particular instance of acquired courage will be only a semblance of real acquired courage. Indeed, he [Aquinas] can identify the 'same' phenomenon (e.g., giving up one's life for one's country) both as a semblance and as a standard. That identification depends on which criteria of value or sort of explanation he uses and thus on which hierarchies he employs.[15]

This complex pattern helps us begin to see how Aquinas's account of courage can be at once very similar and yet significantly different from Aristotle's. Like Aristotle, Aquinas assumes that courage (or fortitude) is a mean between inordinate fear and daring.

> It belongs to the virtue of fortitude to remove any obstacle that withdraws the will from following the reason. Now to be withdrawn from something difficult belongs to the notion of fear, which denotes withdrawal from an evil that entails difficulty. Hence fortitude is chiefly about fear of difficult things, which can withdraw the will from following the reason. And it behooves one not only firmly to bear the assault of these difficulties by restraining fear, but also moderately to withstand them, when, to wit, it is necessary to dispel them altogether in order to free oneself therefrom for the future, which seems under the notion of daring. Therefore fortitude is about fear and daring, as curbing fear and moderating daring. (II-II, 123, 3)

Having already considered the complexities of Aristotle's account of courage, we should not be surprised by this structural similarity. For the meaning of daring and of excessive fear cannot be clear until the practices which correspond to each—or to fortitude itself—have been specified. If Aquinas is good to his word, we should expect that what we should fear and in what we should place our confidence will depend in some way upon charity, which ultimately determines the mean of courage. This turns out to be the case. For according to Aquinas, it is spiritual goods that are truly virtuous people's first concern. Thus hope in God, who promises these goods, cannot but modify our fears about loss of temporal goods. So Yearly comments,

> Aquinas never claims that Christ teaches that temporal goods will appear if spiritual goods are sought. He does claim, however, that spiritual goods should be people's major concern, and they should hope (not presume) that temporal goods will appear. The higher perspective of "a view to the final good for the whole of life" allows people to understand the crucial issue of what really ought to be feared. The major fear courage ultimately should deal with is the fear of not possessing fully the spiritual goods virtuous people pursue and manifest, as Christ's teachings on providence both underline and illuminate.[16]

Of course the pursuit of spiritual goods as well as the pursuit of temporal goods depends upon our having life. Hence death is rightly to be feared as well as avoided.

> It belongs to the notion of virtue that it should regard something extreme: and the most fearful of all bodily evils is death, since it does away with all bodily goods. Wherefore Augustine says (*De Morib. Eccl.* XXII) that "the soul is shaken by its fellow body, with fear of toil and pain, lest the body be stricken and harassed with fear of death lest it be done away and destroyed." Therefore the virtue of fortitude is about the fear of dangers of death. (II-II, 123, 4)

So Aristotle and Aquinas are in agreement that a key locus of courage is our fear of death. Yet we must go on to ask what *kind* of death each thinks we should fear if we are to draw nearer to the thing Aquinas calls fortitude. We might recall, for instance, that Aristotle thought certain deaths, e.g., by drowning, could not be undertaken courageously.[17] And of course, for him it is death on the battlefield while fighting for a noble end that best displays courage.

What does Aquinas think? He follows Aristotle's assumption that fortitude has something to do with death in battle, but adds that "a brave man behaves well in face of danger of any other kind of death; especially since man may be in danger of any kind of death on account of virtue: thus may a man not fail to attend on a sick friend through fear of deadly infection, or not refuse to undertake a journey with some godly object in view through fear of shipwreck or robbers" (II-II, 123, 5).

Quite simply, with these additions and in the texts surrounding them, Aquinas treats fortitude in such a way that its ends are transformed by charity, so that death in battle no longer stands as its paradigm. In this particular text, Aquinas considers death in battle, but he then adds *as equivalents* death while tending to the sick or while undertaking a journey with some godly object. To consider the first, one might ask, what is the noble end of this? and why is it noble? But plainly charity tells us, for charity demands care for the sick and dying, and the risk of one's life in it is courageous, no less than the risk for the common good in battle.

With regard to the second, a "journey with a godly end," where we might face "shipwreck or robbers," Aquinas appears to mean this literally; no doubt the missionary journeys of Paul or the man who journeys from Jerusalem to Jericho in the parable of the good Samaritan echo in the back of his mind as he writes. Yet it is possible, as we have earlier, to take the notion of journey in a more metaphorical way such that it connects to the journey of the Christian life, which is not only difficult but extended through time. In any case, in a journey (as well as in the tending of the sick) the immediacy and excitement of a pitched battle disappears, and the courage required is quieted. Indeed, Aquinas's "fortitude," while used synonymously with "courage," suggests that what is demanded is a kind of endurance in the face of difficulty, danger, or oppression, a steadfastness of purpose and vision that will not be swayed even by threat of death. Hence, for Aquinas, patience and perseverance are integral to the very meaning of courage. To return to the metaphor, this emphasis connects to Aquinas's settled view that the moral life is a journey to God during which we must learn to endure much.[18] In this, patience and perseverance are key. Again Yearley provides a concise account of Aquinas' position: "Perseverance, with its opposed vices of obstinacy and softness (a too easy yielding to pleasure), concerns the need to adhere to the good sought. Patience concerns the need to overcome the sorrow brought by the inevitable loss of some goods."[19]

Wittgenstein was right, the world of the courageous person is different from that of the coward. This is borne out in Aristotle's account when one considers the vision of the soldier who faces death with indifference since he sees no other good. But it is also true that the world of the courageous Christian is different from the world of the courageous pagan. This is so because of their differing visions of the good which exceeds the good of life itself. These differing visions come to bear, ultimately, on the differing paradigms for courage. For Aristotle, as we have seen, this is death in battle. Yet Aquinas has already introduced additional cases as equivalents, which serves to demote death in battle to one of a number of possible ways to die courageously. As for a new paradigm for Aquinas, it is *martyrdom*. He speaks of it, still, as a kind of death in battle, but of course the battle has been transformed, and the persons fighting it, as is shown by the weapons required in it, such as patience and faith.[20] So Christians are required patiently to persevere in the face of persecution, since they have the confidence that enduring wrong is a gift of charity.

> Now it is evident that in martyrdom man is firmly strengthened in the good of virtue, since he cleaves to faith and justice notwithstanding the threatening danger of death, the imminence of which is moreover due to a kind of particular contest with his persecutors. Hence Cyprian says in a sermon: "The crowd of onlookers wondered to see an unearthly battle, and Christ's servants fighting erect, undaunted in speech, with souls unmoved, and strength divine." Wherefore it is evident that martyrdom is an act of fortitude; for which reason the Church reads in the office of Martyrs: They "became valiant in battle." (II-II, 124, 2)

The prominence of martyrdom in Aquinas's account of courage confirms that true courage, as opposed to its semblances, is a gift of the Holy Spirit. Thus the patience of Christians is that which displays the joy of being of service to God (II-II, 136, 3). Such joy is possible because patience is formed by charity. In like manner, courage as a gift of the Spirit protects the martyr from the "dread of dangers" in a distinctive manner:

The Holy Spirit moves the human mind further (than the steadfastness of normal courage), in order that one may reach the end of any
work begun and avoid threatening dangers of any kind. This transcends human nature, for sometimes it does not lie within human
power to attain the end of one's work, or to escape evils or dangers,
since these sometimes press in upon us to the point of death. But the
Holy Spirit achieves this in us when he leads us to eternal life, which
is the end of all good works and the escape from all dangers. And he
pours into our mind a certain confidence that this will be, refusing
to admit the opposing fear.[21]

Put another way, the work of our lives transcends our capacities,
since it demands that we love and serve God. Yet we receive of the
Spirit the strength and courage to persevere in it precisely because we
have been given confidence that God will complete God's work in us
even if our lives are taken by our enemies.

It follows that the fear of death, around which both Aristotle's and
Aquinas's courage take shape, will actually be a different sort of fear
for Christians and pagans. Both fear the loss of the possibility of the
various goods that give our lives form and texture. Yet the good that
life is for, and therefore the good for which it can be courageously
sacrificed, is not for Aquinas the common good of the nation but
rather friendship with God. This good, interestingly, is beyond the
power of human beings to effect; they must learn to accept it as a gift.
Yet this is also the source of their strength, for they trust that God
will bring to completion the work He has begun in them even in the
face of death itself.

It follows that Christians are freed from the anxiety of having to
secure the meaning of their lives in the mode of their death. Indeed,
there is considerable anxiety in death in the battlefield, since the courageous warrior must see himself as carrying the life of his nation on
his shoulders. He dies for its continued life, but if all die like him, all
die in vain. The martyr dies with the hope that her death will
strengthen the church, but it is not quite right to say she dies for the
church. Rather in her death, she imitates Christ.

This is why the martyr can *receive* her death in a way a warrior
cannot. As the warrior dies in the midst of the frenzied whir of battle,
he is active as he dies; as Aristotle would have it, he dies displaying

his prowess in the "noble deeds of war." The martyr dies precisely because she refuses to act as others have specified. Moreover, precisely as she is able to receive death as a consequence of her life's commitments, her martyrdom, while extraordinary, is not different in kind from the other things she has done or suffered throughout her life. In fact, this is an important final difference between the two paradigms of courage. Courage based on martyrdom is no easier than courage based on heroics in battle; it is, however, more accessible.[22] Heroics in battle require not only extraordinary talents but also extraordinary luck at death; indeed, most of those even who serve in war will die, not in this service, but at home or in hospitals, like most of us. For Aristotle such deaths cannot be courageous, since, as he implies (1115a37), like the water that surrounds the drowning man, their illness has made a mockery of their prowess and they cannot display it at death.

By contrast, the martyr's acceptance of her death as a continuing part of her service to God demonstrates how fortitude can infuse our lives and remain even as we die in our weakness. Martyrs, in effect, have to be ready to lose to their persecutors, dying ingloriously. They can do so only because they recognize that neither their life nor their death carries its own (or anyone else's) weight of meaning; rather that is carried by the God who supplies it. Unlike the great heroes of war, martyrs can be followed in daily life, for their courage is none other than an extension of the daily courage we need to carry on as faithful servants of God, which courage we receive as a daily gift of the Spirit. Yearly rightly notes that courageous Christians have confidence that God will secure their ultimate future. But, as he goes on to say, this "confidence includes more than just an assurance about what will happen in the future. They [the courageous] also feel assurance about the meaning of those signs that ensure them that the Holy Spirit moves them and that they are participating in the relationship of friendship with God that characterizes charity."[23]

4. Courage: Christian or American?

One matter remains unresolved. Earlier in this chapter we noted, with the help of Jean Bethke Elshtain, that civic virtue comes armed. For those of us living in America this is especially true, since we have little common history that is not also a history of war. Moreover, as we in our daily lives become ever more distant from the spiritual goods for which we might live, we begin to hunger for the meaning war can bestow or perhaps even for a shot at dying courageously in battle rather than wasting away in an aging body as we lose control over the physical pleasures that have heretofore diverted us from facing our mortality.

But some will say that is just the point. We in America have lost our moral vision precisely as we have lost our courage to fight for what is right and good. A return to virtue may indeed require a new call to arms, but there is no other way to save the soul of our nation. Moreover, as some Christians might add, not only Aristotle but Aquinas (and many other thoughtful Christians) recognized the duty we all have to fight for the common good. Enthusiastic pacifists may wish to gloss it over, but the fact remains that although Aquinas added to Aristotle's list of courageous deaths some of those that occur elsewhere than on the battlefield, he yet retained it as a genuinely courageous act.

It is no part of our purpose to turn Aquinas into a pacifist. Aquinas was not a pacifist, he was a just warrior.[24] Yet Aristotle was not a just warrior. The relevant consideration, then, is not that both Aristotle and Aquinas thought war was permissible, but rather what sort of view each carried about war and therefore about what kind of behavior within it could be called courageous. In this way we would suggest that for Aquinas the transformation of courage worked by charity cannot but change the meaning of a death on the battlefield.

To return briefly to the relevant passage in Aquinas, he remarks that "the dangers of death which occur in battle come to man directly on account of some good, because, to wit, he is defending the common good *by a just fight*" (II-II, 123, 5, emphasis added). This is the first important qualification. The noble good which courage necessarily serves (else it is not courage) is not made noble by the fight itself or by the party involved in the fight (i.e., my city or my country), but rather by the justice of the fight. There is, for Aquinas, no such free-standing category as the "noble acts of war," even though this evidently figures strongly in Aristotle's articulation of the paradigm of courage. For Aquinas, the nobility of the cause in war must be judged independently of our allegiance to one of the parties; consequently, glamorous deaths in battle fighting for an unjust cause cannot be for him acts of courage. There is no hint of this in Aristotle.

Furthermore, Aquinas goes on in this same passage to speak of a "just fight" as falling into two types, each with an illustration. First, there is courage as displayed in battle within a just war, and second, there is the courage displayed in "private combat," as when a judge rules justly even when this places his life or person in considerable peril. By supposing that both of these "just fights" are equally capable of displaying courage, Aquinas places the violent combat of war in relation to other sorts of (nonviolent) combat. In so doing he effectively reorients the courage displayed in war on the new paradigm, namely martyrdom. Courage in war is not courage because it is particularly glamorous or valiant, nor because it involves the "noble acts of war," nor because it is highly honored in city-states, nor because it provides the warrior a unique chance to display his prowess as he dies—all possible reasons suggested by Aristotle's account which assumes its paradigmatic status. Rather courage in battle is courage because in the face of great peril the soldier has persevered in doing what is just—according to a justice now formed by charity.

To sum up the point in a different light, Aquinas offers Christians a courage that will make us patient enough to fight a just war. Indeed, Aristotle's remark that it is unlikely that the truly courageous man will make the very best soldier applies all the more to Aquinas's just warrior, for not only will he know what is at stake in his own death, he will be dogged by the concern that he not kill unjustly. He will not follow the command of his superiors or his country without giving this thought—which means, we think, that precisely as he is courageous according to the courage formed by charity he will be the more likely to subvert the political order as he seeks to serve it by fighting for it.[25] Put ironically, Christian courage will subvert any political order based on courage, that is, upon the courage that derives its intelligibility from the practice of war. That is why Rousseau was right to think that the Christians should be suppressed. Their "acts of courage," even when allegedly in service of the social order, do not sustain it but rather threaten its very foundations.

In reply to his line of argument, it might be suggested that the subversion has already occurred and we are now reaping its benefits with the coming of age of modern representative democracy. The great difference with democracy is that it is a social order that thrives on difference and dissent, and so the peculiar courage of Christians can be tolerated, or even welcomed. Yet this response will not work, for inherent in such an account of the church's relation to democracy is the distinction between the public and private, which—as we have tried to detail in our conversation with John Casey—cannot but marginalize courage of any sort. Indeed, that distinction is itself the principal agent of the destruction of any coherent account of civic virtue in liberal societies.

Here we return once again to Elshtain's armed civic virtue and so to a form of the earlier suggestion that any virtue is better than none, even if it arms us. For a non-liberal Christian (like Richard John Neuhaus), while the revival of civic virtue may bring only a semblance of courage (and of the other virtues) to social orders like America, a semblance of virtue, as Aquinas himself saw, can teach true virtue. Hence, those formed by the courage necessary to face death well will be more easily led to the fuller account of courage offered by Christians.

This is a powerful suggestion and one reason why we are initially disposed to take those who have fought in war with great seriousness. However, there is no reason—in fact, there is reason to the contrary—to think that it is the job of the Christian churches to shore up virtue's semblances for the sake of the wider society in which they live.[26] They may articulate the connections, but this will remain possible only as they speak clearly of, and clearly live, the true virtues that are formed by charity. This is not just a matter of the division of labor, but of truth, for without true courage the semblance of courage cannot be known as it truly is, namely, a semblance. Moreover, at no time can Christians assume that their articulation of true courage will be received as such in the wider society. Besides showing us the shape of true courage, this is another thing the martyrs have taught us. The martyrs must yet stand as a reminder to us all, and particularly to those American Christians who would revive it, that the spirit of civic virtue can and has killed many Christians, and more Jews, all in the name of the common good.

Practicing Patience:
How Christians Should Be Sick

1. The Terms of Our Professions

In our current setting there is something of a rush to call any and every line of work a profession. A number of interesting consequences have followed from this, including that the term "professional" has broken free of older ties in our language to the originating idea of a calling for a special service to the common good. This is not to say, however, that the term "professional" has lost its moral power. If anything it has gained more, albeit a different kind. For there is now no more stinging charge against an aspiring inductee into any one of a legion of careers we call professions that he or she has acted "unprofessionally."

What counts as unprofessional behavior varies, of course, but in all cases it has some connection with how the professional has treated his "client." Indeed, it is this term that has seized the day, becoming a virtual pair with the ubiquitous "professional." Their intertwining is not, however, entirely complete, a fact that gives us our subject for this final chapter. For in the practice of medicine, even though some physicians may treat their patients as clients, or, worse, customers, they yet call them "patients." Indeed, as we shall attempt to show, the retention of "patients" in medicine and the continued practice of patience by patients is key to the good practice of medicine.

When we fix on the connection between patience and patients we cannot but feel some discomfort. It is an empirical fact that often patients are extremely impatient. As a society, nothing upsets us more than having to wait for our bodies. Indeed, our bodies are like our cars: they are to serve as we direct without calling attention to themselves (although we may use them to call attention to us). If they do call for our attention, we are quick to anger, with both our bodies and cars, and with those whose job it is to repair them.

This impatience is of interest to us. At the least, and as we shall briefly try to show, it dooms the practice of medicine. More important, however, is the shape of the patience it lacks. Christians are called to be a patient people, in health and in sickness. Indeed, impatience is a crucial sin that carries us into other sins. The shape of Christian patience, then, will be our chief concern in this chapter, although we mean to describe it concretely as it relates to the practice of medicine. If Christians are faithful, they will be, we think, the most patient of patients. As such they will embody the skills necessary for the sustenance of the practice of medicine.

2. The God that Failed:
The Pathos of Medicine in Modernity

The title *The God That Failed* originally was used for a book of essays by former Communists describing how they became Communists and why and how they lost their faith in communism.[1] Arthur Koestler, one of the essayists, notes that communism, like all true faiths, "involves a revolt against the believer's social environment, and the projection into the future of an ideal derived from the remote past. All utopias are fed from the sources of mythology; the social engineer's blueprints are merely revised editions of the ancient text."[2] For many today, medicine is to be viewed analogously. As they suggest, modern medicine is fueled by the utopian presumption that illness can be cured or tamed by skill and science. As such, medicine represents another utopia, another god that has failed.

According to its critics, as a failed god medicine is not the mode of liberation it professes to be but rather a legitimating ideology that allows some people to control others in the name of liberation. Moreover, like most effective forms of control, the power that medicine exercises is covert, since it stems from and is secured by its invisibility. As such, medicine is but another of the supervisory strategies so prevalent in modern political regimes.[3] Insofar as we desire what medicine teaches us to desire, we willingly shape our lives to become pliant medical subjects. The very understanding of our bodies, our "biology," produces and reproduces us to be good servants of the medical regime.[4]

As for the rise of medical ethics in the last twenty-five years, say the critics, it is but icing on the ideological cake. Just as princes once surrounded themselves with priests whose function it was to legitimate their power to rule, so physicians now employ "ethicists" for structurally similar purposes. A strange creature that only modernity could produce, the "ethicist" may imagine himself to be the patient's advocate against the power of the physician when he champions—as he is doing with increasing frequency—the "autonomy" of the patient. Ironically, however, the stress on autonomy turns out to produce just the kind of ahistorical account of moral agency that so effectively disguises medicine's power over us. Indeed, it is the job of the "ethicist" to devise rules and guidelines that, while ostensively helping us to resolve hard decisions about life and death, in the end convince us that our lives are nothing without such "decisions."[5]

One device we have found effective in teaching students something of the power the church once held over people's lives is to ask them to reflect on how it feels to experience the amazingly technical, administrative, and bureaucratic complexity of a major medical center. Those of us unfortunate enough to have found ourselves patients in such centers recognize deep feelings of powerlessness in the face of such a faceless giant, feelings that more often than not are followed by an overwhelming sense that we must please those "caring" for us or else they will hurt us. Indeed, the hierarchial politics of such medical centers are enough to make the description "Byzantine" inadequate. Medicine, in fact, has become more powerful and pervasive in our lives than the church ever was and surely far more powerful than it is today. This may explain why the current attack against medicine appears ready to exceed the furor of the revolt against the church. It is perhaps the only sort of revolt that makes sense in modernity now that the church is far too weak as an institution to make revolt against it worthwhile.

Despite our deep sympathies with the shape of this revolt against medicine, however, we cannot entirely credit its story. Those currently in revolt against medicine in our society overestimate the intensity of public antipathy toward medicine and its servant, medical ethics. In fact, the revolt has had to this point very little effect, since the questions it has raised can easily be dismissed as extreme moralistic nonsense.

That the revolt is so effortlessly deflated, absorbed, or repudiated may be, as the rebels allege, another sign of medicine's iron grip on our minds. We think, however, that it is a sign of the insufficiency of the moral resources the rebels have brought to bear on medicine as an institution. Modern medicine is not quite a god that failed. It is, rather, a failed substitute for God when God was failed by us. For *modern* medicine was formed by a modern culture that forced upon medicine the impossible role of bandaging the wounds of societies that are built upon the premise that God does not matter.[6] Such social orders, which we rightly call liberal, take as their central problem how to secure cooperation between self-interested individuals who have nothing in common other than their desire to survive. Cooperation is secured by bargains being struck that will presumably secure the best outcomes possible for each individual.[7]

"Liberalism" names those societies wherein it is presupposed that the only thing people have in common is their fear of death, despite the fact that they share no common understanding of death. So liberalism is that cluster of theories about society that are based on the presumption that we must finally each die alone. Our fear of such a death becomes the resource for cooperation as we conspire to create social practices that embody the presumption that holds so many moderns in its grip, namely that there is nothing quite important enough in our lives to risk dying for.[8] Yet, at the same time, we all know we must die. Even more telling, we know that the way we die is the result of the very forms of cooperation (often taking the form of competition) that are created to hide our own deaths from ourselves and from one another. In such social orders, medicine becomes an insurance policy to give us a sense that none of us will have to come to terms with the reality of our death.

Nowhere is this better seen than in the abandonment of the traditional medical imperative "Do no harm" in its correlating form: "When in doubt do not act." If there is a cardinal rule now in medicine it is that in any and every state of uncertainty physicians must nonetheless find something to do. If a physician does not act, her patient will quickly either lose hope in medicine, or, more likely, come to believe her incompetent. Moreover, the imperative to act has driven medical research to discover ever newer and more fantastic modes of intervention, which, while temporarily increasing confidence in a medicine of technological miracles, may in the long run undercut it

---

more deeply. For the risk of error is all the greater and the fall to death all the more jolting since the technological miracles have schooled us in the false hope that death might be avoided altogether. To avoid error, physicians have become increasingly specialized, hoping that by knowing more and more about less and less they will be prone to fewer mistakes, a strategy that ironically results in more mistakes, since, as a matter of fact, the patient happens to be more than the sum of his parts. Unfortunately, he is increasingly cared for by a medicine that is something less than the sum of its specializations.

To position ourselves clearly, we are not distant from the rebels against modern medicine in our diagnosis of its problems. Where we differ profoundly, however, is in the ascription of blame to the institution of medicine for our present state of ill health. No one can or should be blamed. The simple fact is that we are getting precisely the kind of medicine we deserve. Modern medicine exemplifies a secular social order shaped by mechanistic economic and political arrangements, arrangements which are in turn shaped by the metaphysical presumption that our existence has no purpose other than what we arbitrarily create.

In such a world it makes perfect sense to call physicians "health professionals" and patients "clients." Nevertheless, modern medicine has stuck with the anachronisms—which we think demonstrates the true pathos of medicine. For in fact the practice of medicine was formed under a quite different set of presumptions than those now so widely held. This is why at least some physicians still presume that they are to care for a patient even though they cannot cure, or even alleviate to any significant extent, the patient's malady.[9] This kind of behavior makes little sense if physicians are there for the sole purpose of repairing our bodies when they don't serve us as we like. Medical care, moreover, is still governed by the presumption that patients are to be cared for in a manner independent of and preceding all other considerations concerning their worth to the wider society.

This pathos—whereby physicians and patients yet engage in practices that are unintelligible within our predominant modern self-descriptions—is one of the reasons that medicine has seemed such a fertile ground for theological reflection. At the least, some of the practices of medicine continue to form a space where theological claims retain a semblance of intelligibility and persuasiveness. Ironically however, theologians, propelled by the worry of their increasing irrelevancy to the newer trends in medicine and elsewhere, have been quick to shed their theological garments and join the ranks of the philosophical ethicists.[10] In this rush next to nothing has been said about the peculiar fact that medicine still calls its patients "patients." But what could it mean to be called "patient" given the impatience which so imbues the modern practice of medicine and the social order it serves?

3. The Christian Virtue of Patience

In this book we have been reviewing the recent retrieval of the virtues in modern ethics; this retrieval has even more recently begun to affect thinking in medical ethics.[11] However, it is not clear that medicine provides the kind of soil in which the virtues can take firm root. For while medicine usually gives us birth and surrounds us as we die, it does not form or mold us in the time in between. Indeed, when we meet medicine full in the face it comes to us as we or those we love are sick or dying. If, therefore, medicine attempts to form us into virtuous people on its own turf it will inevitably fail, for it will be too little too late. Indeed, if the first time we are called on to exercise patience is as patients, we will surely be unable, for there is no worse time to learn patience than when one is sick. So, if we are to understand the vital importance of patience as a virtue, we cannot begin by considering it in the context of medicine. For us, this will mean that before we can say much about being patient patients we will need to take the time to look at how and why patience is integral to the Christian life.

As a strategy this has its liabilities. For if the virtues in general have been ignored in modern Christian ethics, the virtue of patience has especially been ignored.[12] Happily, however, patience played a prominent role in much earlier Christian accounts of the moral life. It is to these we now turn for needed help in considering the shape of Christian patience.

Saint Cyprian begins his "On the Good of Patience" by observing that philosophers also claim to pursue the virtue of patience, but "their patience is as false as is their wisdom." How can anyone be either wise or patient unless he knows the wisdom and patience of God? In contrast, Christians

> are philosophers not in words but in deeds; we exhibit our wisdom not by our dress, but by truth; we know virtues by their practice rather than through boasting of them; we do not speak great things but we live them. Therefore, as servants and worshipers of God, let us show by spiritual homage the patience that we learn from heavenly teachings. For that virtue we have in common with God. In Him patience has its beginning, and from Him as its source it takes its splendor and dignity. The origin and greatness of patience proceeds from God its Author. The quality that is dear to God ought to be loved by man.[13]

According to Cyprian, God's patience is clearly shown by the way he endures profane temples, replete with earthly images and idolatrous rites meant to insult God's majesty and honor. Yet nowhere is God's patience more clearly exemplified than in the life of Christ. Tertullian likewise observes that the patience of God made it possible for him to be conceived in a mother's womb, await a time for birth, gradually grow up, and even when grown be less than eager to receive recognition, having himself baptized by his own servant. Throughout his ministry he cared for the ungrateful and even refrained from pointing out the betrayer who was part of his own company. "Moreover, while He is being betrayed, while He is being led up 'as a sheep for a victim' (for 'so He no more opens His mouth than a lamb under the power of the shearer'), He to whom, had He willed it, legions of angels would at one word have presented themselves from the heavens, approved not the avenging sword of even one disciple."[14]

Tertullian and Cyprian alike make much of Matthew 5:43–48, where the refusal to return evil for evil is highlighted as in the very character of God, and, through imitation, the way the sons and daughters of God are made perfect. As Tertullian says, "In this principal precept the universal discipline of patience is succinctly comprised, since evil-doing is not conceded even when it is deserved."[15] Such patience is not only in the mind, according to Tertullian, but in the body, for just as Christ exhibited it in his body, so do we. By the affliction of the flesh, a victim is able to appease the Lord by means of the sacrifice of humiliation. By making a libation to the Lord of sordid raiment, together with scantiness of food, content with simple diet and the pure drink of water in conjoining fasts to all this; this *bodily* patience adds a grace to our prayers for good, a strength of our prayers against evil; this opens the ears of Christ our God, dissipates severity, elicits clemency.[16]

Thus, that which springs from a virtue of the mind is perfected in the flesh, and, finally, by the patience of the flesh, does battle under persecution.[17]

For the fathers of the church, bodily patience puts suicide out of the question. Job is the great exemplar in this regard as he resists his wife's suggestion that he should curse God and die. Augustine calls upon those who would kill themselves under persecution to look to "this man," meaning both Job and Christ. Like true martyrs who neither seek death nor invite it prematurely, we ought to bear all patiently rather than "to dare death impatiently." According to Augustine, all that can be said to those who have killed themselves under persecution is "Woe unto them which have lost patience!"[18]

Following Tertullian and Cyprian, Augustine maintains that only patience shaped by Christ is true patience. As he says, "properly speaking those are patient who would rather bear evils without inflicting them, than inflict them without bearing them. As for those who bear evils that they may inflict evil, their patience is neither marvelous nor praiseworthy, for it is not patience at all; we may marvel at their hardness of heart, but we must refuse to call them patient."[19] Such patience cannot come from "the strength of the human will,"[20] but rather must come from the Holy Spirit. Behind it, of course, is the greatest of all the Spirit's gifts, namely charity.

[W]ithout [love] in us there cannot be true patience, because in good men it is the love of God which endureth all things, in bad men the lust of the world. But this love is in us by the Holy Spirit which was given us. Whence, of Whom cometh in us love, of Him cometh patience. But the lust of the world, when it patiently bears the burdens of any manner of calamity, boasts of the strength of its own will, like as of the stupor of disease, not robustness of health. This boasting is insane: it is not the language of patience, but of dotage. A will like this in that degree seems more patient of bitter ills, in which it is more greedy of temporal good things, because more empty of eternal.[21]

Following the fathers before him, Aquinas maintained that true patience comes from God. Like them, he was aware that many people display the semblance of patience without the gift of the Spirit. Yet patience taken as a "natural virtue" cannot be shaped by the appropriate sadness and joy constitutive of Christian patience. For Aquinas a true understanding of our place as creatures must include an insuperable sadness and dejection about our condition. Christ's suffering on the cross exemplifies the sorrow that must be present in every Christian's life.[22] Christians must "be saddened by their own frailty, by the suffering present in the world, and by their inability to change either fundamentally."[23]

From Aquinas's perspective, the problem is how to prevent the sadness, which we appropriately feel, from becoming depression, despair, or apathy. And this falls to patience. "Patience is to ensure that we do not abandon virtue's good through dejection of this kind."[24] It makes us capable of being rightly saddened without succumbing to the temptation to give up hope. A patience-formed sadness can be held together with joy, because each is the effect of charity. Holding such a joy we rightly "grieve over what opposes this participation in the divine good in ourselves, or in our neighbors, whom we love as ourselves."[25]

Lee Yearley suggests that Aquinas's account of patience combines two different, even apparently paradoxical, attitudes. Christians must judge their earthly life according to the standard evident in God's goodness, yet they must also adhere to the future good of possible union with God and the present good evident in God's manifestations in the world and in people's lives. Neither side of such an attitude can be lost. We must persist in sadness, yet it must not be allowed to overwhelm the pursuit of the good, the accurate recognition of its forms, and a correct belief about the world's ultimate character. "This attitude is distinctive enough that it can arise, Aquinas thinks, only from the theological virtues. Charity's friendship with God is most crucial, but the attitude manifest in patience also rests on faith and displays the mean between presumption and despair that appears in hope."[26]

Like all the virtues that come from charity, Christian patience is a gift. As we noted earlier with courage, there are always semblances of the virtues produced apart from charity; patience in particular is frequently confused with its semblances. For example, there is a kind of tempered optimism in which people "either rest too confidently on their past experiences of overcoming dejection or manifest a phlegmatic or unreflective disposition at inappropriate times. Their optimism, then, reflects a flawed hope that is close to dullness or presumption. It displays an intemperate attitude that expresses itself in the naive belief that all will turn out for the best."[27] Christians have no such wan hope, sustained as we are by a patience that looks to our misfortunes, even the misfortune of our illness and death, as part of our service to one another as God's people.

4. Christian Patience and Patients

The matter of whether true patience can be had without God is particularly relevant to our own time and especially to the medicine practiced within it. We suspect that those committed to living in the world without God will find no time for the patience described by the likes of Cyprian, Tertullian, Augustine, and Aquinas. Indeed, we moderns fill our lives with what Albert Borgmann characterizes as a kind of addiction to hyperactivity. Believing that we live in a world of infinite possibilities, we find ourselves constantly striving, restless for what, we are not sure.[28] We call our restlessness freedom, but more often than not our freedom seems more like fate, especially when we get what we have strived for only to discover that it does not satisfy— thus the peculiar combination in modern life of an attitude of metaphysical indeterminism with Stoic fatalism.

All this is what Christians might call impatience; we should not be surprised to discover it, for we live in a world governed by sin. Indeed, Tertullian went so far as to attribute the creation of impatience to the devil, since he could not endure the patience God exemplified in creation. According to Tertullian, the devil passed to Eve that same impatience when, through his speech, he "breathed on her a spirit infected with impatience: so certain is it that she would have never sinned at all, if she had honoured the divine edict by maintaining her patience to the end."[29] She passed her impatience on to Adam, which in turn produced impatient sons. The very impatience that "had immersed Adam and Eve in death, taught their son, too, to begin with murder."[30] That murder was the fruit of impatience, as Cain impatiently refused his God-given obligation to his brother.

Surely medical care is one of God's gifts which it is our prerogative to use as a hedge against the impatience of the world. To care for one another when we cannot cure is one of the many ways we serve one another patiently. To be committed to alleviating the other's pain in a manner that makes all other considerations irrelevant makes no sense if we have not been made to be patient people. Yet as we tried earlier to display, the powers of impatience have breathed heavily on the practice of modern medicine, leading it to promise more than it can or should deliver. Indeed, in the frustration of being unable to meet impatient expectations, we are threatened with a medicine that, in the name of relieving suffering, kills.

We Christians are, of course, as implicated in this strange reversal as our non-Christian neighbors. But these issues are far too serious to play "Who is to blame?" The challenge is rather whether Christians have any contribution to make that would help us discover the proper limits of our care of one another through the office of medicine. It is not the unique task of Christians to suggest new and better theories about medical care, though some Christians engaged in that care undoubtedly have contributions to make. Rather, if Christians have anything to offer, it is to be patients who embody the virtue of Christian patience.[31]

To be patient when we are sick requires first that we learn how to practice patience when we are not sick. God has given us ample resources for recovering the practice of patience. First and foremost, we have been given our bodies, which will not let us do whatever we think we should be able to do.[32] We are our bodies and, as such, we are creatures destined to die. The trick is to learn to love the great good things our bodies make possible without hating our bodies, if for no other reason than that the death of our bodies is our own death. To practice the patience of the body is to be put on the way to holiness as we learn that we are not our own creations.

Secondly, we have been given one another. To learn to live with the unavoidability of the other is to learn to be patient. Such patience comes not just from our inability to have the other do our will; more profoundly, it arises with the love that the presence of the other can and does create in us. Our loves, like our bodies, signal our deaths. And such love—if it is not to be fearful of its loss, a very difficult thing—must be patient. Moreover, patience sustains and strengthens love, for it opens to us the time we need to tell our own story with another's story intertwined and to tell it together with that other. So told, the story in fact constitutes our love.

Thirdly, we have been given time and space for the acquisition of habits that come from worthy activities such as growing food, building shelters, spinning cloth, writing poems, playing baseball, or having children. Such activities not only take time but they create it by forcing us to take first one step and then another. These activities will outlive us, so long as we take the time to pass them on to future generations through shared activities and stories. So too, patience gives us the ability to engage in these activities with our children, to teach by doing, and to tell them worthy stories worthily so that we and they may be rightly entertained.[33]

These resources, these practices of patience, are not simply "there" but arise within the narrative of God's patient care of the world, which is but another way of insisting, with Aquinas, that it is impossible to have patience without charity—that is, without friendship with God. Put simply, our ability to take the time to enjoy God's world, when we are well as when we are sick, depends on our recognition that it is indeed God's world.

When we are sick, reminders of joy may seem to be the gestures of a false courage. Indeed, the Christian is charged with the responsibility of speaking truthfully about the sadness that riddles our lives. As Aquinas maintained, sadness must be recognized and lived with. But the acknowledgment of such sadness, upheld by patience, becomes integral to the Christian gift for sustaining the ill and those who care for them. Hence, those formed by the virtue of patience can be patients who do not believe that life is an end in itself. The patient patient knows—and can teach others, including physicians—that the enemy is neither the illness nor the death it intimates, but rather the fatalism these tempt us to as we meet our "bad luck"[34] with impatience.

If Christians could be such patient patients—and there is every reason to think that we can—we might well stand as witnesses to our non-Christian neighbor of the truth of the story of God's patient care of God's creatures. We might find we have something to say, not only about how illness and death can be met with grace and courage, but also about how those called to be physicians and nurses might care patiently for their patients, and perhaps even about the kind of training they will need to become capable of this high calling. To do this Christians will need to risk being different, but that should not be beyond a people who, having learned the patience of God, can find the time, even in the midst of a frenzied world, to give themselves over to such worthy work.

Notes

1. On Being Temporally Happy

1. Our sense of ambiguity about happiness is captured best by two scenes from the movie *Tender Mercies*. In the first, Mac Sledge is seen hoeing weeds in his garden, directly after his daughter has died. His new wife, who has helped him recover some sense of dignity, stands silently at the edge of the garden. Mac, without looking at her, says several times, "I don't believe in happiness." She makes no attempt to persuade him otherwise. Yet the movie closes with Mac throwing a football with his young stepson as if nothing else mattered. Like Mac, we do not believe in happiness, but we do believe in throwing footballs with stepsons. The problem is knowing how to describe the latter as a way of life.

2. Aristotle, *Nicomachean Ethics,* trans. Martin Ostwald (Indianapolis: Bobbs-Merrill, 1962). All references will appear in the text. Occasionally we shall use Sir David Ross's translation, revised by J. L. Ackrill and J. O. Urmson (New York: Oxford University Press, 1980), which use we shall note in the text.

3. Martha Nussbaum has effectively explored Aristotle's reliance upon "appearances" in her *The Fragility of Goodness: Luck and Ethics in Greek Tragedy and Philosophy* (Cambridge: Cambridge University Press, 1986), a work we discuss extensively in chapter 5. As she says, "Aristotle asks us to look at our practices, seeing, in the different areas, what sorts of judges we do, in fact, trust. This judgment about whom we trust and when seems to come, like the appearances, from us. We turn to doctors because we do, in fact, rely on doctors. This reliance, Aristotle insists, does not need to be justified by producing a further judge to certify the judge; it is sufficiently 'justified' by the facts of what we do" (p. 248).

4. J. L. Ackrill argues persuasively from the text what we do here by example, namely that Aristotle is better interpreted as holding an "inclusive" rather than singular doctrine of *eudaimonia.* By this he means that "*eudaimonia,* being absolutely final and genuinely self-sufficient, is more desirable than anything else in that it *includes* everything desirable in itself. It is best, and better than anything else, not in the way that bacon is better than eggs and than tomatoes (and therefore the best *of the three* to choose), but in the way that bacon, eggs and tomatoes is a better breakfast than either bacon or eggs or tomatoes—and indeed the best breakfast without qualification." "Aristotle on *Eudaimonia,*" in *Essays on Aristotle's Ethics,* ed. Amelie Rorty (Berkeley: University of California Press, 1980), p. 21. (The essays in this volume to-

179

gether make up one of the best commentaries on Aristotle's ethics available.) Similarly, in his *Reason and Human Good in Aristotle* (Cambridge: Harvard University Press, 1975), p. 99, John Cooper notes that in the *Nicomachean Ethics* (1097b16–209) *eudaimonia* involves "a number of good things rather than as demonstrated by a single end, on the ground that flourishing must be the consummately best thing, whereas any quantity of concrete good things can be bettered by the addition to it of some quantity, however small, of another good thing, however slight."

Stephen White has provided the most thorough account of these matters in his *Sovereign Virtue: Aristotle on the Relation between Happiness and Prosperity* (Stanford: Stanford University Press, 1992), pp. 88–108. One of the great virtues of White's account of Aristotle is his locating Aristotle's discussions about such matters within the context of his day. His contrast of Aristotle's views with those of Solon are particularly enlightening.

5. From J. L. Ackrill: "The word *eudaimonia* has a force not at all like 'happiness,' 'comfort,' or 'pleasure,' but more like 'the best possible life' (where 'best' is not a narrowly moral sense)" (p. 24).

6. See Georgios Anagnostopoulous, "Aristotle on Function and Attributive Nature of the Good," in *The Greeks and the Good Life*, ed. David Depew (Fullerton: California State University Press, 1980), p. 96.

7. See for example Bernard Williams's comments in *Morality: An Introduction to Ethics* (New York: Harper and Row, 1972), p. 65.

8. See Ralph McInerny, *Ethical Thomistica* (Washington, D.C.: Catholic University Press, 1982), p. 22. Aquinas, we suspect, suggests the heart of Aristotle's view when he says, "In man it is one thing that he is a mortal rational animal, and another that he is an animal capable of laughter. We must, therefore, consider that every delight is a kind of proper accident resulting from happiness or from some *part* of happiness, since the reason that a man is delighted is that he has some fitting good, either in reality, or in hope, or at least in memory," *Summa Theologiae* I–II, as translated by Fathers of the English Dominican Province (Westminster, Md.: Christian Classics, 1981). All subsequent quotations from Aquinas are from this translation.

9. These are the issues that are at the heart of Nussbaum's *The Fragility of Goodness*, which we have mentioned and which we discuss in considerable detail in chapter 5. See also White's *Sovereign Virtue* for the most balanced account to date of Aristotle's understanding of the relation of happiness and fortune.

10. See Nancy Sherman, *The Fabric of Character: Aristotle's Theory of Virtue* (Oxford: Clarendon Press, 1989), pp. 75–76. Sherman rightly emphasizes the temporal as integral to Aristotle's account of the moral life. She suggests that Aristotle's understanding of the temporal constraint on rationality is not simply that a given end requires the setting of true intentions which constrain immediate action, since few of our rational desires are so simply displayed. Our moral life is constituted by a network of ends so that we are constrained not merely by the isolated pursuit of separate ends over time, "but by a desire to see these ends optimally coordinated in some coherent pattern in and

through time. This integration problem emerges when one begins to consider how to live in an ordered way."

11. There is an important distinction to be drawn between the kind of luck we experience as integral to our moral projects and that which is just "dumb." Thus, the courageous know that by being such they may have to expose themselves to unexpected dangers, but they cannot "expect" to get ill. Having gotten ill, however, they may be expected to respond to it with courage, thus turning their fate into destiny. But Aristotle raises here the very possibility that our ability to develop character may be a matter of luck. Of course that is exactly the possibility that Kant wanted to avoid as he labored to ground morality in rationality *qua* rationality, thus insuring that anyone had the capacity to be "moral." In contrast, Aristotle and, we think, Christians cannot avoid acknowledging that the moral life is a contingent matter. That is why Christian witness is such an imperative, for without the example of the other we die.

12. Of course crucial to such retrospective judgment is forgiveness. We are unable to make our past our own unless we are capable of accepting forgiveness for what we have done even when we were not "fully responsible." Yet forgiveness is a troubling notion for Aristotle, for to be capable of accepting forgiveness seems to make us vulnerable to the very aspects of our lives that threaten self-sufficiency. For further reflections on these matters, see Hauerwas, "Constancy and Forgiveness: The Novel as a School for Virtue," *Dispatches from the Front: Theological Engagements with the Secular* (Durham: Duke University Press, 1994), pp. 31–57.

13. One of us (Hauerwas) has said that the primary relationship between Christianity and marriage, particularly when the latter is understood as life-long fidelity, is that they are both meant to teach you that life is not about happiness. Both involve the undertaking of a commitment that we could not understand prior to the living out of that commitment. But, ironically, they both also teach us that true happiness is possible only retrospectively.

14. John Wesley, in his "An Earnest Appeal to Men of Reason and Religion," suggested that one of the most important questions you can ask anyone is "Are you happy?" assuming that the question of the rationality of religion was not separable from questions of happiness. For he says, "You eat, and drink, and sleep, and dress, and dance, and sit down to play. You are carried abroad. You are at the masquerade, the theatre, the opera house, the park, the levee, the drawing-room. What do you do there? Why, sometimes you talk; sometimes you look at one another. And what are you to do tomorrow, the next day, the next week, the next year? You are to eat, drink, and sleep, and dance, and dress, and play again. . . . Are you, can you, or any reasonable man, be satisfied with this? You are not. It is not possible you should. But what else can you do? You would have something better to employ your time; but you know not where to find it upon earth. And, indeed, it is obvious that the earth, as it is now constituted, even with the help of all European arts, does not afford sufficient employment to take up half the waking hours of its inhabitants. What then can you do? How can you employ the time that lies

so heavy upon your hands? This very thing which you seek declare we unto you. The thing you want is the religion we preach. That alone leaves no time upon our hands. It fills up all the blank spaces of life." *The Works of John Wesley* (Grand Rapids: Baker Book House, 1978), 8:18–19.

2. The Virtues of Happiness

1. On this point, see Aquinas's discussion of the compatibility of sorrow and virtue, *Summa Theologiae* I-II, 59, 3.

2. As we note throughout this book, the last decade has brought to the surface a fair number of critics who are disposed to criticize "modern moral philosophy's" approach to ethics in a wholesale manner. See, for example, Edmund Pincoffs's attack on quandary ethics in his *Quandaries and Virtues: Against Reductivism in Ethics* (Lawrence: University of Kansas Press, 1986). A question now in the minds of many is whether some compromise or synthesis is possible between the critics and the views they criticize. Something like this question is the main subject of the 1988 edition of *Midwest Studies in Philosophy: Ethical Theory: Character and Virtue,* ed. Peter French, Theodore Uehling, and Howard Wettstein (Notre Dame, Ind.: University of Notre Dame Press, 1988). We are less sanguine than most of the authors in that collection. Frequently they seem to assume that the questions about the moral life addressed by the virtues are the same sort of questions already presumed within a framework of a morality of principles. Hence, virtues can be added to principles to round out an already well established modern view about the nature of the "moral life." In particular, the essays by Kurt Baier, Richard Regan, and Michael Slote in this volume illustrate this tendency. (For a particularly useful presentation of the objections to virtue theory as well as a response to those objections, see David Solomon's essay "Internal Objections to Virtue Ethics," in this volume, pp. 248–441.) As Alasdair MacIntyre's work makes clear, however, any attempt to recover the significance of the virtues will challenge the very paradigms of rationality and correlative political presumptions that have shaped modern accounts of the moral life.

In a section of his recent book (intriguingly entitled "Why I am not a Communitarian"), Ronald Beiner argues that the communitarian/liberalism debate over which so much academic ink has been spilt turns out to be far more friendly than it at first appears since "the protagonists on both sides of the argument tend to be what I think one can fairly label liberal social democrats." *What's the Matter with Liberalism?* (Los Angeles: University of California Press, 1992), p. 15. (Notably and perceptively, Beiner excludes MacIntyre from this troop, for MacIntyre is at odds not just with the liberal lack of "community" but with modernity itself. See Beiner, p. 30.)

As Beiner suggests, the communitarians have merely opened the door for the liberal theorists they criticize to claim that their theories indeed arise within a history. Yes, they admit, there is an "us" who inhabit the modern social world, and this is the *community* for which we theorize with our liberal theory. (Rawls effectively does this in his "Kantian Constructivism in Moral Theory: The Dewey Lectures," *Journal of Philosophy* 77, no. 9 [Sept. 1980]: 519 ff.) Modern moral philosophers might embrace "virtue" in the same way. This point underlies our own concern, not so much to defend "virtue" per se, but to speak specifically as Christians in defense of specifically Christian virtues. (See chapter 4.)

3. As Aristotle notes, "Now for most men their pleasures are in conflict with one another because they are not by nature pleasant, but the lovers of what is noble find pleasant those things that are by their nature pleasant" (1099a17, Ross). Of course not all "moral dilemmas" will arise out of conflicting pleasures, but not a few do. So, if a man is in a dilemma about whether to cheat to win a contest that will bring much adulation, he demonstrates his corruption by his dilemma.

4. As Aristotle says, to act virtuously, or on a mean, "to the right person, to the right extent, at the right time, with the right motive, and in the right way, *that* is not for everyone, nor is it easy; wherefore goodness is both rare and laudable and noble" (1109a30, Ross). While Aristotle is ready to trust to popular opinion on many a subject, he does not suppose that most people live lives of virtue. If we begin with the assumption that in morality we must develop a description of a way of life all people are likely to live (or are even capable of it), we will not get very far with the virtues, especially the Christian virtues.

5. MacIntyre emphasizes the importance of constancy by noting that it presupposes the notion of the unity of a human life and, correlatively, that the very concept of a "whole human life" makes sense. The ethical life, he notes, presupposes that "the commitments and responsibilities to the future springing from past episodes in which obligations were conceived and debts assumed unite the present to past and to future in such a way as to make of a human life a unity." He argues that by the time of Jane Austen, whom MacIntyre thinks to be the last great Christian Aristotelian, such unity could no longer be treated as the mere presupposition of the moral life. "It has itself to be continually reaffirmed and its reaffirmation in deed rather than in word is the virtue which Jane Austen calls constancy. Constancy is crucial in at least two novels, *Mansfield Park* and *Persuasion,* in each of which it is a central virtue of the heroine. . . . [W]ithout constancy all the other virtues to some degree lose their point. Constancy is reinforced by and reinforces the Christian virtue of patience, but it is not the same as patience, just as patience which is reinforced by and reinforces the Aristotelian virtue of courage, is not the same as courage. For just as patience necessarily involves recognition of the character of the world, of a kind which courage does not necessarily require, so constancy requires a recognition of a particular kind of threat to the integrity of the personality in the peculiarly modern social world, a recognition which patience does not necessarily require" (*After Virtue,* Notre Dame, Ind.: University of Notre Dame Press, 2d ed., 1984, p. 242).

6. For a good depiction, if not defense, of Aristotle's "great-souled man" see White, *Sovereign Virtue,* pp. 247–71. White uses "dignity" as the most appropriate term to describe such a person.

7. In this light it is possible to make some sense of Kierkegaard's otherwise puzzling claim that the saint is in no way distinguished by his outward action from the sinner. One might interpret him to mean that it is only the attitude or the "intention" of the actor in her action which determines her saintliness, which would make "being a saint" nothing but a predication of a certain sort of inwardness in one's acting. The alternative we can now suggest is that the fact that someone is a saint *determines* for us what her action really is—at the same time that we can also say that we know her to be a saint by her actions. The "outwardness," now, of her specific action, X, is to be understood as the description which might be rendered of it by some computer-like observer tracking her bodily movements.

The puzzle here is how to say that that action X is done by saint Y makes it different from action X′ done by non-saint Z without falling into the view that the difference lies only in Y's attitude or "intention" in doing X. But of course the puzzle has really been created by the modern bifurcation between actions and actors. (And here Kierkegaard has not been of help.) G. E. M. Anscombe has done as much as anyone to begin to reorient us, especially as she shows us that "intention" is wrongly thought of as merely the agent's private and inward orientation to his act. (See Anscombe's *Intention* [Ithaca: Cornell University Press, 1963].) MacIntyre's recourse to "intelligible action" over "action" as the more fundamental unit of meaning also starts us off helpfully, although evidently much more remains to be said. See MacIntyre, *After Virtue,* p. 195 ff., and Charles Pinches, "Action," *Encyclopedia of Bioethics,* rev. ed. (New York: Macmillan, 1995), I, pp. 56–63.

8. We suspect an Aristotelian account is closer to the way Christians ought to think about justice than accounts such as John Rawls's. (See his *A Theory of Justice* [Cambridge, Mass.: Harvard University Press, 1971].) For Aristotle no account of justice is possible that does not require that we have the virtue of justice. Rawls, on the other hand, writes to make justice possible for a social system based upon the presupposition that people need only be self-interested. For example, MacIntyre notes that Hobbes translates Aristotle's *pleonexis* as "a desire of more than their share." Yet Aristotle understood *pleonexis* to be neither more nor less than *acquisitiveness.* Nor can this be translated as greed, as T. H. Irwin (in his translation of the *Ethics*) does. MacIntyre argues that "what such translations of '*pleonexis*' conceal from us is the extent of the difference between Aristotle's standpoint on the virtues and vices, and more especially his standpoint on justice and the dominant standpoint of peculiarly modern societies. For the adherents of that standpoint recognize that acquisitiveness is a character trait indispensable to continuous and limitless economic growth, and one of their central beliefs is that continuous and limitless economic growth is a fundamental good. That a systematically lower standard of living ought to be preferred to a systematically higher standard of living is a thought incompatible with either the economics or the politics

of peculiarly modern societies. So prices and wages have come to be understood as unrelated—and indeed in a modern economy could not be related—to desert in terms of labor, and the notion of a just price or a just wage in modern terms makes no sense. But a community which was guided by Aristotelian norms would not only have to view acquisitiveness as a vice but would have to set strict limits to growth insofar as that is necessary to preserve or enhance a distribution of goods according to desert" (MacIntyre, *Whose Justice? Which Rationality?* [Notre Dame, Ind., University of Notre Dame Press, 1988], p. 112).

9. Committed Lutheran Gilbert Meilaender, himself a proponent of virtue thinking, sounds this cautionary note at the beginning of his *The Theory and Practice of Virtue* (Notre Dame: University of Notre Dame Press, 1984). "[B]efore Christian ethicists latch too quickly onto an ethic of virtue, it is important to remember that an emphasis on character may sit uneasily with some strands of Christian beliefs. No theologian has urged this point more forcefully than Luther. The virtues are, many have wanted to say, 'good for us.' A sketch of the virtues is a picture of a fulfilled life, of the successful realization of a self. Such an approach cannot without difficulty be incorporated into a vision of the world which has at its center a crucified God—which takes, that is, not self-realization but self-sacrifice as its central theme. Furthermore, the very notion of character seems to suggest—has suggested at least since Aristotle—habitual behavior, abilities within our power, an acquired possession. And this in turn may be difficult to reconcile with the Christian emphasis on grace, the sense of the sinner's constant need of forgiveness, and the belief that we can have no claims upon the freedom of God" (p. x).

10. We use the language of "allegiance" and "following" rather than "imitate" to mark the distance between Jesus and our lives. Such a distance is not that which is created by time but rather is theological. We are not called to be Jesus, but rather we are called to be what God has made possible through Jesus' life, death, and resurrection. "*Imitatio Christi*" is a motif necessary for the Christian life, but our imitation reflects Christ's work that needs no repeating.

11. MacIntyre, *After Virtue,* p. 176.

3. Companions on the Way:
The Necessity of Friendship

1. Interestingly, the subject of friendship is beginning to receive renewed attention by philosophers and theologians. Gilbert Meilaender's book *Friendship: A Study in Theological Ethics* (Notre Dame, Ind.: University of Notre Dame Press, 1981) was a pioneering study of the topic. As we have come to expect, Meilaender's book is gracefully written and filled with his usual insightfulness. We must admit, however, that we are not convinced that Meilaender's account of the tension between *agape* and *philia* is correct, since we think

such accounts of *agape* finally owe more to Kant than to the gospel. Of equal note is Paul Wadell's *Friendship and the Moral Life* (Notre Dame: University of Notre Dame Press, 1989). Wadell's book not only has good accounts of Aristotle and Aquinas on friendship but also deals with the question of our friendship with God. Laurence Blum's *Friendship, Altruism, and Morality* (London: Routledge and Kegan Paul, 1980) was an important book in philosophy on friendship. Blum has continued to develop the importance of friendship in his *Moral Perception and Particularity* (Cambridge: Cambridge University Press, 1994).

All three accounts in some way or another refer back to Aristotle's account, which remains seminal. For a classic discussion of Aristotle's view, a discussion upon which we sometimes depend, see John Cooper, "Aristotle on Friendship," in *Essays on Aristotle's Ethics,* ed. Amelie Rorty, pp. 301–40.

2. This is not to say Aristotle thinks of self-sufficiency in these terms. As Amelie Rorty argues, "It has been thought that there is some problem in Aristotle's making friendship necessary to the well-lived life on the one hand, while at the same time emphasizing the priority of self-sufficient, self-contained *energeiai* on the other" (1169b3–13). Self-sufficiency has of course nothing to do with isolation or even with self-development. A self-sufficient life is one whose activities are intrinsically worthy, have their ends in themselves, are worth choosing regardless of what may come of them. Aristotle is not concerned to justify friendship because it is conducive to or promotes self-development but because it is part of a self-contained, fully realized life (1097b1–20). See "The Place of Contemplation in Aristotle's *Nicomachean Ethics*," in *Essays on Aristotle's Ethics,* ed. Rorty, p. 389. See also Sherman's discussion in *The Fabric of Character,* pp. 130–31.

3. Aristotle is often criticized for his views on the inferior status of slaves and women, but he does not exclude the possibility of friendship between slaves (who are not by nature slaves) and women. Certainly he manifests his society's views on these matters, but it is also the case that his account is open to radical innovation through his analysis of friendship. Martha Nussbaum also thinks Aristotle's method in ethics makes him open to radical reconsideration of such issues. See *Fragility of Goodness,* p. 258. See also Nancy Sherman's very interesting discussion of this issue in *The Fabric of Character,* pp. 153–55.

As we imply in the text, the "equality" which characterizes perfect friendship is of character rather than of station. Indeed, friendship may be able to teach us better than any other relation how "equality" of social status is a false equality, since it does little to insure equality in virtue.

4. We find this last quote from Aristotle poignant in the light of our own political situation. Modernity involves the attempt to make political community possible between strangers. As a result, our polities are constantly tempted to fascist excesses because the state must supply the community that is missing. In effect, the only political alternative we have is friendship, particularly the friendship we call "church." The difficulty is that, given our po-

litical presuppositions, that form of friendship is not recognized as political but rather is said to be part of the "private" realm. One of the great social challenges for the church today is to discover how we can be a community that provides for the flourishing of friendship in a manner that can challenge the "politics" of our time.

5. The central problem of modern moral theory—that is, how to resolve the tension between egoism and altruism—is simply unknown to Aristotle. What we can now see is the very problem of egoism and altruism is not an eternal dilemma caused by something called the human condition, but rather is the result of changed social presumptions and practices that Aristotle could only see as corrupt. We are sure, moreover, Aristotle would be right to so understand the matter. See our extended discussion of Nussbaum in chapter 5.

White provides his usual lucid account of Aristotle on the issue of self-love. He notes that the problem, as Aristotle sees it, of the bad loving themselves is that they do so in a manner "that drives them away from themselves," in other words, the major core of what we call egoism is self-alienation. *Sovereign Virtue,* p. 299.

6. See our extended discussion of Nussbaum in chapter 5.

7. We suspect part of Aristotle's difficulty in this respect is related to the absence of any specific and empirical account of moral development. Such an account would have to deal with the particularities of our histories as integral to our moral formation and so to the peculiarities that are sustained in our different moral characters. The conceptual resources to give an account of our biographical situatedness was simply not available to Aristotle. To the extent one can extract from Aristotle an adequate account of moral development, Sherman has certainly done so in her *The Fabric of Character,* pp. 157–99. Of course, as MacIntyre makes clear in *Whose Justice? Which Rationality?* this issue becomes even more complex as soon as the Christian notion of sin is introduced (pp. 146–59).

8. This saying is recorded in the New Testament (Acts 20:35), where the author of Acts attributes it to Paul, who attributes it to Jesus, although it is to be found otherwise neither in the gospels nor in Paul's letters. The point Paul is making is that he has not asked for money to support his preaching efforts. This he did in part to demonstrate that we should exert ourselves in supporting the weak, as if to say that we should demand less for ourselves in our plenty, giving instead to those who were in far greater need. Demanding less for ourselves *is* a Christian sentiment; but this is not the same as magnanimity, which looks to insure that more are in our debt than in our indebtedness.

9. To say that Jesus *commands* is not to say he coerces. We consider this distinction at length in chapter 8.

10. Helen Oppenheimer, *The Hope of Happiness* (London: S.C.M., 1983), p. 131.

11. As Augustine says: "Blessed is the man who loves you, who loves his friend in you, and his enemy because of you" (*Confessions* IV, 9). Loving the

friend "in God" does not make the friendship instrumental (we do not love God in the friend) but rather frees our love to weather the storms of fortune, as in this particular case when Augustine's friend dies.

12. The debate regarding the unity of the virtues is both important and interesting. In *After Virtue* MacIntyre implies that he disbelieves in this unity, on the grounds that a Nazi can legitimately be called courageous even while severely lacking in so many other virtues. In a recent captivating discussion written partly in response to MacIntyre, Ronald Beiner notes that in order to understand Aristotle's interest in the unity of the virtues one must simply recall that he supposes that the virtues have a point, namely to conduce to *eudaimonia*. Detached from this framework we lose any reason or even sense for calling them virtues. So the virtues unite around happiness, and particularly around practical wisdom since it is the man of practical wisdom who alone is capable of it. See Beiner, *What's the Matter with Liberalism?* (Berkeley: University of California Press, 1992), pp. 48–59. He argues as well that "similarity" in way of life need not be implied by the unity thesis, since, as Aristotle sees, there is no one particular good or even set of goods that is the happy life; all sorts of different lives can be happy, and their characters retain difference in their shared happiness.

It is important to say that we do not mean to deny the unity thesis flat out. As we say in the text, we must concur that friends form each other to their own likeness—otherwise instruction in virtue would seem impossible. But to begin with Beiner's point, as we see it, Aristotle's view of friendship, while stopping short of cloning, will tend to progressively minimize differences. Granted, friends will remain different in stature, in temperament, in family origin, and so on. But these differences will tend to become ever more incidental, as we can imagine skin color or even social standing becoming quite quickly an incidental difference in a good friendship, as they are overshadowed by the common virtues and goals of its participants.

We need a way to describe at least some of these differences as non-incidental and resilient, but we do not find it in Aristotle. As we suggest, the New Testament language of gifts of the Spirit is much better equipped here. First, it does not presume all virtues are received in the same way and intimates, as Aquinas later codifies, that some gifts (for Christians all of the virtues are gifts) are not so much acquired by habituation and learned in a friendship in which one is presented a model after which to follow, but rather they are directly bestowed by God—"infused" as Aquinas would have it. Further, these bestowed gifts are given to specific and singular individuals for the benefit of the larger community. Their authoritative exercise of them requires that others in the community both acknowledge their special gift and, further, define their own happiness not at all as an individual achievement, but as something to which the whole community strives (for Christians, the kingdom of God).

Of course whenever Paul discusses the spiritual gifts he also mentions that there are some virtues we all must have. In 1 Corinthians, in fact, the discussion of gifts leads directly to his extended discussion and eulogy of love (chapters 12 and 13). As he puts it, the gifts are to no avail unless they are upheld by love. In this regard, if Christians do go on to affirm an ultimate unity of the virtues, they do best to follow Aquinas rather than Aristotle, who finally calls charity (not prudence) the form of the virtues. Charity or a charity-informed prudence by its very nature cannot exclude the other as another. (See our discussion of the relation between charity and prudence in chapter 6.) It is essentially a communal virtue, something Christians believe must be had together, and something as well that they cannot call complete until the full outbreak of God's kingdom.

4. The Renewal of Virtue and the Peace of Christ

1. See chapter 10, "Morality, the Peculiar Institution," in Bernard Williams, *Ethics and the Limits of Philosophy* (Cambridge, Mass.: Harvard University Press, 1985).

2. See further John Milbank, "Can Morality be Christian?" *Studies in Christian Ethics* 8, no. 1 (1995): 45–59.

3. Foot uses this strategy in her well-known "Euthanasia," first printed in *Philosophy and Public Affairs* 6 (1977): 85–112. Of course her various essays, many reprinted in *Virtues and Vices* (Berkeley: University of California Press, 1978) were instrumental in encouraging the revival in virtue thinking among philosophers. Our critical comments about both her and Frankena's work must be qualified by our gratitude to them for considering the importance of the virtues in an earlier time, when doing so was less popular.

4. William Frankena, "Pritchard and the Ethics of Virtue" in *Perspectives on Morality: Essays by William K. Frankena,* ed. K. E. Goodpaster (Notre Dame: University of Notre Dame Press, 1976), p. 158.

5. See particularly chapters 1 and 2 in Pincoffs, *Quandaries and Virtues.* The strong contrast between Aristotle and Kant assumed in recent moral philosophy is at once explored and challenged in *Aristotle, Kant, and the Stoics: Rethinking Happiness and Duty,* ed. Stephen Engstrom and Jennifer Whiting (Cambridge: Cambridge University Press, 1996). We regret this book appeared too late for us to include here a discussion of the issues raised by the wonderful essays in this collection.

6. Ibid., p. 82. "Preference of persons" is, of course, the key, as that language reinforces the liberal illusion that the life of each person is constituted through his or her self-generating choices. As a result the significance of how our lives are constituted by the histories, communities, and traditions in which we find ourselves is entirely lost.

7. Ibid., p. 163.

8. Bernard Williams, himself not much disposed to "religious moralities," offers a counterpoint to Pincoffs's presumptions. "I do not think it quite right . . . to say, as many do, that even if God existed, this could give no special and acceptable reason for subscribing to morality. If God existed, there might well be special, and acceptable, reasons for subscribing to morality. The

trouble is that the attempt to formulate those reasons in better than the crudest outline runs into the impossibility of thinking coherently about God. The trouble with religious morality comes not from morality's being inescapably pure, but from religion's being incurably unintelligible." Williams, *Morality: An Introduction to Ethics* (New York: Harper and Row, 1972), p. 78. Christians should much rather have their religious faith rejected because it makes no sense than to be excluded from discussions about morality because of the psychological damage they could do to those of their flock who might sometime fall away.

9. Milbank, *Theology and Social Theory: Beyond Secular Reason* (Oxford: Blackwell, 1990). Page references to this work will be placed in parentheses in the body of the paper.

10. See *Three Rival Versions of Moral Enquiry* (Notre Dame: University of Notre Dame Press, 1990).

11. Milbank rightly understands MacIntyre's return to Aquinas as an extension of the return to Aristotle, not so much because of what Aquinas says but because of the way MacIntyre reads him. It is revealing that while MacIntyre mentions Aquinas in *After Virtue,* the book turns on the chapter entitled "Aristotle or Nietzsche?" (Only in *Whose Justice? Which Rationality?* does Aquinas become a truly central figure.) These two really serious options for modern ethics remain in *Three Rival Versions* what they were in *After Virtue:* genealogy (Nietzsche) or tradition (Aristotle-Aquinas). MacIntyre sides, of course, with the second, but in so doing, and in setting up the debate in the way he has, he does not give Aquinas, the alleged hero of *Whose Justice? Which Rationality?*, room to significantly disagree with Aristotle. He "transcends" him, of course, but remains in his line, in his tradition. And so Christianity remains in the line of the Greeks. This is a convenient scheme if one is writing a philosophical history, but it may very well entirely leave out Jewish and Christian scripture, not to mention Aquinas's rooting in it.

In this regard it is worth noting that the very question "Nietzsche or Aristotle?" is an abstraction that must be resisted on MacIntyre's own grounds, for as a question it underwrites the liberal notion that we finally must be able to stand back from all tradition so that we can choose one, or parts of several. Yet if MacIntyre is otherwise right, that is what we cannot do, since the very presuppositions of such a choice are determined by our tradition. The question mark in "Nietzsche or Aristotle?" must be charitably interpreted as ironic, since MacIntyre's whole project is to show that it is a liberal illusion to think that we can simply choose between traditions. One suspects that part of MacIntyre's antagonism toward Burke derives not only from Burke's denial of his Irish heritage to "make it" among the English, but because MacIntyre, like Burke, can be interpreted as simply recommending the importance of tradition *qua* tradition. Indeed, the abstraction "tradition," which Burke embraces and MacIntyre attempts to avoid, may indicate that the one touting it is no longer part of a tradition in good working order. It is a tribute to the profundity of MacIntyre's project that he resists any Burkean interpretation, although, as we mean to suggest in this chapter, he needs to resist it less with protestations, more with concrete theological reflection, which is the lifeblood of the tradition he has reentered. (We are indebted to David Matzko for calling our attention to the irony of MacIntyre's question mark in *After Virtue*.)

12. Bernard Williams concurs with this assessment of our times, but puts the point more poignantly. Much like Martha Nussbaum, in his *Shame and Necessity* (Berkeley: University of California Press, 1993), Williams seeks to illumine our current moral situation by comparing and contrasting how the Greeks understood their world and how we understand ours. As he puts it: "We are in an ethical condition that lies not only beyond Christianity but beyond its Kantian and Hegelian legacies. We have an ambivalent sense of what human beings have achieved, and have hopes for how they might live (in particular, in the form of a still powerful ideal that they should live without lies). We know that the world was not made for us, nor we for the world, that our history tells no purposive story, and that there is no position outside the world or outside history from which we might hope to authenticate our activities. We have to acknowledge the hideous costs of many human achievements that we value, including the reflective sense itself, and recognize that there is no redemptive Hegelian history or universal Leibnizian cost-benefit analysis to show that it will come out well enough in the end. In important ways, we are, in our ethical situation, more like human beings in antiquity than as Western people have been in the meantime. More particularly, we are like those who, from the fifth century and earlier, have left traces of a consciousness that had not been touched by Plato's and Aristotle's attempt to make our ethical relations to the world fully intelligible" (p. 166). In general, we think such a characterization is accurate, but as Christians we cannot believe our existence has no purpose.

13. It may be objected that politics always is some kind of politics of war, and it has been so under the aegis of the liberalism of the last two centuries in the West as much as at any other time. The only reply we have to such an observation, besides admitting the objection's power, is to point to Christianity as a radical political alternative to the politics of war and to note, concomitantly, that for the new politics to seriously challenge that of war it cannot avoid martyrdom, nor can it in good conscience predict that the world will necessarily be less violent because peace has come to it. This politics of peace, of course, is not sustained by the nation-state but by the church—and the church at certain times and places. However, it remains an interesting question how much the politics of war of modern nations-states, which emerged from Christian Europe, enjoyed the mitigating effects of the politics of peace that the Christian church provided, albeit in a bastardized form. This question is unanswerable at present, but will not remain so forever, even if none of us remains to ask it when it could receive an answer.

14. This is especially plain in *Three Rival Versions of Moral Enquiry,* where genealogical proponents compete with those who speak with the voice of tradition, all for the prize of dialectical superiority. The last chapter, "Reconceiving the University as an Institution and the Lecture as a Genre," uses this competition as the basis for a new vision of the university, a place of "con-

strained disagreements." But of course the competition must be managed when it involves the clash between the opposing faculties of one university or even between the two faculties of Tradition University and Genealogical University. This management, however, is doomed on MacIntyre's own terms, and not solely because, as he admits, it involves an extremely utopian picture of the university. For from whence comes the manager? Is he a Kantian re-creation: a universal, untraditioned rationality? Who besides the encylopaedist would accept him? Or is he a Thomist of MacIntyre's ilk? (I.e., must the genealogical university have a traditioned provost?) If so, one wonders about the genuineness of this conflict: why wouldn't the genealogist subvert it, especially since MacIntyre's forces already hold the power when the alleged conflict begins? Of course, MacIntyre on his own terms rightly does not exclude war as a possibility for Christians and non-Christians alike. Like him we believe we cannot and should not avoid conflict. However, as Christians we simply cannot engage in armed conflict because of our understanding of Christian discipleship. That is to say, we are Christological pacifists.

15. Charles Taylor's account of modernity in *Sources of the Self* (Cambridge: Harvard University Press, 1989) represents something like this understanding. Entirely absent from Taylor's account, however, is any sense of *church*, requiring that his account of how the moral goods from the Christian past can be revived must emphasize the individual who accesses these goods through the "personal resonance" of epiphanic art. (See especially the concluding chapter of Taylor's work for this proposal for reviving our moral sources.)

16. Nietzsche understood that the presumption, so common among his contemporaries, that "morality" could cast off its Christian moorings and remain unchanged was destined for a fall. "They got rid of the Christian God, and now feel obligated to cling all the more firmly to Christian morality: this is *English* consistency. . . . With us it is different. When one gives up Christian belief one thereby deprives oneself of the *right* to Christian morality. For the latter is absolutely *not* self-evident: one must make this point clear again and again, in spite of English shallowpates." *Twilight of the Idols* (New York: Penguin, 1968), p. 69.

17. *ST* I-II, 65, 4. The question of the interrelation of the virtues is related to questions of how the virtues are individuated. This in turn depends on the practices and traditions of *actual communities.* In this regard, one of our difficulties in writing about "Christian virtues," and charity in particular, is how such a classification can look like another "position about ethics." To make our view of charity less abstract, it should be said that it cannot be understood separately from christological considerations. The kind of friendship God shares with us is mediated as well as displayed through the cross and resurrection. Charity cannot, therefore, be but another term for love. Rather charity requires depiction through a community of forgiveness. Moreover, charity as the "form" of the virtues does not mean that other virtues are secondary. For example, charity is such only when it is shaped by the humility and patience of a peaceable people. If charity is the form of God's

peace, then those who would be that peace must learn to be patient, living as they do in a violent world. So charity forms our patience, but it is also true that patience forms charity. Thus Aquinas says that the virtues in a sense "flow" into one another. (Interestingly he notes that the vices do not spill over into one another as do the virtues, since a bad person is essentially disordered.)

18. For a compelling and thorough account of the significant differences between (Aristotle's) formation and (Aquinas's) transformation, see L. Gregory Jones, *Transformed Judgment* (Notre Dame: University of Notre Dame Press, 1990).

5. Friendship and Fragility

1. Nussbaum, *The Fragility of Goodness* (Cambridge: Cambridge University Press, 1986). We include page references to Nussbaum's book in parentheses throughout the text of this chapter.

2. *The Fragility of Goodness* includes numerous interludes and appendices which complicate the simple interpretation just given, i.e., that Aristotle synthesizes the tragedians and Plato. Aristotle is hardly Nussbaum's hero, as we shall later see. Nevertheless, the simple tripartite structure forms the book's inquiry, and there is an important sense in which this builds up to and culminates in Nussbaum's treatment of Aristotle even if (as we shall also see) what she says in the chapters about him must be qualified by the appendix on that section and by the book's final chapter on Euripides' *Hecuba.*

3. *Nicomachean Ethics,* 1155a22–27. The translation is Ross's.

4. Hauerwas, "Can Aristotle be a Liberal? or Nussbaum on Luck," *Soundings* 72, 4 (winter, 1989): 675–91.

5. MacIntyre, *After Virtue,* p. 156.

6. In an incisive and gracious response to an earlier version of this chapter by Pinches, Nussbaum confirmed that this is both what she meant and also in fact what she did in 1988.

7. John Cooper, "Aristotle on Friendship," in *Essays on Aristotle's Ethics,* ed. Amelie Rorty, pp. 301–10.

8. Ibid., p. 332.

9. Paul Wadell, *Friendship and the Moral Life* (Notre Dame: University of Notre Dame Press, 1991), p. 49.

10. This paper appears as "Serpents in the Soul: A Reading of Seneca's *Medea*" in *The Therapy of Desire: Theory and Practice in Hellenistic Ethics* (Princeton: Princeton University Press, 1994), pp. 439–83. The quotations cited, originally taken by Pinches as notes from that address, remain the same, although in her printed essay Nussbaum does not as clearly state that they are to be taken as a *revision* of the thesis of *The Fragility of Goodness.*

11. Here we can make plain another complexity in the structure of *Fragility.* Nussbaum uses Plato's middle period dialogues to display the philosopher as stone, as he who hopes to insulate *eudaimonia* from any contingency.

However, she treats the *Phaedrus* as Plato's later recantation of this project. Somewhat unfortunately, the treatment of the *Phaedrus* is placed before the final third section on Aristotle and, since it is linked by author (i.e., Plato) to the decidedly nonfragile vision of *eudaimonia* Nussbaum means to reject, we anticipate its overcoming in the section on Aristotle. Yet as this quote illustrates, Nussbaum favors the Plato of the *Phaedrus* not only over the Plato of the *Protagoras* or the *Republic,* but also over Aristotle.

12. For a recent and generally enlightening discussion of the relation between *agape* and *philia* in Christian ethics, see Edward Collins Vacek, S.J., *Love Human and Divine: The Heart of Christian Ethics* (Washington, D.C.: Georgetown University Press, 1994). Vacek helpfully makes what has been a typically abstract discussion of love concrete by attending, with help from Aquinas, to the structure of the emotions. Over against theologians like Anders Nygren or Gene Outka, he holds that not *agape* but *philia* is actually the primary form of love for Christians. We see our brief discussion in this chapter as suggesting that the choice of one over the other is a false one.

13. Wadell, *Friendship and the Moral Life,* p. 115.

14. Nussbaum means initially to respond in defense of Aristotle to Williams's criticism, although as her language three pages later suggests, she seems also to accept a good bit of its force.

15. This feature of friendship is determinative for C. S. Lewis's well known and subtle treatment in *The Four Loves* (New York: Harcourt Brace Jovanovich, 1960), pp. 87–127. Lewis is well aware of the accompanying danger of insularity we mention here. As he argues, in this way friendship might become uniquely susceptible to pride and is "unable to save itself" until it finds its home in God, who graciously chooses the friends for each other. Lewis's insights about pride and friendship are helpful, and similar to the points we develop in the next chapter about pagan friendship.

16. Thomas Ogletree, *Hospitality to the Stranger* (Philadelphia: Fortress, 1985), pp. 2–3.

17. For a wonderful exploration of these issues see Ralph C. Wood, *The Comedy of Redemption: Christian Faith and Cosmic Vision in Four American Novelists* (Notre Dame: University of Notre Dame Press, 1988). Wood maintains that "Jesus' death and resurrection render human existence comic in both its roots and ramifications. Christian faith is comic . . . in the profoundest sense of the word. It is about eschatological laughter and hope. In the life, crucifixion, and final victory of Jesus, it discerns a decisive turning of human history" (p. 1). Though sympathetic to Wood's arguments, we remain agnostic concerning the use of genre categories for the display of Christian theology.

18. As we have already emphasized, God's love is ultimately transformative of the self. This constitutes the crucial factor that makes friendship with God, in which Christian friendship is rooted, anything but supportive of the status quo. As Paul Wadell puts it, "We cannot love God and remain unchanged. To love God in charity is to become like God in goodness. There is a terrible vulnerability in any love because to love is to become like the one we love. There is a loss of control in this, indeed, a loss of self, because to love

is to lose one kind of self and take on another. Nowhere is this transformation more drastic than in charity. Charity fosters vulnerability to God, an openness so exhaustive that we ultimately become defenseless before the love that is our life" (p. 138). Nussbaum rightly sees the transformative force in love, but on the Christian account she wrongly supposes true love can transform us into monsters, although the rejection or perversion of true love may very well bring this change.

19. Hauerwas, "Can Aristotle be a Liberal," p. 689.

20. The term "living-with" employed by Nussbaum can stand for Christians as an appropriate description of what full humanity entails if it is understood to include "suffering-with." As we tried to suggest in section 1, the "living-with" of Aristotelian friendship does not include suffering-with, for one must heroically suffer alone.

21. Reinhold Niebuhr, *Beyond Tragedy* (New York: Scribner's, 1965), pp. 155–56.

22. We do not mean to suggest that the possibility of redemption and reconciliation is only available to Christians. Indeed, Christians learned of this possibility first as Jews, who followed the God who forgave his people Israel even as they betrayed their joint covenant. Rather, we mean to say that forgiveness and reconciliation become real alternatives to revenge for human relationships just as this reconciling God exists and enters the arena of human interaction.

6. Pagan Virtue and Christian Friendship

1. MacIntyre can be included in company with Nussbaum if we are right, following Milbank, to think that his vision of virtue, at least in *After Virtue,* remains closer to Athens than Jerusalem. MacIntyre is once again to be given credit for pointing out clearly how all philosophical theories, even our specialized and professionalized modern ones like emotivism, presumes a sociology. It is consistent with this insight that he ends *After Virtue* with talk of small communities of virtue, pocket communities hiding away under the great raiment of barbarism which, MacIntyre alleges, has been ruling us for some time. There we await another—doubtless very different—St. Benedict (p. 263). A question to be put to MacIntyre is this one: How will the new St. Benedict differ from the old?

2. John Casey, *Pagan Virtue* (Oxford: Clarendon Press, 1990). Subsequent page citations from this work will appear in parentheses in the body of the text.

3. *The Nicomachean Ethics,* 1123b28–30, Ross, trans.

4. Casey's rendering of Nietzsche seems influenced by MacIntyre's individualistic reading in *After Virtue.* It is possible to attribute to Nietzsche another sort of politics. Alexander Nehamas argues that Nietzsche's life should be understood as a moral model of sorts, not one to be replicated—for this would inhibit rather than enhance creativity—but to be followed in the man-

ner of great literature. A community of free spirits could be one imaginable result. Furthermore, as Nehamas points out, Nietzsche does not propose that those of the superior type treat their inferiors cruelly. To the contrary, they will be tender to them, dutifully acknowledging their function. As such, we may even be able to envision a Nietzschean city. Alexander Nehamas, *Nietzsche: Life as Literature* (Cambridge: Harvard University Press, 1985), p. 216.

5. Peter Berger, "On the Obsolescence of the Concept of Honor," in *Revisions: Changing Perspectives in World Philosophy,* edited by Stanley Hauerwas and Alasdair MacIntyre (Notre Dame: University of Notre Dame Press, 1983), pp. 172–81.

6. Since temperance is the only one of the cardinal virtues about which we have no comment, one might wonder if Casey's temperance also requires community. The answer is that it does, primarily by its connection to practical wisdom. As Casey would have it, temperance rightly channels the *amour propre,* which, while vital, if left unchecked creates in us a certain blindness which resists practical wisdom. Put plainly, the sort of control we hope to achieve of the *amour propre* could not be determined outside of a community of wisdom, and so temperance also requires community. See Casey, pp. 128–35.

7. See Michael Oakeshott, *On Human Conduct* (New York: Oxford University Press, 1975), pp. 257–63, 272–74.

8. Our discussion of Nussbaum's use of John Cooper on Aristotle's friendship in the previous chapter is relevant here. Casey's treatment of friendship depends on Nussbaum's reading of Aristotle (see pp. 185–89) as well as upon Oakeshott's.

9. Nietzsche rightly saw the connections—forfeited in any modern "universal" morality—between a noble or master morality, the specificity of duties to oneself and one's class, and the glorification of a particular cultural history. The master has duties to himself and to friends who share those specific and noble traits which justify their mutual elevation above the slave. Likewise, the master sees these same traits in his ancestors and honors them all the more since he recognizes his historical dependence upon them. "It is the powerful who *understand* how to honor: this is their art, their realm of invention. The profound reverence for age and tradition—all law rests in this double reverence—the faith and prejudice in favor of ancestors and disfavor of those yet to come are typical of the morality of the powerful; and when the men of 'modern ideas,' conversely, believe almost instinctively in 'progress' and 'the future' and more and more lack respect for age, this in itself would sufficiently betray the ignoble origin of these ideas." *Beyond Good and Evil,* trans. by Walter Kaufmann (New York: Vintage Books, 1966), sec. 260.

10. As noted in the previous chapter, MacIntyre's response to the remark from E. M. Forster about choosing between loyalty to one's country or one's friend is relevant here. As we are suggesting, pagan friendship of the sort we are discussing could not have Forster's dilemma.

11. See the *Summa Theologiae* I-II, 46, 6 and II-II, 158, 1. Christian thinkers knew that without the passions, virtue is impossible. See for example

Robert Wilken's chapter "Loving God With a Holy Passion" in his *Remembering the Christian Past* (Grand Rapids: Eerdmans, 1995), pp. 145–63. For a good account of Aquinas on the Passions, see G. Simon Harak, S.J., *Virtuous Passions: The Formation of Christian Character* (New York: Paulist Press, 1993).

12. *De Officiis* 1, 35, quoted in Joseph Pieper, *The Four Cardinal Virtues* (Notre Dame: University of Notre Dame Press, 1966), p. 122.

13. Pieper, *The Four Cardinal Virtues*, p. 123.

14. *ST* I-II, 58, 4.

15. The phrase is Bernard Williams's. See *Ethics and the Limits of Philosophy* (Cambridge: Harvard University Press, 1985), p. 18.

16. Pieper, p. 125. For a helpful elaboration of this point see Nicholas Wolterstorff, "The Migration of Theistic Arguments: From Natural Theology to Evidentialist Apologetics," in *Rationality, Religious Belief and Moral Commitment*, edited by Robert Audi and William Wainwright (Ithaca: Cornell University Press, 1986), pp. 38–81.

17. *The Four Cardinal Virtues*, p. 25. Quoted material is from Aquinas's *"Quaesto disputata de virtutibus in communi,"* 6.

18. See *ST* II-II, 47,6. The tradition of interpretation of Aquinas which understands prudence only as about means is detailed by Daniel Nelson, *The Priority of Prudence: Virtue and Natural Law in Aquinas and the Implications for Modern Ethics* (State College, Pa.: Pennsylvania State University Press, 1992), pp. 1–22. Nelson's own interpretation, with which we concur, grants priority to prudence. For the best account of practical wisdom available see Joseph Dunne, *Back to the Rough Ground: 'Phonesis' and 'Techne' in Modern Philosophy and Aristotle* (Notre Dame: University of Notre Dame Press, 1993).

19. Jean Porter, *The Recovery of Virtue* (Louisville: Westminster/John Knox Press, 1990), p. 161.

20. Ibid., p. 162.

21. Ibid., p. 164. Porter goes on to say that "the virtue of justice demands that objective relationships of equality be maintained among individuals and between individuals in the community itself. It is relatively easy to determine what those relationships should look like, concretely, among individuals. But the right relationship between desert, merit or need, and the distribution of the shared goods of the community is a more difficult question. . . ." Yet it seems as hard or harder to determine what are just relationships between individuals as to settle broader political matters of just distribution. Moreover, Porter's comment could be taken to mean that justice does not demand the guidance of prudence as it settles on what are just relations among individuals. However, as Pieper notes, "[t]he essence of the 'good of reason' is conferred in the directive cognition of prudence. In the virtue of justice, this good of reason becomes transformed into actual existence" (*The Four Cardinal Virtues*, p. 125). In its characteristic work in "actual existence" justice always depends on the vision of prudence.

22. Aquinas considers prudence in its parts in II-II, 49, shortly following the discussion of "prudence in itself" in II-II, 47, to which we just referred. The discussion in question 47 connecting prudence to political prudence

seems to involve its extension: political prudence, while rightly called prudence, is marked off from what we normally refer to as "prudence" by what matters it considers, namely those having to do with governance. So it is that having prudence does not entail any specific kind of political prudence, since what political prudence one has depends entirely on the society in which one lives and whether one is among its governed or governing. In question 49, however, it is clear that for any prudence to be called prudence, it must have the parts, one of which is *docilitas*. In this way, it is right to say that *docilitas* is more vital to our understanding of Aquinas's prudence than its connection, emphasized by Porter, to political prudence. Put simply, whereas there is a prudence that is not political prudence, yet there is no prudence that does not involve *docilitas*.

An emphasis upon this point cannot but cause a significant reorientation in both philosophical and theological ethics, for it requires us to concentrate on moral education within a community. This is one of the consequences of Daniel Nelson's attempt to break the stranglehold of the "Natural Lawyers" upon Aquinas's ethics for, unlike an innate natural law, prudence must be learned. As he puts it: "It is prudence, of course, that is right reason about action and that governs our choices to a right end. These choices cannot be predetermined because 'the means to the end, in human concerns, far from being fixed, are of manifold variety of persons and affairs' (Aquinas, I-II, 58, 4). As a result, knowledge about how to choose is not natural but must be learned" (Nelson, *The Priority of Prudence,* p. 103). Nelson runs out of space before he can develop this insight.

23. Had Casey been clearer and more particular, the contrast between Christian and pagan wisdom might have stood out in greater relief, to their mutual benefit. Plainer differentiation might have fostered agreement of a certain sort. For example, in the two communities the *mode* of passing down wisdom in song or text will bear certain essential similarities; and some of the songs and texts (and therefore the wisdom) might be shared. Furthermore important disagreements might have clearly emerged, as they ought.

24. Alasdair MacIntyre, *Whose Justice? Which Rationality?* p. 196.

25. *ST* I-II, 65, 5.

26. The idea that the world exists for one's city may seem barbarous; in Cicero's case it is precisely the opposite. As his case plainly illustrates, specific concentration upon the good of one's city often includes its moral reform and further refinement. Especially when justice/friendship is placed at the center of the city's life, then what is good for the city, now extended to others beyond its bounds (perhaps by force), will be good for the world. (One can see on this point and others a fairly strong connection between Casey's views and Cicero's, who explicitly acknowledges the ascendancy of justice among the cardinal virtues. See his *De Officiis,* III, 28.)

27. *ST* II-II, 23, 6.

28. *ST* I-II, 66, 6, 1.

29. *ST* I-II, 65, 2.

30. *ST* II-II, 26, 6.

ıul Wadell calls Aquinas's proposal that we can be friends with God
ıst blasphemous claim." The great difference between ourselves and
God requires that "if we are to have friendship with God, there must be a
way that we are made to 'fit' this God. God is our happiness, but God is
absolutely beyond us" (*Friendship and the Moral Life*, p. 125). So friendship
with God requires (indeed, it *is*) our transformation. "To participate in the
friendship of God is to be changed according to it, gradually to be remade
according to the Spirit of Love" (p. 127). Prudence is thus transformed, both
in what it sees and how it sees.

32. C. S. Lewis distinguishes two sorts of pride, "Olympian," which exults
in the friends' shared high-mindedness and in the resulting distance sepa-
rating them from others, and "Titanic," which is "restive, militant and em-
bittered" rather than "tranquil and tolerant," as is Olympian (*The Four Loves*
[London: Collins, 1960], p. 120). If we use these classifications, the pagan
pride we have been discussing would be Olympian, for the paganism we are
imagining retains the degree of nobility which is no part of Lewis's Titanic
pride. The latter seems closer to the description offered by Aquinas which
involves an active turning from God. "[P]ride denotes aversion from God
simply through being unwilling to be subject to God and His rule" (II-II, 162,
6). Ancient pagan pride, Olympian pride, may be better understood as different from the sin Christians call pride (as Aquinas describes it), for it is
developed in ignorance of God, not so much in aversion. In another way,
however, it is as serious an error, since it constructs an almost impenetrable
defense against conversion by hardening a self or community against voices
from the outside and so against any retelling of the story of the self or community in relation to the God Christians call the one true God.

7. On Developing Hopeful Virtues

1. For a full-blown attempt to show how the Bible can be explicated in
terms of the virtues, see Benjamin Farley, *In Praise of Virtue: An Explication of
the Biblical Virtues in a Christian Context* (Grand Rapids: Eerdmans, 1995).

2. Karl Barth, *Church Dogmatics*, II/2 (Edinburgh: T. and T. Clark, 1957),
pp. 644–45.

3. Ibid., p. 612.

4. Gilbert Meilaender, *The Limits of Love: Some Theological Explorations*
(University Park: Pennsylvania State University Press, 1987), p. 35. The earlier and more complete version of the essay from which this quote was originally taken can be found in "The Place of Ethics in the Theological Task,"
Currents in Theology and Mission 6 (1979): 199.

5. Ibid., pp. 35 and 199 respectively.

6. Meilaender, *The Limits of Love*, p. 36. For an account of justification we
unreservedly endorse see David Yeago, "The Promise of God and the Desires
of Our Hearts: Prolegomena to a Lutheran Retrieval of Classical Spiritual Theology," *Lutheran Forum* 30, 2 (May 1996), pp. 21–30. Yeago puts it right when

he observes, "The *content* of the gospel is *not* justification, *not* forgiveness, *not* acceptance; the content of the gospel, what it talks about, what it promises, is Jesus Christ" (27). See also, David Yeago, "Gnosticism, Antinomianism, and Reformation Theology: Reflections on the Costs of a Construal," *Pro Ecclesia* 2, 1 (winter 1993), pp. 37–49.

7. Edmund Pincoffs, *Quandaries and Virtues: Against Reductionism in Ethics,* p. 162.

8. Alasdair MacIntyre, *After Virtue,* pp. 204–25. In *Whose Justice? Which Rationality?* MacIntyre argues not only that the virtues are tradition-specific but so also are the desires. "We are apt to suppose under the influence of this type of modern view that desires are psychologically basic items, largely, even if not entirely, invariant in their function between cultures. This is a mistake. The role and function of desires in the self-understanding of human beings vary from culture to culture with the way in which their projects and aspirations, expressions of need and claims upon others, are organized and articulated in the public social world" (p. 21). If MacIntyre is right about this, and we believe he is, any attempt to construe the virtues in terms of the formation of "invariant" desires and/or passions is rendered problematic. For a somewhat different perspective see Paul Lewis, "Rethinking Emotion and the Moral Life in Light of Thomas Aquinas and Jonathan Edwards" (Ph.D. diss., Duke University, 1991).

9. J. Christiaan Beker, *Paul's Apocalyptic Gospel: The Coming Triumph of God* (Philadelphia: Fortress Press, 1982), p. 30.

10. Robert Roberts, "Virtues and Rules," *Philosophy and Phenomenological Research* 5, 2 (1991): 325 ff.

11. Robert Roberts, "Therapies and the Grammar of a Virtue," in *The Grammar of the Heart: New Essays in Moral Philosophy and Theology,* ed. Richard H. Bell (San Francisco: Harper and Row, 1988), pp. 14–15.

12. Thomas Aquinas, *ST* II-II, 17, 1.

13. Masochism is a troubling concept, as we by no means wish to endorse the presumption that the acceptance of suffering is pathological, although in certain instances it may be. The therapeutic context which produces a notion like masochism often presumes accounts of human existence that entail that all suffering is "bad."

14. For more extended reflection on these matters see Hauerwas's *Naming the Silences: God, Medicine and the Problem of Evil* (Grand Rapids: Eerdmans, 1990). This does not mean that suffering is closer to the absurd, but rather that bearing the "pointlessness" of some kinds of suffering becomes part of our service to God.

15. Earlier in chapter 5 we claimed that this is what Christians do—they rage against fortune. But of course there, as here, the deeper question involves whether Christians can use the language of fortune at all. And clearly they cannot use it indiscriminately, since they acknowledge God is both the creator and sustenance of the universe. When Christians "rage against fortune" they do so less against fortune herself (as does, say, Camus's Dr. Rieux in *The Plague*), more so against the hegemony of "fortune" as the last word.

16. For a powerful account of sainthood that develops this theme see David Matzko, *Hazarding Theology: Theological Descriptions and Particular Lives* (Ph.D. diss., Duke University, 1992).

17. We are indebted to Alasdair MacIntyre for this way of putting the point. For a more developed account of character see Hauerwas, *Character and the Christian Life: A Study in Theological Ethics* (Notre Dame: University of Notre Dame Press, 1994).

18. *After Virtue,* p. 208.

19. *ST* I-II, 114, 6.

20. Ibid., I-II, 114, 2.

21. Robert Sokolowski, *The God of Faith and Reason* (Notre Dame: University of Notre Dame Press, 1982), p. 78.

22. Ibid., p. 82.

23. Aquinas makes the interesting point that the infused moral virtues may encounter difficulty in acting as they contend with dispositions remaining from previous acts. Since the acquired virtues result from previous acts, they are not so likely to have this difficulty. The implication seems to be that we are held back from living as the infused virtues direct us precisely because we have another history which yet holds us in its sway. *ST* I-II, 65, 3.

24. For the development of the idea that the Christian moral life involves finding our life as part of God's life see Hauerwas's *The Peaceable Kingdom: A Primer in Christian Ethics* (Notre Dame: University of Notre Dame Press, 1983). See L. Gregory Jones, *Embodying Forgiveness: A Theological Analysis* (Grand Rapids: Eerdmans, 1995) for a compelling account of forgiveness as a practice.

8. Is Obedience a Virtue

1. See *Nicomachean Ethics,* 1103a11ff. (We use Ross's translation throughout this chapter.) As Aristotle concludes that section: "It makes no small difference, then, whether we form habits of one kind or another from our very youth; it makes a great difference, or rather *all* the difference."

2. Ibid., 1128b15–17. For the most profound account as well as defense of shame see Bernard Williams, *Shame and Necessity* (Berkeley: University of California Press, 1993). Williams's entire project involves trying to help us understand what a "shame culture" must have been like, see in particular chapter 4 for a close analysis of shame in comparison to guilt.

3. Nowell-Smith, "Morality: Religious and Secular," *Readings in the Philosophy of Religion,* ed. Baruch Brody (Englewood Cliffs, N.J.: Prentice-Hall, 1974), p. 583.

4. Ibid., p. 588.

5. E. D. Watt, *Authority* (New York: St. Martins Press, 1983), p. 31.

6. In their own distinctive vocabulary, Christians will call this idolatry, perhaps the most far-reaching of all sins. Idolatry is in some sense an element in all sin, and as such it takes on many forms. Yet, as Augustine would have

it, there is dim glow of the good in all forms, since idolatry is a perversion of the worship we rightly owe to God.

7. *On the Hundredth Anniversary of "Rerum Novarum"* (Boston: Daughters of St. Paul, 1991), p. 59. John Paul's accent on obedience to *truth* suggests that as we obey we can never shut off our minds, since truth is something to be known as well as followed. As Robert Wilken rightly reminds us, modern notions of authority assume that authority has to do with will. In contrast, Christians, and in particular Augustine, thought authority had to do with the understanding. Authority, in other words, gains its intelligibility as a practice in the context of teaching—that is, the student trusts a teacher who gives reasons to illumine that which is taught. Robert Wilken, *Remembering the Christian Past* (Grand Rapids: Eerdmans, 1995), pp. 173–80. See also Herbert McCabe's similar reflections on the nature of obedience in his *God Matters* (Springfield, Ill.: Templegate Publishers, 1987), pp. 226–34.

8. *On the Hundredth Anniversary of "Rerum Novarum,"* p. 41.

9. It may be responded that a person can be "followed" as well as a law or principle. For example, Christians speak of "following Jesus." There is an evident difference, however, between following a principle and following a person. When we follow a principle we do what the principle explicitly says, whereas following a person implies more than doing what he says (although it includes that); it means to travel the way he travels, doing so as he did. The term "apply" is more helpful for displaying the difference, for applying a law or principle is a way of following it, whereas we do not "apply" Jesus as we follow him.

Of course it is true that Jesus issues commands, and in its narrower sense obedience to Jesus is obedience to his commands. However, and this is the central point, the reason Christians obey Jesus' commands—which reason, following Watt's earlier suggestions, is a necessary part of the obedience itself—is not in the command itself but in our trust in the person commanding, in this case Jesus. (This is part of the logic of commands, as Julius Kovesi has made plain in his wonderfully lucid but largely neglected discussion of the logic of commands, rules, and regulations. See his *Moral Notions* (New York: Routledge & Kegan Paul, 1967), especially pp. 66–91.) Indeed, this is the implication of the familiar remark of Jesus in John's Gospel: "If you love me, you will obey what I command" (14:15). The commanding done in this passage, however, is suggestively linked with a subsequent passage from the same discourse that we discussed in chapter 6. There Jesus adds: "You are my friends if you do what I command. I no longer call you servants, because a servant does not know his master's business. Instead I have called you friends, for everything that I learned from my Father I have made known to you" (15:14–15). Apparently, then, obeying the commands of Jesus, whom we have grown to love, initiates in us a process of development that brings us gradually closer to true knowledge of why he commanded them in the first place. Herbert McCabe observes, "Obedience for us (Dominicans) is not a denial of self but a discovery of self. For—to say it again—obedience is not the suppression of our will in favor of someone else's, it is learning to live in community, in solidarity, which is simply learning to live. Of course, to discover yourself is to unlearn as well as to learn; it is to abandon a notion of yourself that you had before in favor of a new and deeper one" (*God Matters*, p. 231).

10. Alasdair MacIntyre, *A Short History of Ethics* (New York: Macmillan, 1966), p. 194.

11. This is one of the reasons that the categorical imperative must supply its own reason for being. As we have been developing the point, one must have a reason for following a command, but the reason is to be found not in the command itself but in our trust in the commander. Interestingly, the presence of a relationship with the real commander provides considerable help in our following it. "Knowing our commander as we do," someone might say "I think we can suppose that this is what she meant for us to do when she issued that command." With the categorical imperative the impersonality of the "commander"—which is "reason itself," or "myself as a rational being"—guarantees that we will receive no such help. As anyone who has taught the *Foundations of the Metaphysics of Morals* knows, Kant's application of the imperative to questions like suicide or whether we should repay our debts must be offered before we can have any sort of clear idea about what acting "as though the maxim of your action were by your will to become a universal law" could mean. (*Foundations of the Metaphysics of Morals*, trans. Lewis White Beck (Indianapolis: Bobbs-Merrill, 1959), p. 39 [421].) Of course, then arises the debate about whether the implications Kant draws about suicide, for instance (422), are consistent with the imperative as abstractly stated.

12. Two helpful anthologies containing essays by contemporary divine command theorists as well as the older sources upon which they typically draw are *Divine Command Morality: Historical and Contemporary Readings*, ed. Janine Marie Idziak (Lewiston, N.Y.: Edwin Mellon Press, 1978) and *Divine Commands and Morality*, ed. Paul Helm, Oxford Readings in Philosophy (Oxford: Oxford University Press, 1981).

13. The question of what sort of god does the commanding has by no means been absent from the debate about the merits of divine command theories of morality; in fact it is central to the discussion of Robert M. Adams's version, perhaps the most discussed. Moreover, Adams has shown himself ready to change his theory in consideration of this debate. See his *The Virtue of Faith* (New York: Oxford University Press, 1987), which includes a number of essays about his divine command theory originally published in response to objections about whether and how much it matters that the divine commands are issued by a god we know of from within the context of the Jewish and Christian traditions. (An especially intriguing response which Adams considered carefully in his "Divine Command Metaethics Modified Again," originally published in the *Journal of Religious Ethics* 7, 1 (spring 1979): 66–79, was Jeffrey Stout's "Metaethics and the Death of Meaning: Adams's Tantalizing Closing," *Journal of Religious Ethics* 6 (spring 1978): 1–18. For more recent entries in the ongoing debate, see MacIntyre's "Which God Ought We to Obey and Why?" *Faith and Philosophy* 3, 4 (October 1986): 359–71 (which

we consider below in the text) and Stephen Sullivan's "Robert Adams's Theistic Argument from the Nature of Morality," *Journal of Religious Ethics* 21 (fall 1993): 303–12. Adams responds directly to Sullivan in "Prospects for a Metaethical Argument for Theism: A Response to Stephen J. Sullivan" in the same issue of the *JRE,* pp. 313–18.

We have taken the bold and perhaps foolish step of classing all recent divine command theories of ethics in the context of what MacIntyre calls the Enlightenment project—which, as he has argued, was bound to fail (see *After Virtue,* especially pp. 49–59). Somewhat cavalierly, we try to display the difficulties of all these theories by attacking Kant. (For a fuller but no less cavalier attempt to connect the divine command theories of ethics with Kant see Hauerwas's "Athens May Be a Long Way from Jerusalem But Prussia Is Even Further," *Asbury Theological Journal* 45, 1 [1990]: 59–63. That essay was written in response to Philip Quinn's response to Hauerwas's "Happiness, the Life of Virtue and Friendship: Theological Reflections on Aristotelian Themes," printed in that same issue. Those essays were the grist for the mill which produced the first section of this book.) More than a direct attack on Kant, what we here attempt to show is that the kind of obedience presumed by his (and the divine command theorists') account of morality is impoverished or, as we say, "flattened."

In that regard, Avi Sagi and Daniel Statman have recently made the intriguing observation that divine command theories of morality have proved not the least bit attractive to Jewish thinkers. (This is especially startling given that Jews, after all, were the first to begin talking about God's commands!) Sagi and Statman's explanation is relevant to the matter at hand, namely that the image of God standing behind the divine command theories—which they call "voluntaristic"—is incompatible with the thicker and also more "rational" picture that has always informed Jewish thought. See "Divine Command Morality and Jewish Tradition," *Journal of Religious Ethics* 23 (spring 1995): 39–67.

14. MacIntyre, "Which God Ought We to Obey and Why?" p. 363.

15. Ibid., p. 365.

16. Christians sometimes use the term "obedience" as *constitutive* of the whole of their life before God. This is because the end of the Christian life is to know God's will and do it. The narrower and more frequent use applies, as Aquinas defines it, to the obedient response to God's specific commands, tacit or expressed. Both senses, we are suggesting, do not stand alone but make sense only when placed in the context of the narrative of a gracious God whose care for us elicits our obedience.

17. *ST* II-II, 161, 1.

18. *ST* II-II, 104, 2.

19. Richard J. Mouw, *The God Who Commands* (Notre Dame: University of Notre Dame Press, 1990), p. 173. This quote appears in chapter 8 of Mouw's book which bears the title "The Triune Commander."

20. Athanasius, *Against the Arians* I, 33. Taken from *Documents in Early*

Christian Thought, ed. Maurice Wiles and Mark Santer (New York: Cambridge University Press, 1975), p. 30.

21. See for instance Richard Swinburne's *The Coherence of Theism* (Oxford: Clarendon Press: 1977), especially pp. 200–208.

22. While true, it is not especially uplifting to note that Jesus' comments cohere with the developmental account of the acquisition of the virtues offered in other sections of this book. The experience of parental love and care, as well as guidance offered early in life, cannot but profoundly influence a person's subsequent lived understanding (or lack thereof) of God's love. In fact there are some among us who offer our children stones instead of bread, snakes instead of fish. It is only by God's special grace, perhaps in the form of a community that offers love to these children who have never known it, that they can be reborn into a life in which the virtues and the descriptions that carry them can have any force at all.

23. Locke, *Second Treatise of Government,* ed. C. B. Macpherson (Indianapolis: Hackett, 1980), p. 31 [55].

24. See John Howard Yoder's chapter bearing that title in *The Politics of Jesus* (Grand Rapids: Eerdmans, 1972), pp. 163–92.

9. Courage Exemplified

1. John Rawls, *A Theory of Justice* (Cambridge, Mass.: Harvard University Press, 1971).

2. For a more thorough critique of Rawls's project see Michael Sandel, *Liberalism and the Limits of Justice* (Cambridge: Cambridge University Press, 1982) and George Parkin Grant, *English-Speaking Justice* (Notre Dame: University of Notre Dame Press, 1985).

3. Jean Bethke Elshtain, "Citizenship and Armed Civic Virtue: Some Questions on the Commitment to Public Life," in *Community in America: The Challenge of Habits of the Heart,* ed. Charles H. Reynolds and Ralph Norman (Berkeley: University of California Press, 1988), p. 50.

4. Hegel perhaps best understood this as he saw that without war bourgeois life would be a "bog" in which the citizens of the liberal state would lack the means to rise above their own self-interest. For Hegel, without war the state cannot become the embodiment of the universal. For a good exposition of Hegel's views see Michael Gillespie, "Death and Desire: War and Bourgeoisification in the Thought of Hegel," in *Understanding the Political Spirit: Philosophical Investigations from Socrates to Nietzsche* (New Haven: Yale University Press, 1988), 153–79.

5. Elshtain, p. 51.

6. Ibid.

7. By placing "courage" in quotation marks we mean to suggest that all "courages" are not created equal, nor, for that matter, are any of the virtues. Investigation of the full implications of such a claim is complex, and we have

not anywhere in this book treated the question with the rigor it deserves. At the least such an investigation would require inquiry concerning how the virtues are individuated or if and how they are unified. As usual, MacIntyre makes some fascinating suggestions about these matters in *After Virtue*. He criticizes Aquinas for trying to provide an exhaustive and consistent classificatory scheme of the virtues because such a scheme betrays the empirical character of much of the knowledge of the virtues. "[W]e learn what kind of quality truthfulness or courage is, what its practice amounts to, what obstacles it creates and what it avoids and so on, only in key part by observing its practice in others and in ourselves. And since we have to be educated into the virtues and most of us are incompletely and unevenly educated in them for a good part of our lives, there is necessarily a kind of empirical untidiness in the way that our knowledge of the virtues is ordered, more particularly in respect of how the practice of each relates to the practice of all the others" (p. 178). This problem bedevils not only Aquinas, but also Aristotle, who continued the Platonic assumption of the unity of the virtues, thus committing himself to the corollary that the virtuous person must have all the virtues at once. There certainly seems something right about the insistence on the interrelation of the virtues, since, for example, courage depends to some degree on temperance. Yet as MacIntyre suggests, strong accounts of the unity of the virtues have difficulty accounting for their acquisition over time.

MacIntyre notes that, because of his insistence on the unity of the virtues, P. T. Geach is led to deny that a devoted Nazi can possess the virtue of courage. MacIntyre resists this because the moral re-education of the Nazi would not require relearning everything, since he already knows what cowardice in the face of harm amounts to, even if his notion of what harm or danger might involve, and why it should be borne, would need to be transformed by humility and charity.

MacIntyre also rightly notes, however, that an account of the virtues cannot be generated from practices alone. The virtues, both for their identification and their relation, require a narrative that displays what a concrete human life looks like in a community of such lives. Thus we can see the importance of the paradigms through which courage is exemplified.

    8. We are using the translation of the *Nichomachean Ethics* by Martin Ostwald (Indianapolis: Bobbs-Merrill, 1962). All references will appear in the text.

    9. It is important to see how Aristotle, and later Aquinas, assumes the descriptions of actions are separable from the character of the agent. That certain actions are always wrong is but a way of saying that no virtuous person could ever envision so acting. Accounts of the virtues do not exclude rules of prohibited actions, but they may very well insist as well that rules (laws) against such actions injure the practices of the community necessary for sustaining virtuous people. (See MacIntyre's comments in *After Virtue*, pp. 149–52.) For an important discussion of the relation of these matters to Roman Catholic moral disputes see Martin Rhonheimer, " 'Intrinsically Evil

Acts' and the Moral Viewpoint: Clarifying a Central Teaching of *Veritatis Splendor,*" *Thomist* 58, 1 (1994): 1–39.

10. Aristotle's reflections on Sparta are especially interesting, given his account of courage and its relation to war in the *Ethics*. He observed that the Spartans, because of their skill and training for war, "remained secure as long as they were at war; but they collapsed as soon as they acquired an empire. They did not know how to use the leisure which peace brought; and they had never accustomed themselves to any discipline other and better than that of war." *The Politics of Aristotle,* trans. Ernest Barker (New York: Oxford University Press, 1958), p. 29 [1271b2–6]. See also Steven White's *Sovereign Virtue: Aristotle on the Relation between Happiness and Prosperity,* pp. 219–46. We are indebted to White for helping us see the significance of Aristotle's criticism of Sparta for understanding courage. Had Aristotle pressed these criticisms systematically, letting them inform his account more deeply, we suspect he could have escaped many of the criticisms we attempt to articulate in this chapter.

11. Lee Yearley, *Mencius and Aquinas: Theories of Virtue and Conceptions of Courage* (Albany: State University of New York Press, 1990), p. 37.

12. *ST* II-II, 123, 1, 2. From this point all references to the *Summa* will be included in the text.

13. Yearley, p. 18.

14. MacIntyre rightly observes that Aquinas's appropriation of Aristotle involves fitting together the inheritance from heroic cultures with a Christianized culture but also with specifically biblical virtues. "Aquinas in his treatise on the virtues treats them in terms of what had become the conventional scheme of the cardinal virtues (prudence, justice, temperance, courage) and the trio of theological virtues. But what then of, for example, patience? Aquinas quotes the Epistle of St. James: 'Patience has its perfect work' (*S. Th.,* qu. LXI art. 3) and considers whether patience should not therefore be listed as a principal virtue. But then Cicero is quoted against St. James, and it is argued that all the other virtues are contained within the four cardinal virtues. Yet if this is so Aquinas cannot of course mean by the Latin names of the cardinal virtues entirely what Aristotle meant by their Greek equivalents, since one or more of the cardinal virtues must contain within itself both patience and another biblical virtue which Aquinas explicitly acknowledges, namely humility. Yet in the only place in Aristotle's account of the virtues where anything resembling humility is mentioned, it is a vice, and patience is not mentioned at all by Aristotle." *After Virtue,* p. 177.

15. Yearley, p. 33.

16. Ibid., p. 129.

17. That Aristotle uses the example of drowning is in itself interesting. One can easily imagine a case in which the courageous person dies in battle by drowning. For example, he is storming the deck of an enemy's ship, slips and falls to his watery grave. Is this a courageous death? Aristotle provides no analysis, but we could imagine it. In such a death the cause is not the

battle itself but rather the water; it is not the thrust of the opponent's sword that finishes the man off but rather the vast and indifferent sea. He therefore does not die fighting but is swallowed by a sea against which his struggling is petty and hopeless. Of course with some imagination we can construct a case where a man drowns while fighting, perhaps with his rival in a choke-hold. If there is a casuistry of the "noble acts of war," it would be interestingly applied here. (For example, how did the two of them happen to get into the water?) If a problem arose it would likely center on the question of whether the man died while displaying his prowess, for, again, who can display prowess against the sea?

18. MacIntyre argues that medieval thinkers did not have the modern conception of history as discontinuous discovery and rediscovery of what history is, but that is in part because medieval thinkers took the basic historical scheme of the Bible to be one within which they could rest assured. On this kind of medieval view the virtues are therefore those qualities which enable human beings to survive evils on their historical journey. See *After Virtue*, p. 176.

19. Yearley, p. 130.

20. The use of the military imagery to apply within the arena of the Christian life is, of course, hardly of Aquinas's invention; it infuses the Bible. Unfortunately this has been frequently narrowed to refer to "the defense of the faith," which allows for a transference of militarism rather than its transformation. This is plainly refuted in Ephesians 6, where Christians are urged to "take up the whole armor of God," which includes the shoes that "will make you ready to proclaim the gospel of peace." Moreover, Isaiah's oft-repeated hope for a day when the nations "shall beat their swords into plowshares, their spears into pruning hooks" (Isaiah 2:4) suggests not so much the utter ceasing of a certain kind of activity, but rather its transformation, as evidenced by its changed weaponry, and so too the purposes of those who wield it.

21. Aquinas, II-II, 139, 1 as quoted in Yearley, p. 141.

22. Peter Geach resists R. M. Hare's view that courage is largely a thing of the past on the ground that Hare has assumed, with Plato and Aristotle, that courage had mainly to do with conduct on the battlefield. Quite to the contrary, as Geach asserts, the "ordinary course of the world, even in times of peace, is so ordered that men regularly need some courage; courage to endure, courage to face the worst." As we are alleging in the text, Geach takes the courage of the martyrs to be accessible to us all, and castigates those who would use the term "heroic virtue" as applied traditionally by the church to the martyrs as a reason to suppose "it is not to be expected of ordinary folk." (Understanding "heroic virtue" in this way is, he thinks, a "cunning snare of Hell's Philological Arm.") Accordingly, in an ironic twist, he urges that the answer "to the plea 'I'm no hero' the reply may be made: 'You are a hero, in the Greek sense of the word: a son not just of mortal parents, but of God.'" See *The Virtues* (New York: Cambridge University Press, 1977), pp. 153–54.

23. Yearley, p. 141.

24. While we think just warriors are wrong, they might not be—another way of saying that we think the just-war position as articulated by an Augustine or a Paul Ramsey is a significant challenge to our own Christian pacifism and is theological to its core. Just warriors and pacifists within the Christian church must be committed to continued engagements which teach them not only to recognize their differences but also their similarities, similarities that make them far more alike one another than the standard realists' accounts of war which rule our contemporary culture and which have taken a firm hold in the church. For a concrete display of how this engagement might go, see Hauerwas and Ramsey's *Speak Up for Just War or Pacifism* (University Park: Pennsylvania State University Press, 1988).

25. Tertullian counsels new believers to abandon military service, not just because of the bloodshed or idolatry which so frequently accompanied it but also because staying in the service as a Christian will mean that "all sorts of quibbling will have to be resorted to in order to avoid offending God, and this is not allowed [for Christians] even outside of military service." *On the Crown,* XI.

26. MacIntyre explores how the semblance of virtue can distort and even render impossible living virtuously in his "How to Seem Virtuous without Actually Being So," *Committee of the Centre for the Study of Cultural Values, Occasional Papers* (Lancaster University, England, 1991), pp. 1–20.

10. Practicing Patience:
How Christians Should Be Sick

1. *The God That Failed,* edited with an introduction by Richard Crossman (New York: Harper and Row, 1963). The book was first published in 1949. It contains essays by Arthur Koestler, Ignazio Silone, Richard Wright, André Gide, Louis Fisher, and Stephen Spender.

2. Ibid., p. 16.

3. See Michel Foucault, *The Birth of the Clinic* (New York: Vantage Books, 1973).

4. For a wonderful set of essays that question the understanding of the body prevalent in modern medicine see *Troubled Bodies: Critical Perspectives on Postmodernism, Medical Ethics, and the Body,* ed. Paul Komersaroff (Durham, N.C.: Duke University Press, 1995). In his introduction Komersaroff observes, "The infiltration of the categories of medicine into the way we think about pregnancy and childbirth, the menopause, sexual relationships and caring for a sick relative, for example—or, for that matter, merely eating, exercising or just lying in the sun—may profoundly transform the quality of these experiences. In these cases, medical modes of thought introduce into previously unproblematic life experiences evaluative criteria that are formulated in purposive-rational terms. That is, they are presented as purely technical values" (p. 3).

5. For an extraordinary account of how "ethics" has served to legitimate the presumptions of modern medicine, see Gerald McKenny, *To Relieve the Human Condition: Bioethic and the Technological Utopianism of Modern Medicine* (Albany: State University of New York Press, 1996). McKenny observes, "A moral discourse which related the health of the body as well as its mortality and its susceptibility to illness and suffering to broader conceptions of a morally worthy life was succeeded by a moral discourse characterized by efforts to eliminate suffering and expand human choice and thereby overcome the human subjections to natural necessity or fate. The result is that standard bioethics moves within the orbit of the technological utopianism of what I call the Baconian project, and its agenda and content are designed to resolve certain issues and problems that arise within that project." McKenny identifies the "Baconian project" with the attempt to eliminate suffering and to expand the realm of human choice through technology.

6. Colin Gunton is to be commended for his attempt to read modernity in this fashion. See his *The One, the Three, and the Many: God, Creation, and the Culture of Modernity* (Cambridge: Cambridge University Press, 1993). We are sympathetic to Gunton's account, though we may have a different reading of who have been and currently are friends and enemies. John Milbank's *Theology and Social Theory,* which we used extensively in chapter 4, provides an important contrast to Gunton. Gunton suggests that Milbank is insufficiently trinitarian and, as a result, fails to see that "modernity" did not begin with nominalism and the Reformation but is rooted earlier (p. 55).

We lack the learning to enter into such debates, but it is clear to us that the hard problem with which both Gunton and Milbank are struggling is how to narrate the "secular" theologically. Secular modes of discourse are now so powerful that theological claims no longer seem to do any work—thus we fail to supply what MacIntyre says we must, that is, a *theological* critique of secular culture and morality.

Few have accomplished this task better than Cardinal John Henry Newman. According to Robert Pattison, Newman regarded what most people take as the character of liberalism—that is, a movement for individual rights, free markets, and material progress—as only the trappings of liberalism. For Newman, liberalism's political program was but a symptom of the heretical belief that shaped its basic principles. Liberalism was only a modern version of the Socinianism of the Reformation and that was but a version of the Arian heresy of the fourth century. According to Newman, what offended the Arians about Nicaea and Constantinople was not that the church declared the Son to be "the same in nature" as the Father, but that anything at all was declared about God. The Arians denied our knowledge of God in Christ and as a result became the first liberals.

In the face of the limits of language and our inability to express the truth fully within its parameters, truth must finally be constructed as a contest of wills. Pattison, a liberal, admires Newman because "he was the last good mind in which the dogmatic principle still excited all the ideological excitement of seventeenth-century controversy. As a result, he denominated ancient theological errors and modern social theories indifferently by the interchangeable names Arianism, Socinianism, Hoadlyism, and liberalism. Newman is the missing link between the belief of the old world and the ideology of the new. As he seemed absurd to his brother, so must he to us; his absurdity is inseparable from his message, which is that those things that the worldly mind of the modern era considers ridiculous—namely the orthodox assertion that belief has a real object, that truth is abiding, and that words can dogmatically state truth—are in fact sublime realities." Pattison, *The Great Dissent: John Henry Newman and the Liberal Heresy* (Oxford: Oxford University Press, 1991), p. 143.

7. Obviously the account of such bargains varies from Hobbes, to Locke, to Rousseau, and in our own day, Rawls and Nozick. Such differences matter, but we are concerned with how to articulate how medicine works in social orders so conceived. The current enthusiasm for rational choice methodologies in the social sciences is a wonderful confirmation of bargaining as the central metaphor for social organization today. For a good critique of the inability of rational choice methods to deliver what they promise, at least in political science, see Donald P. Green and Ian Shapiro, *The Pathologies of Rational Choice Theory: A Critique of Applications in Political Science* (New Haven, Conn.: Yale University Press, 1994).

8. This paragraph is a slight rewording of a footnote from Hauerwas's *Naming the Silences: God, Medicine, and Suffering,* p. 123. I (Hauerwas) think it the heart of the argument of that book, though few have recognized the importance I attribute to this point. That is, of course, not the fault of my readers, since I was in truth trying to disguise the main argument of that book. *Naming the Silences* is allegedly a book about the suffering and death of children, and I hope it is at least that. But I also wanted to make the case that medicine has become the theodical project of modernity, part of whose task is to save liberalism. That is why I claimed that the book was really an exercise in political theory. We are here simply trying to articulate in a straightforward fashion what I attempted to do indirectly in that book. *Naming the Silences* has recently been reprinted by Eerdmans under the title *God, Medicine, and Suffering.* Eerdmans thought my original title was hurting the sales of the book. So much for being subtle.

9. We are acutely aware that this puts the issue too simply, since part of the power of modern medicine is constituted by its ability to name the "illnesses" that then become subject to medical intervention. For a more extended (but hardly exhaustive) discussion of these issues see Hauerwas's *Suffering Presence: Theological Reflections on Medicine, the Mentally Handicapped, and the Church* (Notre Dame: University of Notre Dame Press, 1986).

10. In an article in a special issue of the *Journal of Medicine and Philosophy* on theology and medicine edited by Hauerwas and James Gustafson, Alasdair MacIntyre issued the following challenge. "What we ought to expect from contemporary theologians in the area of medical ethics: First—and without this everything else is uninteresting—we ought to expect a clear statement

of what difference it makes to be a Jew or a Christian or a Moslem, rather than a secular thinker, in morality generally. Second . . . we need to hear a theological critique of secular morality and culture. Third, we want to be told what bearing what has been said under the two headings has on the specific problems which arise for modern medicine." ("Theology, Ethics, and the Ethics of Medicine and Health Care: Comments on Papers by Novak, Mouw, Roach, Cahill, and Hartt," *Journal of Medicine and Philosophy* 4 [1979]: 435.) That challenge was issued in 1979. Subsequent developments have made it clear that that issue did little to convince anyone that theology had or has anything distinctively important to say about these matters. MacIntyre challenges theologians to accent their differences, but in this time called modernity most theologians have attempted to downplay them. Their task has been to suggest that Christians believe pretty much what anyone would believe on reflection. For example, the call for theology to be a "public" discourse seems carried by the urge to show that theological convictions do in fact measure up to standards of truthfulness generally recognized in liberal democratic societies. Only if theology meets these standards can Christians enter into the public arena without apology. (For a succinct chronicle of these developments as well as some interesting comments about the rise of recent promising dissent see Scott Giles and Jeffrey Greenman, "Recent Work on Religion and Bioethics: A Review Article," *Biolaw: A Legal and Ethical Reporter on Medicine, Health Care, and Bioengineering* 2, 7–8 [July-August 1994]: 151–60.)

11. See, for example, *Virtue and Medicine: Explorations in the Character of Medicine,* ed. Earl E. Shelp (Dordrecht: D. Reidel, 1985). Karen Lebacqz's essay, "The Virtuous Patient" (pp. 275–88) is particularly relevant for what we are trying to do here. Lebacqz argues that three virtues—fortitude, prudence, and hope—are central to the task of being a patient. Our only difficulty with her account is knowing from whence such virtues come. William May has also developed the importance of the virtues in his "The Virtues in a Professional Setting" in *Medicine and Moral Reasoning,* ed. K. W. M. Tulford, Grant Gillet, and Janet Martin Soskice (Cambridge: Cambridge University Press, 1994), pp. 75–90. For a overview of recent work in medical ethics on the importance of virtue see Hauerwas's, "Virtue and Character" in the new edition of the *Encyclopedia of Bioethics.*

12. Typically out of step with his contemporaries, over twenty years ago John Howard Yoder observed that apparent complicity with evil, which the nonresistant stance allegedly involves, has always been a stumbling block to nonpacifists. In response, Yoder points out that "this attitude, leaving evil to be evil, leaving the sinner free to separate himself from God and sin against man, is part of the nature of *agape* itself, as revealed already in creation. If the cutting phrase of Peguy, '*complice, c'test pire que coupable,*' were true, then God Himself must needs be the guilty one for making man free and again for letting His innocent Son be killed. The modern tendency to equate involvement with guilt should have to apply *par excellence,* if it were valid at all, to the implication of the all-powerful God in the sin of His creatures. God's love for men begins right at the point where He permits sin against Himself

and against man, without crushing the rebel under his own rebellion. The word for this is divine *patience,* not complicity." *The Original Revolution* (Scottdale, Pa.: Herald Press, 1971), pp. 64–65. Drawing on Yoder, Hauerwas argued in *The Peaceable Kingdom: A Primer in Christian Ethics* that hope and patience are central Christian virtues. See especially pp. 102–6.

13. Cyprian, *De Bono Patientia: A Translation with an Introduction and Commentary,* by Sister M. George Edward Conway, S.S.J. (Washington, D.C.: Catholic University Press of America, 1957), p. 65. Cyprian's account of patience closely parallels Tertullian's earlier treatise "On Patience." The latter can be found in volume 3 of *The Ante-Nicene Fathers* (Grand Rapids: Eerdmans, 1989), pp. 707–17. Augustine drew on both Tertullian and Cyprian for his "On Patience," which can be found in *A Library of Fathers of the Holy Catholic Church, Anterior to the Division of the East and West,* trans. Members of the English Church (Oxford: John Henry Parker Press, 1937), pp. 542–62. Sister Conway provides a very helpful comparison of these three treatments of patience. Augustine is careful to explain that just as God is jealous without any darkening of spirit, so He is patient without "thought of passion," p. 544.

14. Tertullian, p. 708.

15. Ibid., p. 711. Cyprian's reflections on Matthew are found on pages 68–69.

16. Ibid., p. 715.

17. Cyprian observes that the Christian should not hasten to revenge the pain of persecution, since vengeance is the Lord's. "Therefore, even the martyrs as they cry out and as they hasten to their punishment in the intensity of their suffering are still ordered to wait and to show patience until the appointed time is fulfilled and the number of martyrs is complete," p. 89.

18. Augustine, pp. 550–51.

19. Ibid., p. 544. Aquinas uses this quote to counter the claim that patience is not a virtue, since it can sometimes be found in wicked men. See *ST* II-II, 136, 1.

20. Augustine, p. 551.

21. Ibid., pp. 557–58. Augustine, like all the Christian fathers, makes constant appeals to scripture in support of this argument—I Corinthians 13:4 being, of course, the central text. Charity must form patience, but it is equally the case that charity needs patience. In a remarkable passage Cyprian says, "Charity is the bond of brotherhood, the foundation of peace, the steadfastness and firmness of unity; it is greater than both hope and faith; it excels both good works and suffering for the faith; and, as an eternal virtue, it will abide with us forever in the kingdom of heaven. Take patience away from it, and thus forsaken, it will not last; take away the substance of enduring and tolerating, and it attempts to last with no roots or strength. Accordingly, the apostle when he was speaking about charity joined forbearance and patience to it, saying: Charity is magnanimous, charity is kind, charity does not envy, is not puffed up, is not provoked, thinks no evil, loves all things, believes all things, hopes all things, endures all things. By this he showed that charity can persevere steadfastly because it has learned how to endure all things. And

in another place he says: bearing with one another in love, taking every care to preserve the unity of the Spirit in the union of peace. He proved that neither unity nor peace can be preserved unless brothers cherish one another with mutual forbearance and preserve the bond of unity with patience as intermediary" (p. 81).

22. We are indebted once again to Lee Yearley's wonderful *Mencius and Aquinas: Theories of Virtue and Conceptions of Courage,* particularly pp. 136–43. Crucial for understanding Aquinas's views is the significance of his account of the passions and, in particular, sadness as a passion. See *ST* I-II, 35–39. Yearley rightly observes that Aquinas thinks his understanding of the place of sadness in the Christian life is the crucial difference between Stoicism and Christianity. The Christian cannot seek to be free of sadness, for without the appropriate sadness we lack the ability to be joyful.

The Stoics' understanding of the passions was much more complex than they are usually given credit. See, for example, Martha Nussbaum's treatment of Stoicism in *The Therapy of Desire: Theory and Practice in Hellenistic Ethics,* pp. 359–438. Nussbaum, quoting Seneca, observes, " 'Where you take greatest joy you will also have the greatest fear.' Just as there is unity among the virtues, all being forms of correct apprehension of the self-sufficient good, just so there is a unity to the passions—and also to their underlying dispositional states. But this means, too, that there is a unity to the cure of the passions. 'You will cease to fear, if you cease to hope. . . . Both belong to a soul that is hanging in suspense, to a soul that is made anxious by concern with the future.' The world's vulnerable gifts, cherished, give rise to the passionate life; despised, to a life of calm. 'What fortune does not give, she does take away.' " Pp. 388–89. Against such a background the importance of Aquinas's insistence that Christians are the most passionate of people can be understood not only as a claim about what we must be as Christians, but also as a claim about the way the world is. If God, at least the God that Christians worship, does not exist then our joy and our sadness, schooled by our hope, is a lie.

23. Yearley, p. 137. This point should be qualified with the insistence that Thomas's account of patience does not entail passivity. Patience is a necessary component of fortitude, which, as Josef Pieper observes, seems incongruous for many people because for them patience "has come to mean an indiscriminate, self-immolating, crabbed, joyless, and spineless submission to whatever evil is met with or, worse, deliberately sought out. Patience, however, is something quite other than indiscriminate acceptance of any and every evil: 'The patient man is not the one who does not flee from evil, but the one who does not allow himself to be made inordinately sorrowful thereby.' To be patient means to preserve cheerfulness and serenity of mind in spite of injuries that result from the realization of the good. Patience does not imply the exclusion of energetic, forceful activity, but simply, explicitly and solely the exclusion of sadness and confusion of heart. Patience keeps man from the danger that his spirit may be broken by grief and lose its greatness. Patience, therefore, is not the tear-veiled mirror of a 'broken' life (as one might easily assume in

the face of what is frequently presented and praised under this name), but the radiant embodiment of ultimate integrity. In the words of Hildegard of Bingen, patience is 'the pillar which nothing can soften.' And Thomas, following Holy Scripture (Luke 21:19), summarizes with superb precision: "Through patience man possesses his soul.'" *The Four Cardinal Virtues,* p. 129.

24. Aquinas, *ST* II-II, 136, 4, 2. Yearley highlights this wonderful passage.

25. Aquinas, *ST,* II-II, 28, 2. (This is Yearley's translation of this passage.) Crucial for sustaining such joy in the midst of sadness is the kind of materialism required in the Christian belief in the Incarnation and Resurrection. Our belief in the bodily Resurrection—that is, that the Resurrection is not so much a throwing off of our human flesh but rather an exchanging of our present body for a new body so that we may dwell in a new heaven and a new earth—means that Christians' hope that "all manner of things shall be well" can never be a facile optimism that evades the reality of pain. As Jim Fodor observed to one of us (Hauerwas), "simply to encourage people to see things differently, while leaving things as they are, is to reinforce their slavery, the reinforcement of which is all the more insidious precisely because it is disguised as a proclamation of the truth to set us free. Christianity, in other words, is not merely a way of 'regarding,' 'looking at,' or 'interpreting' reality. Christianity is not a 'theory' but a way of life, a way of discipleship. And discipleship is concrete, specific; it occurs—or fails to occur—in particular practices and patterns of engagements, relationships, suffering, and worship. Thus the importance of the practice of 'bodily patience' for guarding against the tendency, all too common among many modern Christians, to affirm 'the primacy of the spiritual' to the neglect of the material conditions of redemption. The practical, material display of Christian virtue necessary for patience is in finding a gift from God and not something we cultivate willfully or from our own strength, apart from God's help. In fact, patience is often something we reluctantly accept, if at all, and then only after a long and painful struggle to acknowledge our creaturely limits and the sense in which most things in our life remain out of our control."

26. Yearley, p. 139.

27. Ibid. Yearley notes that Aquinas did not examine the semblances of patience in the systematic manner in which he explored the semblances of courage. Yet given patience's close relation to endurance, the crucial aspect of courage, Yearly rightly uses the semblances of courage to suggest analogies for how Aquinas might have understood the semblances of patience. Though the comparison of the semblances of patience with true patience (or the semblances of courage with true courage, or the semblances of prudence with true prudence) are usually negative, it is a mistake to assume that positive comparisons are not also a possibility. Since we are God's good creatures we should expect to find in those who are not Christians indications of God's patience. The problem, then, is not that non-Christians fail to exhibit any of the virtues, but that they do and because they do they are just as likely to display them in ways that may be destructive rather than constructive. The Christian advantage is to be part of God's people, which makes us vulnerable

to the judgments of others who have acquired the wisdom necessary to understand the interrelation of the virtues.

28. Albert Borgmann, *Crossing the Postmodern Divide* (Chicago: University of Chicago Press, 1992), pp. 97–102.

29. Tertullian, p. 710. Gerald J. Schiffhorst in a similar fashion argues that in *Paradise Lost* Milton "relies on patience to express the Christian's proper response to the divine will while ironically revealing the anti-heroism of Satan, whose blind impatience reverses what Milton called the 'better fortitude' of patience. Satan's struggle to fight God is undercut by the 'pleasing sorcery' of a false heroism whereas Adam learns to arm himself with patience 'to overcome by suffering' what God will unfold. The centrality of 'patience as the truest fortitude' (*Samson Agonistes,* 654) in revealing this fundamental contrast demonstrates the importance of the virtue in the poem." "Satan's False Heroism in *Paradise Lost* as a Perversion of Patience," *Christianity and Literature* 38, 2 (winter 1984), p. 13.

Schiffhorst provides a very helpful contrast of Christian patience with Stoic indifference by noting the difference between the Christian understanding of providence and the Stoic idea of fortune. He notes that "this basic Christian-pagan distinction helps us recall that Christ's victory over death was a victory over Fortune, and so the virtuous Christian can have everlasting life by imitating Christ's perfect patience. As Miles Coverdale says in his important Elizabethan treatise on patience, 'the impatient man complains against God and ascribes prosperity to his own wisdom, blaming blind Fortune for adversity.' Without ascribing dispassionate Stoic virtues to Satan, we can nevertheless say that his false heroism is rooted in a stubborn pride and that he exhibits all the passions of the impatient man: wrath, despair, grief, and envy," pp. 14–15.

For a wonderful collection of essays on patience, see Gerald J. Schiffhorst, ed., *The Triumph of Patience: Medieval and Renaissance Studies* (Orlando: University Presses of Florida, 1978). Particularly interesting is Elizabeth Kirk's essay entitled, " 'Who Suffreth More Than God?': Narrative Redefinition of Patience in *Patience* and *Piers Plowman*," ibid., pp. 88–105. She not only provides a wonderful commentary on the medieval poet of the Pearl, but ends with a delightful quote from Chaucer's Parson that she thinks contains everything written large in *Patience* and *Piers Plowman:* "Patience, that is another remedie agayns Ire, is a vewru that suffreth swetely every mannes goodness, and is nat wroth for noon harm that is doon to hym. . . . This vertu maketh a man lyk to God, and maketh hym Goddes owene deere child, as seith Crist. This vertu disconfiteth thyn enemy. And therfore seith the wise man, If thow wolt vengukysse thyn enemy, lerne to suffre. . . . And understond wel that obedience is parfit, whan that a man dooth gladly and hastily, with good herte entirely, al that he should do," p. 102.

30. Tertullian, p. 710. As pacifists we find Tertullian's suggestion that our violence lies in our impatience as intriguing as it is persuasive.

31. Our emphasis on patience as the virtue essential to the doctor-patient relationship may appear particularly perverse because it seems to make the

patient even more powerless. There is rightly an asymmetry between the doctor and patient inasmuch as the physician has authority that the patient does not or should not have. However, once it is understood that medicine names an activity in which doctor and patient are jointly involved, patience can work in such a relationship to decrease rather than increase the abuse of power. (In like manner, rethinking the medical relation in the light of the authority and obedience we discussed in chapter 8 should also decrease it.) Crucially both Christian patience and obedience require the church for display. Without the kind of friendship, dependency, trust, and mutual nurturing imbedded in the worship of God, patience and obedience always risks the possibility of becoming malformed. That is why Hauerwas suggested in *Suffering Presence* that institutionalized medicine requires a church for sustaining the kind of presence that physicians, nurses, and others in medical settings provide. The hospital is the best exemplification of the kind of care the church should make possible and sustain, although as we suggested earlier, "the hospital," increasingly detached from the practices of the church which gave it birth, may be on its way to an entirely new sort of existence.

32. We are acutely aware, as anyone must be after the work of Foucault, that appeals to the "body" are anything but unproblematic. Recent historical work helps us better understand why Paul could say that nothing was more "spiritual" than the body. Moreover, understanding the body as peculiarly "spiritual" we think has great potential for helping us reexamine the relation of Christian practices and the practice of medicine. See for example Peter Brown's *The Body and Society: Men, Women and Sexual Renunciation in Early Christianity* (Boston: Faber, 1988) and Dale Martin's *The Corinthian Body* (New Haven: Yale University Press, 1995).

Particularly important is a better understanding of the "therapy of desire" characteristic of Christian practice in contrast to the assumptions of Galen and the other Hellenistic philosophical schools. For example, we need a Christian account parallel to Nussbaum's *The Therapy of Desire*. Brown's book is obviously a good beginning, but one has the feeling that we are just beginning to understand what Augustine and Aquinas grasped far better than we about the nature of the passions. We are indebted to Mr. Thomas Harvey, a graduate student at Duke, for a paper in which he explored how Augustine provided an alternative to Galen's understanding of the body.

33. For a fuller development of how our practices not only take but also create time, see "Taking Time for Peace: The Moral Significance of the Trivial," the final chapter in Hauerwas's *Christian Existence Today: Essays on Church, World, and Living in Between* (Durham: Labyrinth Press, 1988), pp. 253–66.

34. We put quotes around this phrase to indicate its everyday usage but also to mark our unease. As we implied earlier, luck is a Stoic not a Christian notion that implies fortune, which is blind. Christians do not believe the world is ruled by fortune but rather by God's providential care.

Name Index

Abel, 107
Abraham, 141, 145
Ackrill, J. L., 179n., 180n.
Adam, 216n.
Adam and Eve, 175–76
Adams, Robert Merridew, 141, 203n., 204n.
Ambrose, 100
Anagnostopoulos, Georgios, 180n.
Ananaias and Sapphira, 141
Anscombe, G. E. M., 184n.
Aquinas. *See* Thomas Aquinas
Aristotle, x–xi, xii, xiii, xiv, 3–43, 46–51, 62–66, 68–86, 89, 93, 97, 98, 102–5, 114, 118, 128, 130, 131, 151, 154–58, 160–64, 179n., 180n., 181n., 183n., 184n., 186n., 187n., 188n., 189n., 191n., 193n., 194., 201n., 206n., 207n., 208.
Athanasius, 145, 146, 204n.
Augustine, 27, 62, 65, 131, 158, 173, 175, 187–88n., 201n., 202n., 209n., 213n., 217n.
Austen, Jane, 183n.

Baier, Kurt, 182n.
Barth, Karl, 115, 128, 199n.
Beiner, Ronald, 182n., 188n.
Beker, J. Christiaan, 117, 200n.
Bellah, Robert, 55, 238
Benedict, Saint, 195n.
Bennett, William, 55
Berger, Peter, 94, 196n.
Blake, William, 141
Blum, Laurence, 186n.
Borgmann, Albert, 175, 216n.
Brown, Peter, 217n.
Burke, Edmund, 190n.
Bush, George, 74

Cain, 107, 176
Camus, Albert, 200n.

Casey, John, ix, xiii, xiv, xvi, 89–109, 165, 195n., 196n., 198n.
Chaucer, Geoffrey, 216n.
Christ. *See* Jesus of Nazareth
Chrysostom, 57
Cicero, 27, 198n., 207n.
Conway, Sister M. George Edward, 213n.
Cooper, John, 74, 75, 180n., 186n., 193n., 196n.
Coverdale, Miles, 216n.
Cyprian, 160, 171, 172, 173, 175, 213n.

Descartes, René, 101
Dionysus, 84
Dukakis, Michael, 74
Dunne, Joseph, 197n.

Edwards, Jonathan,
Elshtain, Jean Bethke, 150, 151, 162, 165, 205n.
Engstrom, Stephen, 189n.
Euripides, 79, 193n.

Farley, Benjamin, 199n.
Fisher, Louis, 209n.
Fodor, Jim, 215n.
Foot, Phillipa, 57, 59, 60, 189n.
Forster, E. M., 73, 196n.
Foucault, Michel, 209n., 217n.
Francis of Assisi, 137
Frankena, William, 58, 59, 60, 189n.

Galen, 217n.
Geach, Peter T., 206n., 208n.
Gide, André, 209n.
Giles, Scott, 212n.
Gillespie, Michael, 205n.
Gogh, Vincent Van, 23
Grant, George Parkin, 205n.
Green, Donald P., 211n.
Greenman, Jeffrey, 212n.

219

Subject Index

Abortion, 19
Action, 6, 7, 8, 10, 19, 22–23, 127,
 137, 184n., 206n.
  and character, 25
  and narrative, 126
  and virtue, 127
  See also Will
Activity, 9, 98
  and rational element, 9, 10
  energeiai, 186n.
  friendship as common, shared, 49,
   177
  friendship as befitting virtuous, 38
  See also Friendship, Virtue
Analogy, 35, 62, 98, 129, 132, 133,
 145–46
Anger, 90, 91, 92–93, 99–100, 107–8
  and hatred, 92, 107
  and jealousy, 89
  and justice, 100
  and pity, 90
  and reason, 100
  and vision of the good, 99
  as self-assertion, 92
  place in virtuous life, 99
  specificity of, 92–93
  See also Emotion
Appetite, 21, 143. *See also* Desire
Authority, 202n.
  and power, 134, 135, 146, 147
  creation of, 135
  See also Obedience
Autonomy, 131

Body, xi, 119, 155, 166, 173, 209n., 217n.
  and conflict, 72
  and pursuit of truth, 59
  and time, x–xi
  as corporate history of virtue
   friends, 49
  church as, 16, 69

  human, 166, 170, 176
  practices of, 69
  resurrection of, 215n.
  See also Church, Human Existence

Character, 4, 12, 23, 24, 25, 101, 131,
 185n.
  and action, 24
  and friendship, 26
  and history, 12
  and time, 12, 40
  as integrity of self over time, 137
  as narratively constituted, 125
  as natural gift, 25
  as retrospective self-discovery, 125–
   26
  definition of, 125, 126
  responsibility for, 25, 27
  settled, 24, 31, 40
  steadfastness of, 22, 43, 70, 124
  See also Constancy, Friendship, Narrative, Self, Suffering, Time
Charity, xv, 68, 105, 159, 173
  and forgiveness, 192n.
  and mutuality, 68
  and patience, 173, 193n., 213–14n.
  and prudence, 189n.
  and rebuke, 107
  as communion, 106, 189n., 192n.
  as form of all the virtues, xv, 63–
   64, 69, 156–57, 165, 192n.
  as form of God's peace, 193n.
  as friendship with God, 162
  as highest virtue, 106
  caritas, 63, 64, 69, 104, 127
  See also Courage, Love, Prudence
Choice(s), 6, 7, 15, 125, 130, 131,
 211n. *See also* Decision
Christianity:
  appropriation of pagan virtues as a
   threat to, 26–27

223

Ideology, 167–68
Imitation, 40–41, 99, 151, 161, 172,
181n., 185n.
  and courage, 161
  and discipleship, 105, 202n.
  and obedience, 139
Integrity, 29
  as faithfulness for one's story, 137
  See also, Constancy, Narrative, Faithfulness
Intention(s), 126, 140, 184n. *See also*
  Motives

Judgment(s), xvii, 22, 25
  common, 28
  retrospective vs. prospective, 125,
  181n.
  shared, 83
Justice, 24, 27, 58, 91, 92, 96–97, 149,
184n., 197n.
  and friendship, 73, 97, 99, 104
  and prudence, 102, 197n.
  as capstone virtue, 103
Justification:
  and sanctification, 114–17
  narrative display of, 117, 120

Liberalism, xi, xii, xv, 66, 67, 95, 130,
149, 169, 190n., 210–11n.
  and communitarianism, 182–83n.
  and Enlightenment project, 60
  and individualism, 94
  Enlightenment, 59, 60, 89
Liberation. *See* Freedom
Love:
  as *agape*, 82, 85, 185–86n, 212n.
  as *eros*, 80
Luck, 16, 70, 78, 85, 86, 89, 162, 177,
181n., 217n.
  tuche, 70, 72
  See also Stoicism

Magnanimity, 20–21, 25, 28, 29, 41,
46, 181n.
  Aristotle's magnanimous man, 64,
  65, 184n.
Marriage, 15, 137, 181n.
Martyr, Martyrdom, 151, 156, 160–65,
173, 191n., 208n., 213n.

Mean:
  Aristotle's doctrine of, 20–21, 157,
  183n.
  means/end distinction, 7, 8, 18, 101
Medicine (modern), 166–70
  and virtue, 171
  as a failed god, 167, 169
  professionalization of, 166, 170
  revolt against, 168–69
  See also Patience
Memory, 99, 104, 108
  and the saints, 124
  betrayal of, 108
Merit, 126–27
Metaphysics, xii, 9
Modernity, xiii, 81, 103
Moral Development, 4, 130–31
Moral Life:
  Aristotle's heroic vision of, 31–32
  as journey towards happiness, 32
  as journey with friends, 34
  as transformation, 31
  'journey' or 'way' as governing
  motif, 29, 30, 31
  journey and growth, 116
  metaphor of journey versus trip,
  18–20, 22, 23, 28, 31, 116, 126,
  159
  See also Friendship, Human Existence
Motives, 58, 60

Narrative, x, 14, 29, 99, 104, 113, 145,
177, 204n., 206.
  and advent of the new, 83–84
  and Christian account of the virtues, 29
  and self, 92, 93, 127–28
  as necessarily communal, 95
  character of Christian, 45, 47
  preeminence of, 125
  See also Character, Hope, Justification, Self, Sin

Obedience, xv, xvi, 27, 29, 115, 129–
48, 204n.
  and command, 202–3n.
  and consent, 134, 142
  as political virtue, 137, 138